Iceland Travel Guide

Iceland is not a destination, but a journey into the heart of nature's wonders, where fire and ice dance in eternal harmony.

Welcome to your guide to a Luxury Trip to Iceland on a budget!

This travel guide is your step-by-step manual for unlocking luxury hotels, enjoying the best culinary offerings and once-in-a-lifetime luxury experiences in Iceland at a fraction of the usual cost.

Everyone's budget is different, but luxury is typically defined by first or business class seats on the airplane, five-star hotels, chauffeurs, exclusive experiences, and delectable fine dining. Yes, all of these can be enjoyed on a budget.

Finding luxury deals in Iceland simply requires a bit of research and planning, which this book has done for you. We have packedthis book with local insider tips and knowledge to save you tens of thousands.

If the mere mention of the word luxury has you thinking things like "Money doesn't grow on trees," "I don't need anything fancy," "I don't deserve nice things," or "People who take luxury trips are shallow and materialistic/environmentally harmful/lack empathy, etc.," then stop. While we all know travel increases our happiness, research on the effects of luxury travel has proven even better results:

Reduced stress: A study published in the Journal of Travel Research found that individuals who visited luxury hotels reported feeling less stressed than those who in standard hotels.[1]

Increased happiness: A study conducted by the International Journal of Tourism Research found that luxury travel experiences lead to an increase in happiness and overall life satisfaction.[2] Researchers also found that luxury travel experiences can improve individuals' mental health by providing a sense of escape from daily stressors and enhancing feelings of relaxation and rejuvenation.

Enhanced creativity: Researchers found engaging in luxury travel experiences can stimulate creativity and lead to more innovative thinking.[3]

While all of this makes perfect sense; it feels much nicer to stay in a hotel room that's cleaned daily than in an Airbnb where you're cleaning up after yourself. What you might not know is that you can have all of that increased happiness and well-being without emptying your bank account. Does it sound too good to be true? I assure you that by the

---

[1] Wöber, K. W., & Fuchs, M. (2016). The effects of hotel attributes on perceived value and satisfaction. Journal of Travel Research, 55(3), 306-318.

[2] Ladhari, R., Souiden, N., & Dufour, B. (2017). Luxury hotel customers' satisfaction and loyalty: An empirical study. International Journal of Hospitality Management, 63, 1-10.

[3] Kim, S., Kim, S. Y., & Lee, H. R. (2019). Luxury travel, inspiration, and creativity: A qualitative investigation. Tourism Management, 71, 354-366.

end of this book, you'll not only possess insider tips and tricks but also wholeheartedly believe that budget-friendly luxury travel is within everyone's reach.

The Magical Power of Bargains

Have you ever felt the rush of getting a bargain? And then found good fortune just keeps following you?

Let me give you an example. In 2009, I graduated into the worst global recession for generations. One unemployed day, I saw a suit I knew I could get a job in. The suit was £250. Money I didn't have. Imagine my shock when the next day I saw the exact same suit (in my size) in the window of a second-hand shop (thrift store) for £18! I bought the suit and after three months of interviewing, without a single call back, within a week of owning that £18 suit, I was hired on a salary far above my expectations. That's the powerful psychological effect of getting an incredible deal. It builds a sense of excitement and happiness that literally creates miracles.

I have no doubt that the Northern Lights, cascading waterfalls, and geothermal marvels of Iceland will uplift and inspire you but when you add the bargains from this book to your vacation, not only will you save a ton of money; you are guaranteed to enjoy a truly magical trip to Iceland.

Who this book is for and why anyone can enjoy luxury travel on a budget

Did you know you can fly on a private jet for $500? Yes, a fully private jet. Complete with flutes of champagne and reclinable creamy leather seats. Your average billionaire spends $20,000 on the exact same flight. You can get it for $500 when you book private jet empty leg flights.This is just one of thousands of ways you can travel luxuriously on a budget. You see there is a big difference between being cheap and frugal.

When our brain hears the word "budget" it hears deprivation, suffering, agony, even depression. But budget travel need not be synonymous with hostels and pack lunches. You can enjoy an incredible and luxurious trip to Iceland on a budget, just like you can enjoy a private jet flight for 10% of the normal cost when you know how.

Over 20 years of travel has taught me I could have a 20 cent experience that will stir my soul more than a $100 one. Of course, sometimes the reverse is true, my point is, spending money on travel is the best investment you can make but it doesn't have to be at levels set by hotels and attractions with massive ad spends and influencers who are paid small fortunes to get you to buy into something you could have for a fraction of the cost.

This book is for those who love bargains and want to have the cold hard budget busting facts to hand (which is why we've included so many one page charts, which you can use as a quick reference), but otherwise, the book provides plenty of tips to help you shape your own Iceland experience.

We have designed these travel guides to give you a unique planning tool to experience an unforgettable trip without spending the ascribed tourist budget.

This guide focuses on Iceland's unbelievable bargains. Of course, there is little value in traveling to Iceland and not experiencing everything it has to offer. Where possible, we've included super cheap workarounds or listed the experience in the Loved but Costly section.

When it comes to luxury budget travel, it's all about what you know. You can have all the feels without most of the bills. A few days spent planning can save you thousands. Luckily, we've done the planning for you, so you can distill the information in minutes not days, leaving you to focus on what matters: immersing yourself in the sights, sounds and smells of Iceland, meeting awesome new people and feeling relaxed and happy.

This book reads like a good friend has travelled the length and breadth of Iceland and brought you back incredible insider tips.

So, grab a cup of tea or coffee, put your feet up and relax; you're about to enter the world of enjoying Iceland on the Super Cheap. Oh, and don't forget a biscuit. You need energy to plan a trip of a lifetime on a budget.

Discover Iceland

Iceland, a land where the ancient forces of fire and ice converge to create landscapes that defy imagination. From its volcanic origins to its vibrant capital, Reykjavik, every corner of this Nordic island nation is a testament to nature's grandeur and human resilience.

As you step off the plane, you'll be greeted by the crisp, pure air that whispers tales of adventure. Iceland's allure lies in its otherworldly landscapes, where geysers shoot skyward, glaciers stretch endlessly, and waterfalls cascade with unbridled power.

But Iceland is more than just a feast for the senses; it's a journey through time. Traces of Iceland's rich history dating back to the Viking settlers who first braved these shores over a millennium ago can be found throughout the land. Explore historic sites like the UNESCO-listed Þingvellir National Park, where ancient parliaments convened amidst breathtaking natural beauty.

Yet, Iceland is not merely a museum of the past; it's a living canvas where nature paints with bold strokes. Witness the majestic spectacle of the Great Geysir and the awe-inspiring power of Gullfoss waterfall. Venture into Vatnajökull National Park, where glaciers conceal hidden ice caves and tranquil lagoons mirror the vastness of the sky.

And as night falls, prepare to be dazzled by the celestial ballet of the Northern Lights. Iceland's pristine skies provide the perfect backdrop for this enchanting display of green and purple hues, leaving visitors in silent awe.

However, the beauty of Iceland comes at a price. Its isolated location and challenging geography contribute to the higher cost of goods and services. Yet, with strategic planning and local insights, you can experience the magic of Iceland without breaking the bank. It is absolutely true, that the best things in Iceland are FREE. I've included details guidance on whether you should hire a car or not and how to stay totally for free! Let's begin!

Key Facts About Iceland:

- Located in the North Atlantic Ocean.
- The population of Iceland is approximately 366,000 people, with Icelandic as the official language and widespread proficiency in English. Iceland has a small population primarily due to its geographical isolation, harsh climate, and limited arable land. The population of Iceland primarily consists of ethnic Icelanders, who are descendants of Norse settlers who arrived on the island during the Viking Age.
- The currency used is the Icelandic Króna (ISK).
- Notable sectors of the economy include tourism, fishing, and renewable energy, with a focus on geothermal and hydropower sources.

The Weird and Wonderful

Elves and Hidden People:

Icelandic folklore is rich with tales of elves and hidden people. Many locals genuinely believe in the existence of these mystical beings, and construction projects have been altered to avoid disturbing their supposed habitats.

No Mosquitoes:

One of the perks of visiting Iceland is the absence of mosquitoes. Due to the country's cool climate and limited standing water, these pesky insects are virtually nonexistent.

No Trains

Iceland does not have a train system primarily due to its challenging terrain, low population density, and the country's relatively small size.

Banning Beer Until 1989:

Iceland has a curious history with beer. Until 1989, beer was prohibited in the country. The ban was lifted on March 1st of that year, and now Icelanders celebrate "Beer Day" annually on the same date.

Incredible Language Evolution:

The Icelandic language has changed very little over the centuries, making it one of the closest languages to Old Norse. This linguistic preservation allows modern Icelanders to read ancient texts with relative ease.

Naming Committee:

Iceland has a Naming Committee responsible for approving or rejecting names for newborns. The committee ensures that names adhere to Icelandic linguistic traditions and do not pose any issues or conflicts.

Geothermal Bread Baking:

In the geothermal area of Hveragerði, locals utilize the natural heat from the ground to bake bread. They bury dough in the hot sand and let the Earth's geothermal energy do the baking. The result is deliciously unique geothermal bread.

No McDonald's or Starbucks:

Iceland is one of the few countries in the world without a McDonald's or Starbucks. The high cost of operating in the country, combined with a strong emphasis on local and sustainable alternatives, has limited the presence of these global chains.

The World's Oldest Parliament:

Established in 930 AD, the Alþingi in Þingvellir National Park is one of the oldest parliaments in the world. It convened annually, bringing together chieftains to discuss laws and settle disputes.

No Military Forces:

Iceland is one of the few NATO member countries without a standing army. Instead, its defense is handled by the Icelandic Coast Guard and other international defense agreements.

Record-Breaking Waterfalls:

Dettifoss, located in Vatnajökull National Park, is not only Europe's most powerful waterfall but also served as a filming location for the opening scene of the movie "Prometheus."

Ms. Guðrún or Ms. Pétursdóttir?

Iceland maintains another Norse tradition: the practice of using patronyms instead of surnames. An Icelander's given name is followed by their parent's first name (usually the father's), in the genitive case, and the suffix -son or -dóttir, for example, Guðrún Pétursdóttir (Guðrún, Pétur's daughter). Members of the same family can, therefore, have many different "surnames," which can sometimes create confusion for visitors. Due to the patronymic last names Icelanders use, phone books are alphabetized by first name rather than last name. This also applies when addressing an individual. Icelanders would never expect to be addressed as Mr. or Ms. Jónsson/-dóttir no matter how important they might be. Also, titles are generally not used, so being addressed as Ms./Miss/Mrs./Mr. so-and-so would make many an Icelander uncomfortable.

Some of Iceland's Best Bargains

The Blue Lagoon

The Blue Lagoon, nestled in the volcanic landscapes of Grindavík on the Reykjanes Peninsula, is a quintessential Icelandic experience. Formed accidentally in 1976 from runoff water of the nearby Svartsengi geothermal power plant, this geothermal spa boasts a rich history and a unique therapeutic allure.

With starting prices at $65 USD, planning your visit strategically can save you $30 + and enhance your experience. Opting for early morning (before 8am) or late afternoon (after 5pm) visits allows you to enjoy lower prices and a more tranquil atmosphere with fewer crowds. During the peak times, in peak season, it's almost unbearable.

To get there affordably, hop on Bus Route 55 departing from Reykjavik's BSI Bus Terminal for a scenic 40-45 minute journey.

The Blue Lagoon's turquoise-blue waters, heated by volcanic activity beneath the earth's surface, maintain a soothing temperature of 37 to 39 degrees Celsius (98 to 102 degrees Fahrenheit). Rich in minerals like silica and sulfur, the lagoon offers purported therapeutic benefits, particularly for skin conditions like psoriasis. Its proximity to Reykjavik and

Keflavik International Airport makes it a convenient stop for tourists seeking relaxation amidst Iceland's natural wonders.

Alternatives like the Secret Lagoon, Fontana Geothermal Baths, Mývatn Nature Baths, Reykjadalur Hot Springs, and Seljavallalaug offer equally enchanting geothermal experiences at half the price or even for free. This book will explore the free geothermal hot springs in detail further on.

When you arrive go to the tourist information centers for free resources, budget-friendly recommendations, and discount coupons.

Strategies to Experience The Blue Lagoon on a Budget	Description	Cost
Stopover Tour from Keflavik Airport	Many tour operators offer stopover tours from Keflavik Airport to the Blue Lagoon, allowing travelers to visit the lagoon en route to or from the airport. These tours typically include transportation to and from the airport and admission to the Blue Lagoon.	Varies, but often starts from $50-$100 depending on the tour package.
Early Morning Visit (Before 8am)	The Blue Lagoon tends to be less crowded in the early morning hours, offering a more peaceful and serene experience. By visiting before 8am, visitors can enjoy the lagoon's amenities and facilities at a discounted rate.	Discounted rates compared to peak hours, typically starting from $40-$60.
Book in Advance	Booking tickets in advance online can sometimes offer discounts compared to purchasing tickets on-site. Additionally, some travel websites or booking platforms may offer promotional deals or package discounts for the Blue Lagoon.	Savings vary depending on promotions, but can range from 5%-15% off regular admission prices.
Opt for Basic Package	The Blue Lagoon offers different packages with varying levels of amenities and perks. Choosing the basic package provides access to the lagoon itself, along with a silica mud mask. Visitors can save money by opting for the basic package instead of premium packages.	Basic package prices start from around $60-$80.
Utilize Public Transportation	Instead of booking expensive transportation options, such as private shuttles or taxis, travelers can utilize public transportation options to reach the Blue Lagoon, such as buses or shared transfers. Public transportation can be more cost-effective, especially for solo travelers or small groups.	Bus fares vary depending on the departure point, but typically cost around $20-$30 for a round trip.

Exploring the Golden Circle Without a Car or Tour

The Golden Circle is a popular tourist route that covers approximately 300 kilometers (190 miles) looping from Reykjavik into central Iceland and back. It's renowned for showcasing some of Iceland's most stunning natural landscapes and iconic landmarks. A tour starts at $45 but you can explore the Golden Circle in Iceland without a car or a tour, you can still experience its beauty using alternative transportation methods. Here's how:

- **Þingvellir National Park**: To reach Þingvellir National Park by bus, you can take a guided tour or use public transportation. Some tour companies offer day trips from Reykjavik that include transportation to Þingvellir along with other stops on the Golden Circle route. Alternatively, you can use the public bus service operated by Strætó. Bus route 52 runs from Reykjavik to Þingvellir during the summer months, providing easy access to the park.
- **Geysir Geothermal Area**: Similarly, you can reach the Geysir Geothermal Area by joining a guided tour or using public transportation. Many tour operators include a stop at the Geysir Geothermal Area as part of their Golden Circle tours. If you prefer to use public transportation, you can take bus route 52 from Reykjavik to Geysir. From there, it's a short walk to explore the geysers and hot springs.
- **Gullfoss Waterfall**: Gullfoss Waterfall is often the next stop on Golden Circle tours after visiting the Geysir Geothermal Area. Many tour companies include Gullfoss as a highlight of their Golden Circle itinerary. If you're using public transportation, you can take bus route 52 from Geysir to Gullfoss. The bus will drop you off at the Gullfoss parking lot, where you can walk to the viewing platforms overlooking the waterfall.

Cheapest tours

- a. **Reykjavik Excursions Golden Circle Classic Tour**:
  - Starting Price: Around $45 to $50 USD per person.
  - Pros: Affordable, covers main attractions (Thingvellir, Geysir, Gullfoss).
  - Cons: Limited time at each stop, may be crowded during peak seasons.

- b. **Gray Line Iceland Golden Circle Express Tour**:
  - Starting Price: Approximately $55 to $60 USD per person.
  - Pros: Affordable, shorter duration.
  - Cons: Limited time at attractions, less in-depth commentary.
  -

- c. **Gateway to Iceland Golden Circle and Secret Lagoon Tour**:
  - Starting Price: Around $75 to $80 USD per person.
  - Pros: Affordable, includes visit to Secret Lagoon.
  - Cons: Limited time at attractions, may feel rushed.
  -

The good news is, if you plan to rent a car, parking is largely free near attractions in Iceland.

Iceland Discount Passes

Deciding whether Icelandic discount passes are worth it depends on your travel style and itinerary. If you plan extensive travel across Iceland and intend to visit numerous attractions, a discount pass could offer significant savings. However, for shorter stays or more localized exploration, it may not be as beneficial. Consider factors like included attractions, duration of stay, flexibility, comparative costs, and additional perks to determine if the pass aligns with your needs and budget. Research reviews and recommendations for insight into the pass's usability and value. Ultimately, weigh the benefits against your travel priorities to make the best decision for your Icelandic adventure.

Pass/ Membership	Description	Highlights	Starting Prices (in ISK)	Starting Prices (in USD)
Reykjavik City Card	Provides free access to public transportation, museums, and thermal pools in Reykjavik. Also offers discounts on various tours and attractions.	- Free entry to major museums and galleries in Reykjavik. - Unlimited bus rides within the city. - Discounts on tours and activities.	3,900 ISK (24 hours)	$29.67
			6,400 ISK (48 hours)	$48.62
			7,900 ISK (72 hours)	$60.06
Icelandair Stopover Pass	Exclusive to Icelandair passengers, it offers discounts on tours, activities, and services across the country.	- Discounts on various attractions, excursions, and dining. - Access to exclusive offers from partners.	Included for Icelandair passengers during their layover.	Included for Icelandair passengers during their layover.
Blue Lagoon Premium Pass	Grants access to the Blue Lagoon's premium facilities, including the Retreat Spa and private changing rooms.	- Entry to the Blue Lagoon. - Access to the Retreat Spa and private lagoon. - Silica mud mask and use of bathrobe included.	14,900 ISK (standard admission not included)	$113.39
Golden Circle Passport	Covers admission to the key attractions on the Golden Circle route, such as Thingvellir National Park, Geysir, and Gullfoss.	- Entry to Thingvellir, Geysir, and Gullfoss. - Discounts at local businesses along the Golden Circle.	Prices vary; around 11,000 ISK (adults)	Prices vary; around $83.76 (adults)

South Coast Adventure	Offers entry to attractions along the South Coast, including Seljalandsfoss, Skogafoss, and the Black Sand Beach.	- Access to popular South Coast landmarks. - Discounts on tours and services in the area.	Prices vary; around 10,000 ISK (adults)	Prices vary; around $76.05 (adults)

Cheapest Igloos in Iceland

Staying in an igloo in Iceland offers a unique and unforgettable experience that allows you to immerse yourself in the stunning natural beauty of the country while enjoying cozy and comfortable accommodations. Here are some appealing choices:

- **Igloo Lodge** (South Iceland): Starting at $80 USD per night, Igloo Lodge offers affordable igloo accommodations near popular attractions like the Golden Circle.
- **Igloo Village Búðardalur** (West Iceland): Prices begin at around $90 USD per night for basic yet comfortable igloo stays amidst the picturesque landscapes of West Iceland.

Free Northern Lights

Experiencing the Northern Lights in Iceland for free requires a combination of luck, planning, and flexibility. Here's a step-by-step guide:

1. Timing and Season:

Choose the right time of year, typically from late September to early April, when the nights are dark enough to witness the Northern Lights.

2. Dark Sky Areas:

Head to areas with minimal light pollution for optimal visibility. Towns or villages like Vik, Kirkjufell, or Akureyri offer good viewing opportunities.

3. Check Aurora Forecast:

Monitor the Aurora forecast to determine when the Northern Lights are likely to be visible. Numerous online tools and apps provide real-time information on aurora activity.

4. Clear Skies:

Choose nights with clear skies for better visibility. Apps like Vedur or websites like the Icelandic Met Office provide weather forecasts.

5. Public Transportation:

Utilize public transport to reach dark sky areas economically. Buses and coaches connect major towns like Reykjavik to various regions, making it affordable to reach potential Northern Lights spots.

6. Cost of Tours:

While free viewing is possible, guided tours offer expert insights and increase the chances of a successful sighting. Tour costs vary, with prices ranging from 8,000 to 40,000 ISK depending on factors like duration, amenities, and additional activities.

7. Flexible Schedule:

Be flexible with your travel dates to maximize the chances of catching the Northern Lights during a clear night. Stay in a location for a few days to increase your opportunities.

8. Free Viewing Spots:

Explore free viewing spots in and around towns. In Reykjavik, places like Grotta Lighthouse and Oskjuhlid Hill provide dark areas for potential sightings.

9. Aurora Hunting Apps:

Use Aurora hunting apps or websites to locate the best spots for free viewing. These tools can guide you to locations with optimal visibility based on real-time data.

10. Safety and Warmth:

Dress warmly, as Icelandic nights can be chilly. Ensure your safety by choosing easily accessible locations, especially if you're relying on public transport.

11. Be Patient:

The Northern Lights are a natural phenomenon, and patience is key. Spend time in your chosen location, and if conditions are right, you might be rewarded with a spectacular display.

While free viewing is possible, investing in a guided tour can enhance the experience. Consider factors such as transportation convenience, duration, and additional activities when selecting a tour. With careful planning and a bit of luck, you can witness the enchanting Northern Lights in Iceland without breaking the bank.

DIY Game of Thrones Tour

Prices for guided Game of Thrones tours in Iceland can range from $100 to $300 USD per person for a half-day or full-day tour but if you have a car or use the bus you can create your own adventure through the stunning Icelandic landscapes that brought the world of Game of Thrones to life. Here's your guide:

Here's your itinerary:

- **Þingvellir National Park**:
  - Game of Thrones Location: North of the Wall scenes.
  - DIY Tip: Wander through Almannagjá gorge and Þingvallavatn Lake.
  - Access: Take the Golden Circle bus tour from Reykjavik.
  - Entrance Fee: None.
- **Dimmuborgir**:
  - Game of Thrones Location: Mance Rayder's Wildling camp.
  - DIY Tip: Stroll through the eerie lava formations.
  - Access: Take a bus from Reykjavik to Akureyri, then transfer to a local bus or tour to Lake Mývatn.
  - Entrance Fee: None.
- **Hverir Geothermal Area**:
  - Game of Thrones Location: Beyond the Wall scenes.
  - DIY Tip: Witness bubbling mud pots and steam vents.
  - Access: Same route as Dimmuborgir, near Lake Mývatn.
  - Entrance Fee: None.
- **Reynisfjara Black Sand Beach**:
  - Game of Thrones Location: Eastwatch-by-the-Sea.
  - DIY Tip: Marvel at the black sand beach and basalt columns.
  - Access: Take a bus from Reykjavik to Vík.
  - Entrance Fee: None.
- **Þórufoss Waterfall**:
  - Game of Thrones Location: The "Frozen Lake" scenes.
  - DIY Tip: Hike to Þórufoss for a tranquil setting.
  - Access: Take the Golden Circle bus tour or a public bus to Selfoss.
  - Entrance Fee: None.
- **Akureyri**:
  - Game of Thrones Location: Various scenes filmed in the North.
  - DIY Tip: Explore the charming town known as the "capital of the North."
  - Access: Take a bus from Reykjavik to Akureyri.
  - Entrance Fee: None for exploring the town.
- **Kirkjufell Mountain**:
  - Game of Thrones Location: The "Arrowhead Mountain."
  - DIY Tip: Capture the iconic silhouette of Kirkjufell.
  - Access: Take a bus from Reykjavik to Grundarfjörður.
  - Entrance Fee: None for viewing the mountain.

Visiting Waterfalls

Iceland is renowned for its stunning natural landscapes, and waterfalls are among its most captivating features. The exact number of waterfalls in Iceland is challenging to determine precisely because new ones can be discovered, especially in remote areas. Additionally, seasonal variations and changes in water flow can influence the visibility of waterfalls.

Indulging in Waterfall Tours in Iceland doesn't have to drain your wallet. Here's a guide on experiencing the luxury of Iceland's stunning waterfalls while staying budget-savvy:

1. Free Waterfalls:

- Here are some stunning waterfalls in Iceland that you can visit for free:
- Seljalandsfoss: Located in the south of Iceland, this waterfall is famous for its unique path that allows you to walk behind the cascading water.
- Skógafoss: Another iconic waterfall in the south, Skógafoss is known for its powerful flow and the rainbow that often forms in its mist.
- Gullfoss: Found in the Golden Circle route, Gullfoss is one of Iceland's most famous waterfalls, cascading in two tiers into a deep canyon.
- Svartifoss: Situated in Vatnajökull National Park, Svartifoss is renowned for its basalt columns surrounding the waterfall, creating a stunning backdrop.

- Dettifoss: Located in the northeast of Iceland, Dettifoss is Europe's most powerful waterfall, thundering down a rugged canyon.
- Goðafoss: Known as the "Waterfall of the Gods," Goðafoss is located in the north of Iceland and offers a picturesque setting with its horseshoe-shaped cascade.
- Kirkjufellsfoss: Found near the iconic Kirkjufell mountain on the Snæfellsnes Peninsula, Kirkjufellsfoss is a charming waterfall often photographed with its stunning backdrop.
- Hraunfossar: Situated in western Iceland, Hraunfossar is unique as it flows out of a lava field, creating a series of cascades streaming into the Hvítá River.
- Dynjandi: Located in the Westfjords, Dynjandi is a stunning tiered waterfall that resembles a bridal veil when viewed from a distance.
- Glymur: Tucked away in Hvalfjörður fjord, Glymur is Iceland's second-highest waterfall, reached by a scenic hike through a canyon.
-

2. Self-Guided Exploration:

- Save on guided tour costs by exploring waterfalls on your own. Rent a car to visit multiple waterfalls in a day, creating a personalized tour at your own pace.

3. Off-Peak Travel:

- Travel during the shoulder seasons to avoid peak tourist times. This not only reduces the cost of accommodation but also makes for a more intimate experience at the waterfalls without the crowds.

4. Budget-Friendly Tours:

- If you prefer a guided experience, research budget-friendly waterfall tours. Some tour operators offer economical packages that include transportation and visits to multiple waterfalls.

5. Group Discounts:

- Check for group discounts or package deals if you are traveling with friends or joining a group tour. Splitting costs can significantly reduce the overall expense.

6. Hostel Accommodations:

- Opt for budget-friendly accommodations like hostels or guesthouses near popular waterfall destinations. These options provide a comfortable stay without breaking the bank.

7. Pack a Picnic:

- Save on dining expenses by packing a picnic. Many waterfall locations have scenic spots where you can enjoy a meal while surrounded by nature.

8. Utilize Free Trails:

- Take advantage of free hiking trails leading to waterfalls. Some trails offer stunning views and lead to lesser-known waterfalls that are equally captivating.

9. Visit Less Touristy Locations:

- Explore waterfalls in less touristy areas. While the well-known waterfalls are awe-inspiring, Iceland is full of hidden gems waiting to be discovered, often without the crowds.

10. Local Transportation:

- Use local transportation options to reach waterfall sites. Public buses or shuttle services can be more economical than renting a car for those on a tight budget.

11. Visit During Festivals:

- Plan your trip during local festivals, as some may include free events or activities near waterfalls. It's a great way to experience Icelandic culture while enjoying the natural beauty.

Exploring Islands

Iceland has several islands surrounding its coastline, each offering unique attractions and experiences. While some islands are accessible year-round, others have seasonal accessibility. Here are a few notable islands to consider visiting around Iceland, along with tips on how to get to them inexpensively:

- **Vestmannaeyjar (Westman Islands):**
  - **How to Get There:** Take a ferry or a domestic flight from Reykjavik to Vestmannaeyjar.
  - **Ferry Prices:** Prices vary, but a round-trip ferry ticket can cost around $30 - $50 USD per person.
  - **Flight Prices:** Domestic flights might cost around $80 - $150 USD one way.
- **Flatey:**
  - **How to Get There:** Flatey is accessible by ferry from Stykkishólmur or Brjánslækur.
  - **Ferry Prices:** The ferry from Stykkishólmur to Flatey might cost around $15 - $20 USD.
  - **Travel Tip:** Flatey is a small island with no cars, providing a peaceful and serene atmosphere.
- **Grímsey:**
  - **How to Get There:** Grímsey is accessible by ferry from Dalvík or by a domestic flight from Akureyri.
  - **Ferry Prices:** The ferry from Dalvík to Grímsey might cost around $50 - $70 USD.
  - **Flight Prices:** Domestic flights to Grímsey can cost around $100 - $150 USD one way.
- **Drangey:**
  - **How to Get There:** Drangey is accessible by boat from the town of Sauðárkrókur.
  - **Boat Tour Prices:** Boat tours to Drangey may cost around $60 - $80 USD per person.
  - **Travel Tip:** Drangey is a birdwatcher's paradise, known for its steep cliffs and bird colonies.
- **Flatey (Breiðafjörður):**
  - **How to Get There:** Flatey in Breiðafjörður is accessible by ferry from Stykkishólmur.
  - **Ferry Prices:** The ferry from Stykkishólmur to Flatey might cost around $25 - $40 USD.
  - **Travel Tip:** Breiðafjörður is famous for its vast intertidal zone and diverse birdlife.
- **Hrísey:**
  - **How to Get There:** Hrísey is accessible by ferry from Dalvík.
  - **Ferry Prices:** The ferry from Dalvík to Hrísey might cost around $20 - $30 USD.
  - **Travel Tip:** Hrísey is known for its tranquility, hiking trails, and birdwatching opportunities.

Tips for Affordable Island Travel:

- **Book in Advance:** Ferry and flight prices can vary, so booking in advance often yields lower prices.
- **Travel Off-Peak:** Consider visiting during the off-peak season for potential discounts on transportation and accommodations.
- **Pack Snacks:** Bring your own snacks to save money on food during your island visit.
- **Camp or Stay in Budget Accommodations:** If you plan to stay overnight, consider camping or staying in budget accommodations to save on lodging costs.

Animal Encounters

Iceland's wildlife is as rugged and resilient as its landscapes, shaped by harsh conditions and human influence alike. Iceland offers unique animal encounter experiences, allowing you to appreciate the country's diverse wildlife. Here are some notable free animal encounters:

- **Puffin Watching**: While boat tours offer close-up views, you can also spot puffins from coastal viewpoints such as the cliffs near Dyrhólaey or Látrabjarg. These spots offer fantastic views of puffin colonies without any cost.
- **Whale Watching**: From certain coastal areas like Reykjavik or Husavik, you can often catch glimpses of whales from shore, especially during the summer months when they are more active. Keep an eye out for spouts and fins breaking the surface.
- **Seal Watching**: Coastal areas like Jökulsárlón Glacier Lagoon or Vatnsnes Peninsula offer opportunities to spot seals lounging on icebergs or sunbathing on the shore. Access to these spots is free, and you can enjoy the sights at your own pace.
- **Arctic Fox Watching**: Explore the Hornstrandir Nature Reserve in the Westfjords independently, as there are no entrance fees. Hike the trails and keep your eyes peeled for sightings of these elusive creatures in their natural habitat.
- **Bird Watching in Lake Mývatn**: Lake Mývatn is easily accessible, with several viewpoints around the lake providing excellent birdwatching opportunities. Bring your binoculars and enjoy observing the diverse bird species that inhabit the area, all for free.

- **Reindeer Spotting in East Iceland**: While reindeer are elusive, you may encounter them in the wilderness of East Iceland, particularly in places like the Eastfjords. Drive through the area and keep a lookout for these majestic animals grazing in the wild.
- **Fox and Rabbit Watching**: Explore the outskirts of Reykjavik or rural areas independently to spot red foxes and rabbits. These animals can often be seen in fields or meadows, and you can enjoy observing them without any cost.
- In Iceland, you can easily see Icelandic horses for free by observing them grazing in pastures along roadsides or in open fields, particularly in rural areas and along the Ring Road (Route 1). Simply driving through the countryside offers opportunities to spot these iconic horses. These sturdy and resilient horses are believed to have been brought to the island by the first Norse settlers during the 9th and 10th centuries, making them one of the oldest and purest breeds in the world.

Always prioritize ethical and responsible wildlife viewing practices, respecting the animals' natural behaviors and environments. Be mindful of seasonal variations in animal activities and consult local guides for the best chances of successful encounters.

The Laugavegur Trail

The Laugavegur Trail offers some of the most breathtaking scenery in Iceland, showcasing diverse landscapes including colorful rhyolite mountains, vast lava fields, bubbling hot springs, and sparkling glacial rivers. Hikers are treated to ever-changing vistas around every corner. And if you book in advance you can get accommodation for $40!

There are huts along the trail, operated by the Icelandic Touring Association (Ferðafélag Íslands or ÚTÍ), are in high demand, especially during the summer months when the trail is typically open. On average, the cost ranges from $40 to $100 USD per person per night.

Here's why booking in advance is essential:

- **Limited Accommodation**: The huts along the Laugavegur Trail have limited capacity, and they fill up quickly during the peak hiking season, typically from June to September. With only a few huts available along the trail, securing a spot in advance ensures you have a place to stay each night of your trek.
- **High Demand**: The Laugavegur Trail is one of the most popular trekking routes in Iceland, known for its breathtaking scenery and unique geological features. As a result, competition for accommodation is fierce, with hikers vying for limited spots in the huts.

- **Peak Season Crowds**: During the summer months, the Laugavegur Trail can become crowded with hikers, both solo trekkers and guided groups. With so many people wanting to experience the trail's beauty, accommodation options can quickly become fully booked if not reserved in advance.

Experience the Elf and hidden people culture in Iceland

Iceland's folklore is rich with tales of elves, hidden people, and mystical creatures that have captured the imagination of locals and visitors alike for centuries. Deeply ingrained in Icelandic culture, belief in elves, also known as "álfar" or "huldufólk" (hidden people), remains surprisingly prevalent in modern society, shaping the way Icelanders interact with their environment and influencing everything from urban planning to road construction.

The folklore surrounding elves and hidden people traces its origins back to ancient Norse mythology and pagan beliefs. According to Icelandic folklore, elves are believed to be supernatural beings, often depicted as small in stature and ethereal in appearance, with the ability to vanish or change their form at will. They are said to dwell in the hidden realms of rocks, mountains, and forests, living in harmony with nature and possessing great wisdom and magical powers.

The hidden people, on the other hand, are described as a parallel society living alongside humans but hidden from mortal eyes. They are believed to inhabit a realm that exists in parallel to our own, often concealed within rocks, hillsides, or other natural formations.

Despite their invisibility to most humans, hidden people are said to interact with the human world, sometimes appearing to offer assistance or guidance, while other times playing mischievous tricks on those who intrude upon their territory.

Throughout Iceland, there are numerous sites associated with elf and hidden people folklore, including "elf rocks" or "elf churches" where these beings are said to reside. One such notable location is Álfhóll (Elf Hill) in the capital city of Reykjavik, a small grassy mound located near the iconic Hallgrímskirkja church. According to legend, Álfhóll is home to a colony of elves who fiercely guard their territory against human intrusion.

Another famous site is the Elf School in Reykjavik, where visitors can learn about Icelandic folklore and the history of elves and hidden people through lectures and guided tours. The school's founder, Magnús Skarphéðinsson, is a prominent advocate for elf and hidden people culture and has dedicated his life to preserving and promoting these beliefs.

There are also several free ways to learn about elf and hidden people culture in Iceland and even visit some sites associated with this folklore. Here are some options:

- **Álfhóll (Elf Hill) in Reykjavik:**
  - Location: Near Hallgrímskirkja church in Reykjavik.
  - Description: Visit this small grassy mound believed to be home to a colony of elves. While access to the hill itself may be restricted, you can still observe it from nearby areas.
  - Booking: No booking required. Simply visit the site during your time in Reykjavik.
- **The Elf School in Reykjavik:**
  - Location: Bjarnarhöfn 4, 110 Reykjavík, Iceland.
  - Description: Attend lectures and guided tours at the Elf School to learn about Icelandic folklore, including elves and hidden people.
  - Booking: To attend lectures or tours, contact the Elf School directly through their website: Elf School.
- **Local Libraries and Museums:**
  - Description: Many libraries and museums in Iceland feature exhibits and resources related to Icelandic folklore, including elf and hidden people culture. Visit your local library or museum to explore books, displays, and other materials on this topic.
  - Booking: No booking required. Check the opening hours of your chosen library or museum before visiting.

Let the government entertain you

Iceland has many government-subsidized activities and events you can enjoy at a discount or for free:

- **Iceland Symphony Orchestra Concerts:** The Iceland Symphony Orchestra regularly performs concerts featuring classical masterpieces, contemporary compositions, and collaborations with renowned soloists and conductors. Tickets for these performances are often subsidized by the government, making them accessible to a wider audience.
- **Reykjavik Art Museum Exhibitions:** The Reykjavik Art Museum showcases contemporary and modern art by Icelandic and international artists. With government funding, the museum offers discounted admission fees for visitors, allowing art enthusiasts to explore its diverse collections without spending a fortune.
- **Reykjavik Culture Night:** Reykjavik Culture Night is an annual event supported by the Icelandic government, featuring a vibrant celebration of Icelandic culture, music, and arts. Visitors can enjoy free concerts, art installations, street performances, and cultural activities throughout the city.
- **National Day Celebrations:** Iceland's National Day, celebrated on June 17th, commemorates the country's independence from Denmark. Government-sponsored festivities include parades, concerts, traditional dance performances, and outdoor events held in public squares and parks across the country.
- **Free Public Lectures at University of Iceland:** The University of Iceland hosts public lectures, seminars, and academic discussions on various topics, including literature, history, science, and politics. These events are open to the public and are often subsidized by government funding.
- **National Parks and Protected Areas:** Iceland's national parks and protected areas, such as Þingvellir National Park and Vatnajökull National Park, receive government support for conservation efforts and visitor facilities. Entrance fees to these natural wonders are relatively low, allowing visitors to explore Iceland's pristine landscapes affordably.
- **Municipal Swimming Pools:** Municipal swimming pools across Iceland receive government subsidies to keep admission fees affordable for residents and visitors. These pools offer geothermally heated swimming facilities, hot tubs, saunas, and steam baths, providing a relaxing and budget-friendly way to unwind.

Enjoy Beer tastings

Beer has a long history in Iceland, dating back to the time of the Vikings. Historians believe that Norse settlers brought the art of brewing to Iceland in the 9th century, using grains such as barley to produce ale. Here are some popular craft beer bars in Reykjavik along with an estimate of the cost for beer tastings:

- **Mikkeller & Friends Reykjavik:**
    - Address: Hverfisgata 12, 101 Reykjavik
    - Beer Tasting Cost: Approximately $15-$25 USD for a flight of 4-6 beers.
- **Skúli Craft Bar:**
    - Address: Aðalstræti 9, 101 Reykjavik
    - Beer Tasting Cost: Around $20-$30 USD for a flight of 4-6 beers.
- **Microbar:**
    - Address: Vesturgata 2, 101 Reykjavik
    - Beer Tasting Cost: Roughly $15-$25 USD for a flight of 4-6 beers.
- **Bryggjan Brugghús:**
    - Address: Grandagarður 8, 101 Reykjavik
    - Beer Tasting Cost: Approximately $20-$35 USD for a flight of 4-6 beers, depending on beer selection and portion sizes.
- **Kaldi Bar:**
    - Address: Laugavegur 20b, 101 Reykjavik
    - Beer Tasting Cost: Around $15-$25 USD for a flight of 4-6 Kaldi beers.
- **Vínbarr:**
    - Address: Vesturgata 7, 101 Reykjavik
    - Beer Tasting Cost: Estimated at $20-$30 USD for a flight of 4-6 craft beers.
- **Ölstofa Kormáks og Skjaldar:**
    - Address: Vegamótastígur 9, 101 Reykjavik
    - Beer Tasting Cost: Roughly $15-$25 USD for a flight of 4-6 beers.

Try Einstök Ölgerð, this Belgian-style witbier is infused with coriander and orange peel, offering a refreshing and citrusy taste. It's one of Iceland's most iconic craft beers and widely available locally.

Cheap Boat Cruises

While specific whale and puffin cruises might run you $100, you can do Harbour cruises from $15. The cheapest harbor tours in Iceland can typically be found in smaller towns with local operators offering shorter excursions. Here are some options to consider:

- **Höfn Harbor Tour:**
    - Location: Höfn, a town in southeastern Iceland known for its picturesque harbor.
    - Prices: Harbor tours in Höfn may start as low as $20 to $30 USD per person for shorter excursions.
- **Stykkishólmur Harbor Tour:**
    - Location: Stykkishólmur, a charming town in western Iceland with a bustling harbor.
    - Prices: Harbor tours in Stykkishólmur may start around $25 to $35 USD per person for basic sightseeing trips.
- **Húsavík Harbor Tour:**
    - Location: Húsavík, often referred to as the whale watching capital of Iceland, located in the north.
    - Prices: While whale watching is the main attraction in Húsavík, some operators offer budget-friendly harbor tours starting at approximately $30 to $40 USD per person.
- **Akureyri Harbor Tour:**
    - Location: Akureyri, the second-largest city in Iceland, situated in the north.
    - Prices: Harbor tours in Akureyri may start around $25 to $35 USD per person for shorter excursions around the scenic Eyjafjörður fjord.

Explore Natural Wonders

Iceland offers a range of natural wonders and outdoor activities that you can enjoy for free or at a subsidized cost. Here are some free or subsidized activities, including visits to national parks:

1. National Parks:

- **Thingvellir National Park:** Entrance to Thingvellir is free. The park is known for its historical and geological significance, including the meeting point of the North American and Eurasian tectonic plates.
- **Vatnajokull National Park:** While some areas within the park may require a fee for specific activities, there are parts, such as Skaftafell, where you can explore nature for free.

While some national parks may have more direct bus routes than others, they are all accessible by bus. However, the frequency of bus services and the proximity of bus stops to the park entrances may vary. It's essential to check the bus schedules and routes beforehand. Use Strateo to check.

National Park	Highlights	Entry Fee	How to Get There by Bus
Þingvellir	UNESCO World Heritage Site, tectonic plate boundary, Almannagjá gorge, Öxarárfoss waterfall	Free	Bus Route 52 from Reykjavik
Snæfellsjökull	Iconic glacier-capped volcano, diverse landscapes, Snæfellsjökull Glacier	Free	Bus Route 57 from Reykjavik
Vatnajökull	Largest national park in Europe, Vatnajökull Glacier, diverse ecosystems, waterfalls	Free	Various routes from Reykjavik or major towns
Snæfellsjökull	Stunning coastal scenery, birdwatching, hiking trails, volcanic landscapes	Free	Bus Route 57 from Reykjavik
Jökulsárgljúfur	Ásbyrgi Canyon, Dettifoss waterfall, Hljóðaklettar rock formations, diverse birdlife	Free	Bus Route 62 from Reykjavik
Þórsmörk	Glacial valleys, hiking trails, Þórsmörk Nature Reserve, Fimmvörðuháls Pass	Free	Bus Route 51 from Reykjavik
Snæfellsnes Peninsula	Kirkjufell Mountain, Snæfellsjökull National Park, coastal cliffs, lava fields	Free	Bus Route 58 from Reykjavik

2. Waterfalls and Scenic Stops:

- **Gullfoss:** This iconic waterfall is free to view. Enjoy the stunning double cascade without any entrance fee.
- **Seljalandsfoss and Skogafoss:** Both waterfalls are freely accessible. You can explore the area around them without any cost.

3. Hiking Trails:

- **Laugavegur and Fimmvorduhals Trails:** These long-distance hiking trails offer breathtaking landscapes and are free to hike. Keep in mind that overnight camping might have associated fees in certain areas.
-

5. Hot Springs and Geothermal Areas:

- **Reykjadalur Hot Springs:** A popular spot for a natural hot spring bath, and the hike to get there is free. Be aware that parking might have a small fee.
- **Hveragerdi Geothermal Park:** Explore the geothermal park in Hveragerdi, known for hot springs and mud pots. Access is typically free.

6. Coastal Areas:

- **Reynisfjara Black Sand Beach:** Visit this famous black sand beach for free. Witness the stunning basalt columns and the Reynisdrangar sea stacks.

Go Thrift Shopping

Thrift shopping in Iceland can be a delightful and distinctive experience, offering insight into local fashion trends and a sustainable way to refresh your wardrobe. While Iceland may not have as many thrift stores as some other places, the ones available often provide high-quality items. In Reykjavik, the capital city, you can explore stores such as Red Cross (Rauði krossinn), Salvation Army (Frelsarmálin), and the popular vintage shop Spúútnik for curated selections of second-hand clothing and accessories.

Timing your visit strategically can enhance your thrift shopping experience. Thrift stores may update their inventory with seasonal changes, making transitions between seasons an opportune time to find unique items. Additionally, keep an eye out for sales or promotions, as some thrift stores may offer discounts during specific times of the year.

Beyond dedicated thrift stores, consider exploring local markets and flea markets. Kolaportið in Reykjavik and the Vesturbæjar Flea Market are venues where you can find second-hand items, including clothing, books, and vintage pieces. These markets often contribute to the vibrant and diverse second-hand shopping scene in Iceland.

Quality is a key aspect when thrift shopping in Iceland. The items you find are generally of high quality, and it's advisable to check for any defects or signs of wear to ensure they are in good condition. Thrift stores in Iceland occasionally carry designer or branded clothing at affordable prices.

Look for local designers and traditional Icelandic clothing to add a unique touch to your finds. Thrift stores might showcase pieces by Icelandic designers, contributing to the cultural and creative fabric of the country. Additionally, keep an eye out for traditional Icelandic clothing like lopapeysa, the iconic wool sweater.

Church Hop

The predominant religion in Iceland is Christianity, with the majority of Icelanders being members of the Lutheran Church of Iceland. Here are some of the best churches in Iceland along with their history and noteworthy features inside:

- **Hallgrímskirkja (Hallgrímur's Church) - Reykjavik:**
  - **History:** This iconic Lutheran church is Reykjavik's most famous landmark. Designed by architect Guðjón Samúelsson, its construction began in 1945 and was completed in 1986.
  - **Inside:** Admire the impressive pipe organ, crafted by Johannes Klais of Bonn, Germany. Take the elevator to the top of the tower for breathtaking views of Reykjavik.
- **Akureyrarkirkja (Akureyri Church) - Akureyri:**
  - **History:** This striking church dominates the skyline of Akureyri, Iceland's second-largest city. It was designed by Guðjón Samúelsson and consecrated in 1940.
  - **Inside:** The interior features beautiful stained glass windows and a carved wooden pulpit. Don't miss the large pipe organ, which was added in 1992.
- **Ísafjarðarkirkja (Ísafjörður Church) - Ísafjörður:**
  - **History:** Built in 1859, this church is one of the oldest in Iceland. It is located in the picturesque town of Ísafjörður in the Westfjords region.
  - **Inside:** Admire the elegant simplicity of the interior, with its wooden pews and altarpiece. Look for the historic church bell, which dates back to 1743.
- **Hallgrímskirkja (Hallgrímur's Church) - Sólfarið (The Sun Voyager) - Reykjavik:**
  - **History:** Though not a church, the Sun Voyager sculpture located near Hallgrímskirkja is a notable landmark in Reykjavik. Created by artist Jón Gunnar Árnason, it resembles a Viking ship and symbolizes exploration and discovery.
  - **Inside:** While there is nothing to see inside the sculpture itself, it's worth taking a stroll around it to admire its sleek and striking design.

MORE FREEBIES

Grafarvogur Sculpture Path:

Walk along the sculpture path in Grafarvogur, Reykjavik. Admire outdoor artworks created by Icelandic and international artists.

Horse Watching in Skagafjörður:

Visit Skagafjörður and enjoy watching the Icelandic horses in their natural environment. Many farms allow you to observe the horses for free.

Glymur Waterfall Hike:

Hike to Glymur, Iceland's second-highest waterfall, located in Hvalfjörður. The trail offers breathtaking views without an entrance fee.

Eyrarbakki Village:

Explore the charming village of Eyrarbakki on the south coast. Wander through its historic streets and enjoy the seaside views.

Free Samples at the Icelandic Distillery:

For a distinctive taste of Icelandic spirits without breaking the bank, head to the Icelandic Distillery in Reykjavik. The distillery often offers free tastings, allowing you to sample local drinks and appreciate the unique flavors of Icelandic beverages without the commitment of purchasing an entire bottle.

Rauðasandur (Red Sand Beach):
Discover the breathtaking beauty of Rauðasandur beach in the Westfjords, renowned for its distinctive red sand. Enjoy the stunning scenery without any entrance fees, making it an affordable yet captivating natural attraction to explore in Iceland.

Not free by awesome: Geothermal Bread Baking - $20.

Discover the enchanting hot springs in Hveragerði, where you can engage in an exceptional and budget-friendly activity – baking bread using the natural geothermal heat. This hands-on experience allows you to witness the power of Iceland's geothermal energy while enjoying a unique culinary adventure.

What you need to know before visiting Iceland

Weather and Seasons:

Iceland's weather can be unpredictable, with rain, wind, and sudden changes. Summers boast long daylight hours, while winters experience limited daylight and cold, snowy conditions.

Clothing:

Pack layers, waterproof clothing, and sturdy shoes for diverse weather conditions. In winter, bring warm clothing, including a good jacket, hat, gloves, and insulated boots.

Currency:

The official currency is the Icelandic króna (ISK). Credit and debit cards are widely accepted, but carrying some cash for smaller establishments is advisable.

Language:

Icelandic is the official language, but English is widely spoken. Learning a few basic Icelandic phrases can be appreciated by locals.

Safety:

Iceland is known for being one of the safest countries globally. However, exercise caution, especially when exploring remote areas without data.

Driving and Transportation:

Renting a car is an excellent way to explore, but be aware of challenging driving conditions, especially in winter. Public transportation is limited outside Reykjavik, so plan routes and transportation in advance.

Natural Wonders:

Respect nature and follow Leave No Trace principles. Stay on paths, avoid disturbing wildlife, and be cautious near natural attractions.

Entry Requirements:

Check visa requirements based on your nationality and ensure your passport is valid for at least six months beyond your planned departure date.

Hot Springs and Swimming Pools

When visiting hot springs in Iceland, observe local etiquette by showering before entering without swimwear to maintain cleanliness. Refrain from using soaps or shampoos to preserve water quality and environmental integrity. Keep noise levels low, avoid disruptive activities, and respect others' personal space to create a tranquil atmosphere. Follow posted rules, be considerate of time limits during peak hours, and be mindful of the unique ecosystems surrounding the hot springs. By embracing these practices, you not only contribute to the preservation of Iceland's natural beauty but also ensure a respectful and enjoyable experience for all hot spring visitors.

Emergency Services:

The emergency number in Iceland is 112. Familiarize yourself with local emergency services and healthcare facilities, especially in remote areas.

Wi-Fi and Connectivity:

Urban areas have good internet connectivity, but remote regions may not. Purchase a local SIM card for continuous data access.

Time Zone:

Iceland is in the Greenwich Mean Time (GMT) zone but follows GMT+0 during daylight saving time.

Cultural Respect:

Familiarize yourself with Icelandic customs and traditions. Respect local communities, and ask for permission before photographing individuals.

Plan Ahead:
Iceland's popularity has surged, so plan and book accommodations and tours well in advance, especially during peak seasons. It is best to pack a sheet. Similar to other Scandinavian nations, in Iceland, several hostels may impose an additional charge for the provision of bed sheets.

Medical services:

Tourists in Iceland can access medical services through various channels. In case of an emergency, dial 112 to connect with emergency services, including medical assistance. Major cities and towns have hospitals and health clinics where tourists can seek urgent medical care. Pharmacies are widespread, providing over-the-counter medications and advice. Private medical clinics offer services to residents and tourists, and having comprehensive travel insurance is advisable for reimbursement of medical expenses. Telemedicine services may be available for remote consultations. Tour operators and accommodations can provide information about nearby medical facilities, and carrying the European Health Insurance Card (EHIC) is recommended for citizens of EEA countries. Staying informed about the local healthcare system and any travel advisories is essential for a safe and secure visit to Iceland.

How to Enjoy ALLOCATING Money in Iceland

'Money's greatest intrinsic value—and this can't be overstated—is its ability to give you control over your time.' - Morgan Housel

Notice I have titled the chapter how to enjoy allocating money in Iceland. I'll use saving and allocating interchangeably in the book, but since most people associate saving to feel like a turtleneck, that's too tight, I've chosen to use wealth language. Rich people don't save. They allocate. What's the difference? Saving can feel like something you don't want or wish to do and allocating has your personal will attached to it.

And on that note, it would be helpful if you considered removing the following words and phrase from your vocabulary for planning and enjoying your Iceland trip:

- Wish

- Want

- Maybe someday

These words are part of poverty language. Language is a dominant source of creation. Use it to your advantage. You don't have to wish, want or say maybe someday to Iceland. You can enjoy the same things millionaires enjoy in Iceland without the huge spend.

'People don't like to be sold-but they love to buy.' - Jeffrey Gitomer.

Every good salesperson who understands the quote above places obstacles in the way of their clients' buying. Companies create waiting lists, restaurants pay people to queue outside in order to create demand. People reason if something is so in demand, it must be worth having but that's often just marketing. Take this sales maxim 'People don't like to be sold-but they love to buy and flip it on its head to allocate your money in Iceland on things YOU desire. You love to spend and hate to be sold. That means when something comes your way, it's not 'I can't afford it,' it's 'I don't want it' or maybe 'I don't want it right now'.

Saving money doesn't mean never buying a latte, never taking a taxi, never taking vacations (of course, you bought this book). Only you get to decide on how you spend and on what. Not an advice columnist who thinks you can buy a house if you never eat avocado toast again.

I love what Kate Northrup says about affording something: "If you really wanted it you would figure out a way to get it. If it were that VALUABLE to you, you would make it happen."

I believe if you master the art of allocating money to bargains, it can feel even better than spending it! Bold claim, I know. But here's the truth: Money gives you freedom and options. The more you keep in your account and or invested the more freedom and options you'll have. The principal reason you should save and allocate money is TO BE FREE! Remember, a trip's main purpose is relaxation, rest and enjoyment, aka to feel free.

When you talk to most people about saving money on vacation. They grimace. How awful they proclaim not to go wild on your vacation. If you can't get into a ton of debt enjoying your once-in-a-lifetime vacation, when can you?

When you spend money 'theres's a sudden rush of dopamine which vanishes once the transaction is complete. What happens in the brain when you save money? It increases feelings of security and peace. You don't need to stress life's uncertainties. And having a greater sense of peace can actually help you save more money.' Stressed out people make impulsive financial choices, calm people don't.'

The secret to enjoying saving money on vacation is very simple: never save money from a position of lack. Don't think 'I wish I could afford that'. Choose not to be marketed to. Choose not to consume at a price others set. Don't save money from the flawed premise you don't have enough. Don't waste your time living in the box that society has created, which says saving money on vacation means sacrifice. It doesn't.

Traveling to Iceland can be an expensive endeavor if you don't approach it with a plan, but you have this book which is packed with tips. The biggest other asset is your perspective.

Winning the Vacation Game

The inspiration for these books struck me during a Vipassana meditation retreat. As I contemplated the excitement that precedes a vacation, I couldn't help but wish that we could all carry that same sense of anticipation in our daily lives. It was from this introspection that the concept of indulging in luxurious trips on a budget was born. The driving force behind this idea has always been the prevalence of disregarded inequalities.

A report from the Pew Charitable Trusts unveiled a stark reality: only about 4% of individuals born into the lowest income quintile, the bottom 20%, in the United States manage to ascend to the top income quintile during their lifetime. This trend is mirrored in many parts of Europe, underscoring the immense hurdles faced by those from disadvantaged backgrounds, including myself, in their pursuit of financial security.

To compound this, a comprehensive study conducted by researchers at Stanford University and published in the Journal of Personality and Social Psychology illuminated a compelling connection between career choices, personal fulfillment, and income. It revealed that individuals who prioritize intrinsic factors like passion often find themselves with lower average incomes, highlighting the intricate dynamics at play in the pursuit of one's dreams. Either you're in a low-income career, believing you can't afford to travel, or you're earning well but desperately need a vacation due to your work being mediocre at best. Personally, I believe it's better to do what you love and take time to plan a luxury trip on a budget. Of course, that, in itself, is a luxurious choice not all of us have. I haven't even mentioned Income, education, and systemic inequalities that can lock restrict travel opportunities for many.

Despite these challenging realities, I firmly believe that every individual can have their dream getaway. I am committed to providing practical insights and strategies that empower individuals to turn their dream vacations into a tangible reality without breaking the bank.

Currency Reference

1,000 Icelandic Króna (ISK) is approximately:

- 7.89 USD (United States Dollar)
- 6.69 EUR (Euro)
- 5.70 GBP (British Pound Sterling)

- $10 USD = approximately 1,285 ISK
- $20 USD = approximately 2,570 ISK
- $50 USD = approximately 6,425 ISK
- $100 USD = approximately 12,850 ISK

- £10 GBP = approximately 1,418 ISK
- £20 GBP = approximately 2,836 ISK
- £50 GBP = approximately 7,091 ISK
- £100 GBP = approximately 14,183 ISK

- €10 EUR = approximately 1,061 ISK
- €20 EUR = approximately 2,121 ISK
- €50 EUR = approximately 5,303 ISK
- €100 EUR = approximately 10,606 ISK

How to feel RICH in Iceland

You don't need millions in your bank to **feel rich**. Feeling rich feels different to every person."Researchers have pooled data on the relationship between money and emotions from more than 1.6 million people across 162 countries and found that **wealthier people feel more positive "self-regard emotions" such as confidence, pride and determination."**

Here are things to see, do and taste in Iceland, that will have you overflowing with gratitude for your luxury trip to Iceland.

- Achieving a Michelin Star rating is the most coveted accolade for restaurants but those that obtain a Michelin Star are synonymous with high cost, but in Iceland there is Dill which offers a reasonably priced Michelin Star lunch menu but the Chef's Choice" option at Matarkjallarinn is our pick. It is a restaurant located in the heart of Reykjavik. While it may not have a traditional tasting menu, it offers a "Chef's Choice" option, which is a set menu featuring a selection of dishes chosen by the chef. This can be a more budget-friendly way to experience a variety of flavors.. If fine dining isn't your thing, don't worry further on in the guide you will find a range of delicious cheap eats in Iceland that deserve a Michelin-Star.
- While money can't buy happiness, it can buy cake and isn't that sort of the same thing? Jokes aside, Brauð & Co has turned cakes and pastries into edible art. Visit to taste the most delicious buttery croissant in Iceland.
- While you might not be staying in a penthouse, you can still enjoy the same views. Visit rooftop bars in Iceland, like Ský Restaurant & Bar, located in CenterHotel Arnarhvoll to enjoy incredible sunset views for the price of just one drink. And if you want to continue enjoying libations, head over to Lebowski Bar for a dirt-cheap happy hour, lots of reasonably priced (and delicious) cocktails and cheap delicious snacks.

Those are just some ideas for you to know that visiting Iceland on a budget doesn't have to feel like sacrifice or constriction. Now let's get into the nuts and bolts of Iceland on the super cheap.

How to use this book

Google and TripAdvisor are your on-the-go guides while traveling, a travel guide adds the most value during the planning phase, and if you're without Wi-Fi. Always download the google map for your destination - having an offline map will make using this guide much more comfortable. For ease of use, we've set the book out the way you travel, booking your flights, arriving, how to get around, then on to the money-saving tips. The tips we ordered according to when you need to know the tip to save money, so free tours and combination tickets feature first. We prioritized the rest of the tips by how much money you can save and then by how likely it was that you could find the tip with a google search. Meaning those we think you could find alone are nearer the bottom. I hope you find this layout useful. If you have any ideas about making Super Cheap Insider Guides easier to use, please email me philgattang@gmail.com

A quick note on How We Source Super Cheap Tips
We focus entirely on finding the best bargains. We give each of our collaborators $2,000 to hunt down never-before-seen deals. The type you either only know if you're local or by on the ground research. We spend zero on marketing and a little on designing an excellent cover. We do this yearly, which means we just keep finding more amazing ways for you to have the same experience for less.

Now let's get started with juicing the most pleasure from your trip to Iceland with the least possible money!

Planning your trip

When to visit

Here's a chart outlining the pros and cons of visiting Iceland for every month of the year:

Month	Pros	Cons
January	- Chance to see Northern Lights.	- Short daylight hours. Cold temperatures.
	- Low tourist crowds.	- Limited outdoor activities.
February	- Northern Lights.	- Cold temperatures.
	- Winter activities like ice caves.	- Short days.
March	- Northern Lights.	- Winter weather persists.
	- Increasing daylight hours.	- Ice and snow may limit travel in some areas.
April	- Longer days.	- Lingering winter weather.
	- Emerging spring landscapes.	- Limited greenery.
May	- Warmer temperatures.	- Melting snow may cause muddy conditions.
	- More accessible roads.	- Some attractions may not be fully open.
June	- Midnight Sun.	- Crowds start increasing.
	- Pleasant weather for outdoor activities.	- Accommodation prices rise.
July	- Midnight Sun.	- Peak tourist season.
	- Warm temperatures.	- Higher prices for tours and accommodations.
August	- Midnight Sun.	- Peak tourist season.
	- Wildflowers in bloom.	- Crowded attractions.
September	- Mild temperatures.	- Crowds decrease.
	- Autumn colors begin.	- Some attractions may close.
October	- Chance to see Northern Lights.	- Shorter days.
	- Fewer tourists.	- Colder temperatures.
November	- Northern Lights.	- Shorter days.
	- Fewer tourists.	- Winter weather begins.
December	- Chance to see Northern Lights.	- Short daylight hours. Cold temperatures.
	- Festive atmosphere.	- Limited outdoor activities. Snow and ice.

TOP PLANNING TIPS

1. Visit During the Off-Season:

- Consider traveling during the shoulder seasons (spring and autumn) to take advantage of lower accommodation prices and fewer crowds. Winter is also an option for those interested in the Northern Lights.

2. Book Accommodations in Advance:

- Secure your accommodations well in advance to access better rates. Look for guesthouses, hostels, or budget hotels, and consider options outside major tourist areas.

3. Cook Your Own Meals:

- Save on dining expenses by buying groceries from local supermarkets and cooking your own meals. Many accommodations, especially guesthouses and hostels, provide kitchen facilities.

4. BYOB (Bring Your Own Booze):

- Alcohol is expensive in Iceland. Purchase duty-free alcohol at the airport upon arrival and enjoy drinks in your accommodation before heading out.

5. Use Public Transportation:

- Opt for public transportation, such as buses, instead of renting a car for every day of your trip. It can be more cost-effective, especially if you're staying within Reykjavik.

6. Rent a Campervan:

- If you plan to explore beyond Reykjavik, consider renting a campervan. It provides both accommodation and transportation, saving on hotel costs.

7. Consider camping - it's free!

In Iceland, there are several rental companies where you can rent camping equipment for your outdoor adventures. Here are some popular options:

- Iceland Camping Equipment Rental: This company offers a wide range of camping gear, including tents, sleeping bags, sleeping mats, cooking equipment, and more. They have pickup locations in Reykjavik and Akureyri, and you can also arrange delivery to your accommodation.
- Iceland Camping Gear Rental: With locations in Reykjavik and Keflavik, this rental company provides camping equipment for individuals, families, and groups. Their inventory includes tents, sleeping bags, cooking gear, and accessories like camping chairs and tables.
- Go Campers: Specializing in camper van rentals, Go Campers also offers camping equipment for those who prefer tent camping. They provide tents, sleeping bags, and other essentials as optional add-ons to their camper van rentals.

The season in Iceland and what to pack for each

Iceland experiences four distinct seasons, each offering a unique set of conditions and attractions. Here's a guide on what to pack for each season:

1. Spring (March to May):

- **Weather:** Spring in Iceland is a transitional period. Days become longer, temperatures rise, and nature begins to bloom.
  - **What to Pack:**
  - Light layers, including a waterproof jacket and a mix of long-sleeved shirts and T-shirts.
  - Comfortable walking shoes for exploring.
  - Sunglasses and sunscreen, as daylight hours increase.
  - Hat and gloves, especially for early spring.

2. Summer (June to August):

- **Weather:** Summer is the peak tourist season with long days, milder temperatures, and lush landscapes.
  - **What to Pack:**
  - Light layers, including a mix of T-shirts, long-sleeved shirts, and a waterproof jacket.
  - Comfortable walking shoes for exploring.
  - Sunglasses, sunscreen, and a hat for protection against the Midnight Sun.
  - Swimsuit for hot spring and thermal pool visits.
  - Insect repellent for rural areas.

3. Autumn (September to November):

- **Weather:** Autumn marks the beginning of colder temperatures and shorter days. Fall foliage adds a touch of color to the landscapes.
  - **What to Pack:**
  - Medium-weight layers, including sweaters and a waterproof jacket.
  - Sturdy and comfortable walking shoes.
  - Hat, gloves, and a scarf for cooler temperatures.
  - Camera for capturing the autumn colors.

4. Winter (December to February):

- **Weather:** Winter brings cold temperatures, snow, and limited daylight hours. It's an excellent time for witnessing the Northern Lights.
  - **What to Pack:**
  - Heavyweight, insulated layers, including a warm coat, thermal underwear, and a waterproof jacket.
  - Insulated and waterproof boots suitable for snow.
  - Hat, gloves, and a scarf for protection against the cold.
  - Hand and foot warmers for extra warmth.
  - Camera and tripod for capturing the Northern Lights.

General Packing Tips:

- **All Seasons:**
  - Travel adapter for Icelandic power outlets.
  - Portable power bank for electronic devices.
  - Waterproof backpack or daypack for outdoor excursions.
  - Travel insurance that covers potential medical expenses and unexpected events.
- **Year-Round:**
  - Consider packing a reusable water bottle, as tap water in Iceland is safe to drink.
  - Depending on your preferences, a good pair of binoculars for bird watching or scenic views.
  - Personal toiletries and any necessary medications.

What's On?

Iceland offers a plethora of natural wonders and cultural events throughout the year that tourists can enjoy for free. Here's a month-by-month breakdown:

January:

- **Northern Lights:** The winter months provide excellent opportunities to witness the mesmerizing Northern Lights, or Aurora Borealis. Head away from city lights for the best view.

February:

- **Winter Festivals:** Attend local winter festivals, often featuring music, art, and traditional Icelandic celebrations.

March:

- **Harpa Concert Hall Lights:** Witness the stunning illuminations on Harpa Concert Hall in Reykjavik during the city's dark winter nights.

April:

- **Birdwatching:** April marks the beginning of the birdwatching season, especially in locations like Lake Mývatn, where various bird species start nesting.

May:

- **Museum Night:** Reykjavik hosts a "Museum Night" where museums and galleries offer free entry and extended hours.

June:

- **National Independence Day:** Celebrate Iceland's National Day on June 17th with parades, concerts, and various public events.

July:

- **Reykjavik Culture Night:** Enjoy a day of free events, concerts, and cultural activities throughout Reykjavik.

August:

- **Outdoor Concerts:** Attend outdoor music festivals and concerts, often held in various locations around the country during the summer.

September:

- **Northern Lights Return:** As the nights grow darker, the Northern Lights become visible again.

October:

- **Culture Days:** Participate in various cultural events and activities during Iceland's Culture Days.

November:

- **Airwaves Music Festival:** Attend the Iceland Airwaves Music Festival, featuring both local and international artists.

December:

- **Christmas Markets:** Explore Christmas markets in Reykjavik and other towns, often offering a festive atmosphere and sometimes free concerts.

Free festivals

Name of Festival	Description	Date	Location
Reykjavik Arts Festival	A celebration of visual arts, music, dance, and theater featuring both local and international artists.	May - June	Reykjavik and various locations
Secret Solstice	An annual music festival showcasing a mix of Icelandic and international artists, set against the backdrop of the	June	Laugardalur Valley, Reykjavik
Independence Day (Þjóðhátíðardagurinn)	Celebrating Iceland's independence with various events, including parades, concerts, and traditional activities.	June 17	Nationwide, with significant
Reykjavik Pride	A vibrant LGBTQ+ festival featuring a parade, concerts, and various events promoting equality and diversity.	August	Reykjavik
Reykjavik International Film Festival (RIFF)	Showcasing a diverse selection of international and Icelandic films, with screenings, discussions, and events.	September	Reykjavik
Iceland Airwaves	A music festival showcasing a wide range of genres, from Icelandic indie bands to well-known international acts.	November	Venues across Reykjavik

How to enjoy the major attractions in Iceland with money saving tips or free alternatives

Iceland's major attractions are breathtaking, and while some may come with entrance fees, there are often money-saving tips and free alternatives to help you make the most of your visit. Here's a guide to enjoying Iceland's major attractions on a budget:

1. Golden Circle:

- **Money-Saving Tip:** Rent a car or join a budget-friendly tour to explore the Golden Circle independently.
- **Free Alternative:** Visit Þingvellir National Park, the Geysir geothermal area, and Gullfoss waterfall, all are free to explore.

2. Blue Lagoon:

- **Money-Saving Tip:** Visit the Blue Lagoon during off-peak hours for lower entrance fees. Book tickets well in advance for online discounts.
- **Free Alternative:** Explore the Secret Lagoon or natural hot springs in the Icelandic wilderness for a more budget-friendly geothermal experience.

3. Jökulsárlón Glacier Lagoon:

- **Money-Saving Tip:** Explore the area independently by renting a car instead of booking an expensive tour.
- **Free Alternative:** While not the same as Jökulsárlón, you can see icebergs at Fjallsárlón Glacier Lagoon for free.

4. Skógafoss and Seljalandsfoss Waterfalls:

- **Money-Saving Tip:** Visit these waterfalls as part of a self-driving tour or on a budget-friendly group tour.
- **Free Alternative:** Discover smaller, less-known waterfalls scattered across the Icelandic countryside, often without entrance fees.

5. Vatnajökull National Park:

- **Money-Saving Tip:** Join a more affordable glacier hike or ice cave tour offered by local operators.
- **Free Alternative:** Explore the park's stunning landscapes, including Svartifoss waterfall and Skaftafell, without booking expensive tours.

6. Landmannalaugar:

- **Money-Saving Tip:** Consider a budget-friendly bus tour or self-drive to Landmannalaugar.
- **Free Alternative:** Hike the Laugavegur Trail starting from Þórsmörk to Landmannalaugar for stunning landscapes at no cost.

7. Reykjavik City:

- **Money-Saving Tip:** Walk or use public transportation instead of taxis. Use the Reykjavik City Card for discounted entry to museums and free bus travel.

- **Free Alternative:** Explore the city's street art, stroll around the harbor, and visit Hallgrímskirkja church for free panoramic views.

8. Akureyri and North Iceland:

- **Money-Saving Tip:** Stay in budget accommodations, and explore the area with a rental car.
- **Free Alternative:** Enjoy the Botanical Gardens in Akureyri and visit Goðafoss waterfall without spending on organized tours.

9. Snæfellsnes Peninsula:

- **Money-Saving Tip:** Self-drive or join a budget-friendly bus tour to explore the peninsula.
- **Free Alternative:** Discover the charming villages, black sand beaches, and Snæfellsjökull National Park without joining expensive guided excursions.

Booking Flights

How to Find Heavily Discounted Private Jet Flights to or from Iceland

If you're dreaming of travelling to Iceland on a private jet you can accomplish your dream for a 10th of the cost.

Empty leg flights, also known as empty leg charters or deadhead flights, are flights operated by private jet companies that do not have any passengers on board. These flights occur when a private jet is chartered for a one-way trip, but the jet needs to return to its base or another location without passengers.

Rather than flying empty, private jet companies may offer these empty leg flights for a reduced price to travelers who are flexible and able to fly on short notice. Because the flight is already scheduled and paid for by the original charter, private jet companies are willing to offer these flights at a discounted rate in order to recoup some of the cost.

Empty leg flights can be a cost-effective way to experience the luxury and convenience of private jet travel.

There are several websites that offer empty leg flights for booking. Here are a few:

JetSuiteX: This website offers discounted, last-minute flights on private jets, including empty leg flights.

PrivateFly: This website allows you to search for empty leg flights by location or date. You can also request a quote for a custom flight if you have specific needs.

Victor: This website offers a variety of private jet services, including empty leg flights.

Sky500: This website offers a variety of private jet services, including empty leg flights.

Air Charter Service: This website allows you to search for empty leg flights by location or date. You can also request a quote for a custom flight if you have specific needs.

Keep in mind that empty leg flights are often available at short notice, so it's a good idea to be flexible with your travel plans if you're looking for a deal. It's also important to do your research and read reviews before booking a flight with any company.

RECAP: To book an empty leg flight in Iceland, follow these steps:

1. Research and identify private jet companies and or brokers that offer empty leg flights departing from Iceland. You can use the websites mentioned earlier, such as JetSuiteX, PrivateFly, Victor, Sky500, or Air Charter Service, to search for available flights.

2. Check the availability and pricing of empty leg flights that match your travel dates and destination. Empty leg flights are often available at short notice.

3. Contact the private jet company or broker to inquire about booking the empty leg flight. Be sure to provide your travel details, including your preferred departure and arrival times, number of passengers, and any special requests.

4. Confirm your booking and make payment. Private jet companies and brokers typically require full payment upfront, so be prepared to pay for the flight in advance.

5. Arrive at the airport at least 30 minutes before the scheduled departure time.

6. Check in at the private jet terminal and go through any necessary security checks. Unlike commercial airlines, there is typically no long queue or security checks for private jet flights.

7. Board the private jet and settle into your seat. You will have plenty of space to stretch out and relax, as well as access to amenities such as Wi-Fi, entertainment systems, and refreshments.

How to Find CHEAP FIRST-CLASS Flights to Iceland

Upgrade at the airport

Airlines are extremely reluctant to advertise price drops in first or business class tickets so the best way to secure them is actually at the airport when airlines have no choice but to decrease prices dramatically because otherwise they lose money. Ask about upgrading to business or first-class when you check-in. If you check-in online look around the airport for your airlines branded bidding system.

Use Air-miles

When it comes to accruing air-miles for American citizens **Chase Sapphire Reserve card** ranks top. If you put everything on there and pay it off immediately you will end up getting free flights all the time, aside from taxes.

Get 2-3 chase cards with sign up bonuses, you'll have 200k points in no time and can book with points on multiple airlines when transferring your points to them.

Please note, this is only applicable to those living in the USA. In the Bonus Section we have detailed the best air-mile credit cards for those living in other countries.

How many miles does it take to fly first class?

New York City to Iceland could require anywhere from 70,000 to 120,000 frequent flyer miles, depending on the airline and the time of year you plan to travel.

How to Fly Business Class to Iceland cheaply

TAP Air Portugal is a popular airline that operates flights from New York City to Iceland with the cheapest business class options. In low season this route typically started at around $1,000-$1,500 per person for a round-trip ticket.

The average cost for a round-trip flight from New York City to Iceland typically ranged from around $400 to $1200 for an economy seat, so if travelling business class is important to you, TAP Air Portugal is likely to be the best bang for your buck.

To find the best deals on business class flights to Iceland, follow these steps:

1. Use travel search engines: Start by searching for flights on popular travel search engines like Google Flights, Kayak, or Skyscanner. These sites allow you to compare prices from different airlines and book the cheapest available business option.
2. Sign up for airline newsletters: Airlines often send out exclusive deals and promotions to their email subscribers. Sign up for TAP Air Portugal's newsletter to receive notifications about special offers and discounts on business class flights.
3. Book in advance: Booking your flight well in advance can help you secure a better deal on business class tickets. Aim to book your flight at least two to three months before your travel date.

How to ALWAYS Find Super Cheap Flights to Iceland

If you're just interested in finding the cheapest flight to Iceland here is here to do it!

Luck is just an illusion.

Anyone can find incredible flight deals. If you can be flexible you can save huge amounts of money. In fact, the biggest tip I can give you for finding incredible flight deals is simple: find a flexible job. Don't despair if you can't do that theres still a lot you can do.

Book your flight to Iceland on a Tuesday or Wednesday

Tuesdays and Wednesdays are the cheapest days of the week to fly. You can take a flight to Iceland on a Tuesday or Wednesday for less than half the price you'd pay on a Thursday Friday, Saturday, Sunday or Monday.

Start with Google Flights (but NEVER book through them)

I conduct upwards of 50 flight searches a day for readers. I use google flights first when looking for flights. I put specific departure but broad destination (e.g Europe) and usually find amazing deals.

The great thing about Google Flights is you can search by class. You can pick a specific destination and it will tell you which time is cheapest in which class. Or you can put in dates and you can see which area is cheapest to travel to.

But be aware Google flights does not show the cheapest prices among the flight search engines but it does offer several advantages

1. You can see the cheapest dates for the next 8 weeks. Other search engines will blackout over 70% of the prices.
2. You can put in multiple airports to fly from. Just use a common to separate in the from input.
3. If you're flexible on where you're going Google flights can show you the cheapest destinations.
4. You can set-up price tracking, where Google will email you when prices rise or decline.

Once you have established the cheapest dates to fly go over to skyscanner.net and put those dates in. You will find sky scanner offers the cheapest flights.

Get Alerts when Prices to Iceland are Lowest

Google also has a nice feature which allows you to set up an alert to email you when prices to your destination are at their lowest. So if you don't have fixed dates this feature can save you a fortune.

Baggage add-ons

It may be cheaper and more convenient to send your luggage separately with a service like sendmybag.com Often the luggage sending fee is cheaper than what the airlines charge to check baggage. Visit Lugless.com or luggagefree.com in addition to sendmybag.com for a quotation.

Loading times

Anyone who has attempted to find a cheap flight will know the pain of excruciating long loading times. If you encounter this issue use google flights to find the cheapest dates and then go to skyscanner.net for the lowest price.

Always try to book direct with the airline

Once you have found the cheapest flight go direct to the airlines booking page. This is advantageous because if you need to change your flights or arrange a refund, its much easier to do so, than via a third party booking agent.

That said, sometimes the third party bookers offer cheaper deals than the airline, so you need to make the decision based on how likely you think it is that disruption will impede you making those flights.

More Fight Tricks and Tips

www.secretflying.com/usa-deals offers a range of deals from the USA and other countries. For example you can pick-up a round trip flight non-stop from from the east coast to johannesburg for $350 return on this site

Scott's cheap flights, you can select your home airport and get emails on deals but you pay for an annual subscription. A free workaround is to download Hopper and set search alerts for trips/price drops.

Premium service of Scott's cheap flights.
They sometime have discounted business and first class but in my experience they are few and far between.

JGOOT.com has 5 times as many choices as Scott's cheap flights.

kiwi.com allows you to be able to do radius searches so you can find cheaper flights to general areas.

Finding Error Fares

Travel Pirates (www.travelpirates.com) is a gold-mine for finding error deals. Subscribe to their newsletter. I recently found a reader an airfare from Montreal-Brazil for a $200 round trip (mistake fare!). Of course these error fares are always certain dates, but if you can be flexible you can save a lot of money.

Things you can do that might reduce the fare to Iceland:

- Use a VPN (if the booker knows you booked one-way, the return fare will go up)
- Buy your ticket in a different currency

If all else fails...

If you can't find a cheap flight for your dates I can find one for you. I do not charge for this nor do I send affiliate links. I'll send you a screenshot of the best options I find as airlines attach cookies to flight links. To use this free service please review this guide and send me a screenshot of your review - with your flight hacking request. I aim to reply to you within 12 hours. If it's an urgent request mark the email URGENT in the subject line and I will endeavour to reply ASAP.

A tip for coping with Jet-lag

Jetlag is primarily caused by disruptions to the body's circadian rhythm, which is the internal "biological clock" that regulates many of the body's processes, including sleep-wake cycles. When you travel across multiple time zones, your body's clock is disrupted, leading to symptoms like fatigue, insomnia, and stomach problems.

Eating on your travel destination's time before you travel can help to adjust your body's clock before you arrive, which can help to mitigate the effects of jetlag. This means that if you're traveling to a destination that is several hours ahead of your current time zone, you should try to eat meals at the appropriate times for your destination a few days before you leave. For example, if you're traveling from New York to Iceland, which is seven hours ahead, you could start eating dinner at 9pm EST (which is 3am Iceland time) a few days before your trip.

By adjusting your eating schedule before you travel, you can help to shift your body's clock closer to the destination's time zone, which can make it easier to adjust to the new schedule once you arrive.

Accommodation

Your two biggest expenses when travelling to Iceland are accommodation and food. This section is intended to help you cut these costs dramatically without compromising on those luxury feels:

How to Book a Five-star Hotel consistently on the Cheap in Iceland

The cheapest four and five-star hotel deals are available when you 'blind book'. Blind booking is a type of discounted hotel booking where the guest doesn't know the name of the hotel until after they've booked and paid for the reservation. This allows hotels to offer lower prices without damaging their brand image or cannibalizing their full-price bookings.

Here are some of the best platforms for blind booking a hotel in Iceland:

1. Hotwire - This website offers discounted hotel rates for blind booking. You can choose the star rating, neighborhood, and amenities you want, but the actual hotel name will not be revealed until after you've booked.
2. Priceline - Once you've made the reservation, the hotel name and location will be revealed.
3. Secret Escapes - This website offers luxury hotel deals at discounted rates. You can choose the type of hotel you want and the general location, but the hotel name and exact location will be revealed after you book.
4. Lastminute.com - You can select the star rating and general location, but the hotel name and exact location will be revealed after booking. Using the Top Secret hotels you can find a four star hotel from $60 a night in Iceland - consistently!Most of the hotels featured are in the Grange Group. If in doubt, simply copy and paste the description into Google to find the name before booking.

Cheap hotel chains in Iceland

Iceland is known for having a higher cost of living, and accommodation prices can reflect that. However, there are some hotel chains and budget-friendly options that travelers may consider. Please note that the availability of these options and their affordability may vary depending on the time of year, demand, and other factors. Here are a few hotel chains and budget options in Iceland:

- **Fosshotel:**
    - Fosshotel is a chain of hotels in Iceland with various locations, including Reykjavik and other cities. They offer a range of accommodations, and prices can vary depending on the location and room type.
- **Icelandair Hotels:**
    - Icelandair Hotels is another chain with multiple properties across Iceland. They provide a variety of accommodations, including budget-friendly options.

Unique cheap accommodation

Finding unique and budget-friendly accommodation options in Iceland can add an extra layer of adventure to your trip. Here are some ideas for unique and potentially more affordable places to stay:

- **Farm Stays:**
  - Experience rural life by staying on a farm. Some farmers in Iceland open their homes to guests, providing a unique opportunity to connect with locals and enjoy the countryside.
  - Platforms: Check platforms like Airbnb for farm stay options.
  - Starting Prices: Farm stays can range from $50 to $100 USD per night, depending on the location and amenities.
- **Camping:**
  - Wild camping is FREE!
  - Iceland has numerous campsites, especially during the summer months. Camping is a budget-friendly option, and you'll have the chance to sleep amidst Iceland's stunning landscapes.
  - Platforms: Explore camping options on websites like Camping Iceland.
  - Starting Prices: Camping fees typically range from $10 to $20 USD per person per night.
- **Mountain Huts:**
  - Ideal for hiking or trekking enthusiasts, mountain huts offer basic accommodations in the highlands. They are perfect for those exploring Iceland's interior on foot.
  - Platforms: Check with organizations like the Icelandic Touring Association (Ferðafélag Íslands) for mountain hut bookings.
  - Starting Prices: Mountain hut stays range from $20 to $40 USD per person per night.
- **Cabins and Cottages:**
  - Look for cabins or cottages for rent, especially if you're willing to stay a bit outside of popular tourist areas. You can find more budget-friendly options with a bit of research.
  - Platforms: Search for cabin rentals on websites like Booking.com or VRBO.
  - Starting Prices: Cabin rentals can vary widely but typically start around $80 to $150 USD per night.
- **Unique Airbnb Properties:**
  - Explore Airbnb for unique and affordable stays. Iceland offers converted barns, tiny houses, and other unconventional accommodations that can offer a memorable experience.
  - Platform: Browse listings on Airbnb.
  - Starting Prices: Prices vary depending on the property, but you can find options starting from $50 to $100 USD per night.
- **Icelandic Summerhouses:**
  - Many Icelanders have summerhouses, and some are available for rent. These cozy cottages are often located in picturesque settings and can provide a peaceful retreat.

- Platforms: Look for summerhouse rentals on websites like Bungalo or Visit Iceland.
- Starting Prices: Summerhouse rentals can start from $100 to $200 USD per night, depending on the location and amenities.
- Universities renting out dorms. One university in Iceland that has been known to offer dormitory accommodations to the public is the University of Iceland (Háskóli Íslands). During the summer months, when students are on break, the university may make dormitory rooms available for short-term rentals.

Camping

Wild camping is allowed in many areas of Iceland, but there are important considerations and regulations to keep in mind.

Wild camping in Iceland can be an incredible experience, but it's essential to follow Leave No Trace principles and respect the environment. Here's a general guide:

1. Legalities:

- Wild camping is legal in Iceland, but you must stay at least 150 meters away from homes or other structures.
- National parks and private land require permission; check local regulations.

2. Choosing Campsites:

- Opt for durable surfaces like gravel or sand to minimize environmental impact.
- Respect nature; avoid disturbing wildlife and plant life.

4. Essentials to Pack:

- Sturdy tent designed for windy conditions.
- Warm sleeping bag suitable for Icelandic weather.
- Portable stove and cookware.
- Adequate food and water supplies.
- Warm clothing and waterproof gear.
- Maps, compass, and a GPS device.
- Portable power bank for electronics.
- First aid kit.

You can bring these, or rent insider Iceland.

5. Water Sources:

- Iceland has numerous freshwater sources, but carry a water purification system or boil water to be safe.

6. Waste Management:

- Pack out all waste, including toilet paper. Leave no trace.
- Use designated toilets where available or dig a small hole at least 30 cm deep for human waste.

7. Weather Considerations:

- Icelandic weather is unpredictable; be prepared for rain, wind, and sudden temperature changes.

8. Wildlife Awareness:

- Be cautious of wildlife, especially birds nesting on the ground.

9. Cultural Considerations:

- Respect local customs and traditions.
- Ask for permission if camping on private land.

10. Emergency Preparedness:

- Inform someone of your plans.
- Carry a fully charged phone and know emergency numbers.

11. Road Conditions:

- Ensure your vehicle (if using one) is suitable for F-roads if you plan to venture into the highlands.

Always check for updated information as regulations and conditions can change. Enjoy the stunning landscapes responsibly!

Popular places to wild camp in Iceland

1. Landmannalaugar:

- *Advantages:* Striking landscapes with colorful rhyolite mountains and natural hot springs. Popular starting point for hiking trails like Laugavegur.
- *Disadvantages:* Crowded during peak season, challenging access without a 4x4 vehicle.

2. Thórsmörk:

- *Advantages:* Glacial valleys, river crossings, and proximity to Eyjafjallajökull volcano. Offers hiking trails and stunning scenery.
- *Disadvantages:* Limited access without a 4x4; busy during high season.

3. Hornstrandir Nature Reserve:

- *Advantages:* Remote and pristine nature, rich in wildlife. Excellent for experienced hikers seeking solitude.
- *Disadvantages:* Inaccessible by car; requires a boat or hiking. Limited facilities.

4. Skaftafell National Park:

- *Advantages:* Glacial landscapes, waterfalls, and hiking trails, including the popular Svartifoss. Accessible by car.
- *Disadvantages:* Tourist popularity; can be crowded in peak season.

5. Vatnajökull National Park:

- *Advantages:* Largest national park, diverse landscapes with glaciers, waterfalls, and canyons. Various camping sites.
- *Disadvantages:* Some areas require a 4x4; popular spots may get crowded.

6. Seljalandsfoss:

- *Advantages:* Iconic waterfall with a camping area nearby. Accessible by car, close to the Ring Road.
- *Disadvantages:* Can be busy with tourists; limited privacy.

7. Jökulsárlón Glacier Lagoon:

- *Advantages:* Unique glacial lagoon setting. Easy access by car.
- *Disadvantages:* Tourist popularity; limited wild camping options directly at the lagoon.

8. Þingvellir National Park:

- *Advantages:* Historical and geological significance, part of the Golden Circle. Accessible by car.
- *Disadvantages:* Popular tourist destination; regulated camping areas.

9. East Fjords:

- *Advantages:* Scenic fjords, charming fishing villages. Some accessible by car.
- *Disadvantages:* Limited camping facilities; variable road conditions.

10. Snæfellsnes Peninsula:

- *Advantages:* Diverse landscapes, including a glacier-capped volcano. Accessible by car.
- *Disadvantages:* Popular among tourists; regulated camping areas.

Always check current regulations and conditions, and respect the fragile Icelandic environment while wild camping.

Strategies to Book Five-Star Hotels for Two-Star Prices in Iceland

Use Time

There are two ways to use time. One is to book in advance. Three months will net you the best deal, especially if your visit coincides with an event. The other is to book on the day of your stay. This is a risky move, but if executed well, you can lay your head in a five-star hotel for a 2-star fee.

Before you travel to Iceland, check for big events using a simple google search 'What's on in Iceland', if you find no big events drawing travellers, risk showing up with no accommodation booked (If there are big events on demand exceeds supply and you should avoid using this strategy).If you don't want to risk showing up with no accommodation booked, book a cheap accommodation with free-cancellation.

Before I go into demand-based pricing, take a moment to think about your risk tolerance. By risk, I am not talking about personal safety. No amount of financial savings is worth risking that. What I am talking about is being inconvenienced. Do you deal well with last-minute changes? Can you roll with the punches or do you freak out if something changes? Everyone is different and knowing yourself is the best way to plan a great trip. If you are someone that likes to have everything pre-planned using demand-based pricing to get cheap accommodation will not work for you.

Demand-based pricing

Be they an Airbnb host or hotel manager; no one wants empty rooms. Most will do anything to make some revenue because they still have the same costs to cover whether the room is occupied or not. That's why you will find many hotels drastically slashing room rates for same-day bookings.

How to book five-star hotels for a two-star price

You will not be able to find these discounts when the demand exceeds the supply. So if you're visiting during the peak season, or during an event which has drawn many travellers again don't try this.

1. On the day of your stay, visit booking.com (which offers better discounts than Kayak and agoda.com). Hotel
   Tonight individually checks for any last-minute bookings, but they take a big chunk of the action, so the better deals come from booking.com.
2. The best results come from booking between 2 pm and 4 pm when the risk of losing any revenue with no occupancy is most pronounced, so algorithms supporting hotels slash prices. This is when you can find rates that are not within the "lowest publicly visible" rate.

3. To avoid losing customers to other websites, or cheapening the image of their hotel most will only offer the super cheap rates during a two hour window from 2 pm to 4 pm. Two guests will pay 10x difference in price but it's absolutely vital to the hotel that neither knows it.

Takeaway: To get the lowest price book on the day of stay between 2 pm and 4 pm and extend your search radius to include further afield hotels with good transport connections.

There are several luxury hotels outside of Reykjavik that offer good transport connections to the city, as well as easy access to other nearby attractions. Here are a few options to consider:

> Hotel Kriunes:
> > Location: Located in the town of Hafnarfjörður, about a 15-minute drive from Reykjavik.
> > Transport: The hotel offers free parking for guests, and there are bus stops nearby with direct routes to Reykjavik city center.
> > Starting Prices: Prices start around $80 to $100 USD per night.
> Hotel Hafnarfjall:
> > Location: Situated in Borgarnes, approximately a 1-hour drive from Reykjavik.
> > Transport: The hotel provides free parking, and there are regular buses connecting Borgarnes to Reykjavik.
> > Starting Prices: Rates typically begin at $70 to $90 USD per night.
> Hotel Eldhestar:
> > Location: Located in Hveragerði, about a 40-minute drive from Reykjavik.
> > Transport: The hotel offers free parking, and there are bus services available from Hveragerði to Reykjavik.
> > Starting Prices: Prices start around $90 to $110 USD per night.
> Hotel Klettur:
> > Location: Situated in the town of Akranes, approximately a 45-minute drive from Reykjavik.
> > Transport: The hotel provides free parking, and there are bus connections available from Akranes to Reykjavik.
> > Starting Prices: Rates typically begin at $80 to $100 USD per night.
> Hotel Laxnes:
> > Location: Located in Mosfellsbær, about a 15-minute drive from Reykjavik.
> > Transport: The hotel offers free parking, and there are regular bus services connecting Mosfellsbær to Reykjavik.
> > Starting Prices: Prices start around $70 to $90 USD per night.

These are just a few examples of luxury hotels outside of Iceland's city center with good transport connections to the city and opportunities for last-minute discounts.

Priceline Hack to get a Luxury Hotel on the Cheap

Priceline.com has been around since 1997 and is an incredible site for sourcing luxury Hotels on the cheap in Iceland.

Priceline have a database of the lowest price a hotel will accept for a particular time and date. That amount changes depending on two factors:

1. Demand: More demand high prices.

2. Likelihood of lost revenue: if the room is still available at 3pm the same-day prices will plummet.

Obviously they don't want you to know the lowest price as they make more commission the higher the price you pay.

They offer two good deals to entice you to book with them in Iceland. And the good news is neither require last-minute booking (though the price will decrease the closer to the date you book).

'Firstly, 'price-breakers'. You blind book from a choice of three highly rated hotels which they name. Pricebreakers, travelers are shown three similar, highly-rated hotels, listed under a single low price.' After you book they reveal the name of the hotel.

Secondly, the 'express deals'. These are the last minute deals. You'll be able to see the name of the hotel before you book.

To find the right luxury hotel for you at a cheap price you should plug in the neighbourhoods you want to stay in, an acceptable rating (4 or 5 stars), and filter by the amenities you want.

You can also get an addition discount for your Iceland hotel by booking on their dedicated app.

How to trick travel Algorithms to get the lowest hotel price

Do not believe anyone who says changing your IP address to get cheaper hotels or flights does NOT work. If you don't believe us, download a Tor Network and search for flights and hotels to one destination using your current IP and then the tor network (a tor browser hides your IP address from algorithms. It is commonly used by hackers). You will receive different prices.

The price you see is a decision made by an algorithm that adjusts prices using data points such as past bookings, remaining capacity, average demand and the probability of selling the room or flight later at a higher price. Ifknows you've searched for the area before ip the prices high. To circumvent this, you can either use a different IP address from a cafe or airport or data from an international sim. I use a sim from Three, which provides free data in many countries around the world. When you search from a new IP address, most of the time, and particularly near booking you will get a lower price. Sometimes if your sim comes from a 'rich' country, say the UK or USA, you will see higher rates as the algorithm has learnt people from these countries pay more. The solution is to book from a local wifi connection - but a different one from the one you originally searched from.

Cheapest villages to rent airbnbs in Iceland

- **Vik:** Vik is a small village located on the southern coast of Iceland. It is known for its black sand beaches, dramatic cliffs, and the iconic Reynisfjara beach. The village is surrounded by beautiful natural landscapes, including waterfalls and glaciers. While it's a popular tourist destination, you may find more affordable options compared to larger cities.
- **Hella:** Hella is a village situated in the southern part of Iceland, offering a tranquil setting surrounded by rivers and mountains. It's conveniently located for exploring popular attractions like the Golden Circle. Accommodations in Hella may be more budget-friendly compared to larger cities like Reykjavik.
- **Höfn:** Höfn is a charming fishing village located in the southeastern part of Iceland. It's known for its seafood, stunning coastal scenery, and proximity to Vatnajökull National Park. While it's a bit remote, you might find affordable options for accommodations, and the scenery is well worth the visit.
- **Selfoss:** Selfoss is a town in southern Iceland, situated on the banks of the Ölfusá River. It serves as a gateway to the Golden Circle attractions. Selfoss has a range of accommodation options, and staying here can be more budget-friendly compared to the capital, Reykjavik.

Caution Advised

Iceland is widely a safe destination with low crime rates, offering a secure environment for travelers. However, as with any place, it's important to exercise caution and be mindful of potential hazards. While dangerous areas are relatively uncommon, there are certain situations and locations in Iceland where tourists should proceed with caution.
Coastal Areas pose potential risks, particularly during inclement weather conditions when sudden waves or unexpected weather changes can occur, presenting dangers to unwary visitors. Glacier Areas, although stunning, can be hazardous environments. It's imperative to adhere to safety guidelines and refrain from venturing onto glaciers without appropriate equipment and knowledge.

In Hot Springs and Geothermal Areas, some pools may have boiling or extremely hot water. It's essential to stick to marked paths and exercise caution to prevent accidents. Rural Roads in Winter, especially in remote areas, can be challenging to navigate due to snow and icy conditions. Travelers should check road conditions, use suitable vehicles, and drive with care.

River Crossings, particularly in the highlands, carry inherent risks. Only attempt crossings under appropriate conditions and with vehicles equipped for such terrain. Venturing into Unmarked Trails and Wilderness Areas without proper guidance, equipment, or knowledge of the terrain can be perilous. It's advisable to stick to marked trails and seek advice from locals.

Winter Driving presents its own set of challenges, including icy roads and limited daylight hours. Renting a suitable vehicle, staying informed about road conditions, and driving cautiously are essential precautions. Exploring Caves and Lava Tubes without proper equipment and guidance can be hazardous. It's crucial to always go with a guide and follow safety instructions.

How to get last-minute discounts on owner rented properties

In addition to Airbnb, you can also find owner rented rooms and apartments on www.vrbo.com or HomeAway or a host of others.

Nearly all owners renting accommodation will happily give renters a "last-minute" discount to avoid the space sitting empty, not earning a dime.

Go to Airbnb or another platform and put in today's date. Once you've found something you like start the negotiating by asking for a 25% reduction. A sample message to an Airbnb host might read:

Dear HOST NAME,

I love your apartment. It looks perfect for me. Unfortunately, I'm on a very tight budget. I hope you won't be offended, but I wanted to ask if you would be amenable to offering me a 25% discount for tonight, tomorrow and the following day? I see that you aren't booked. I can assure you, I will leave your place exactly the way I found it. I will put bed linen in the washer and ensure everything is clean for the next guest. I would be delighted to bring you a bottle of wine to thank you for any discount that you could offer.

If this sounds okay, please send me a custom offer, and I will book straight away.

YOUR NAME.

In my experience, a polite, genuine message like this, that proposes reciprocity will be successful 80% of the time. Don't ask for more than 25% off, this person still has to pay the bills and will probably say no as your stay will cost them more in bills than they make. Plus starting higher, can offend the owner and do you want to stay somewhere, where you have offended the host?

In Practice

To use either of these methods, you must travel light. Less stuff means greater mobility, everything is faster and you don't have to check-in or store luggage. If you have a lot of luggage, you're going to have fewer of these opportunities to save on accommodation. Plus travelling light benefits the planet - you're buying, consuming, and transporting less stuff.

Blind-booking

If your risk tolerance does not allow for last-minute booking, you can use blind-booking. Many hotels not wanting to cheapen their brand with known low-prices, choose to operate a blind booking policy. This is where you book without knowing the name of the hotel you're going to stay in until you've made the payment. This is also sometimes used as a marketing strategy where the hotel is seeking to recover from past issues. I've stayed in plenty of blind book hotels. As long as you choose 4 or 5 star hotels, you will find them to be clean, comfortable and safe. priceline.com, Hot Rate® Hotels and Top Secret

Hotels (operated by lastminute.com) offer the best deals.

Hotels.com Loyalty Program

This is currently the best hotel loyalty program with hotels in Iceland. The basic premise is you collect 10 nights and get 1 free. hotels.com price match, so if booking.com has a cheaper price you can get hotel.com, to match. If you intend to travel more than ten nights in a year, its a great choice to get the 11th free.

Don't let time use you.

Rigidity will cost you money. You pay the price you're willing to pay, not the amount itrequires a hotel to deliver. Therefore if you're in town for a big event, saving money on accommodation is nearly impossible so in such cases book three months ahead.

How to trick travel Algorithms to get the lowest hotel price

Do not believe anyone who says changing your IP address to get cheaper hotels or flights does NOT work. If you don't believe us, download a Tor Network and search for flights and hotels to one destination using your current IP and then the tor network (a tor browser hides your IP address from algorithms. It is commonly used by hackers). You will receive different prices.

The price you see is a decision made by an algorithm that adjusts prices using data points such as past bookings, remaining capacity, average demand and the probability of selling the room or flight later at a higher price. Ifknows you've searched for the area before ip the prices high. To circumvent this, you can either use a different IP address from a cafe or airport or data from an international sim. I use a sim from Three, which provides free data in many countries around the world. When you search from a new IP address, most of the time, and particularly near booking you will get a lower price. Sometimes if your sim comes from a 'rich' country, say the UK or USA, you will see higher rates as the algorithm has learnt people from these countries pay more. The solution is to book from a local wifi connection - but a different one from the one you originally searched from.

Saving money on Iceland Food

If you walk-in to any Iceland restaurant without planning you can easily walk out with a bill for $100 plus, so it pays to know how to eat well cheaply. Here are our tips:

Opt for Dagshérbergismatseðill

In Iceland, lunch specials are often referred to as "Dagshérbergi" or "Dagshérbergismatseðill," which translates to "Daily Special" or "Daily Special Menu." These lunch specials are commonly offered by restaurants, cafes, and eateries, particularly during the lunch hours. The concept is similar to prix-fixe menus, providing customers with a set selection of dishes at a fixed price for lunch.
When exploring dining options in Iceland, especially in urban areas like Reykjavik, you may come across signs or menu sections indicating "Dagshérbergi" or "Dagshérbergismatseðill" to highlight the daily lunch specials. These specials often include a variety of courses, including starters, main courses, and sometimes desserts, at a more affordable price compared to ordering à la carte.

In Reykjavik, you'll find a variety of restaurants and cafes offering delicious Dagshérbergi (daily specials) that cater to different tastes and preferences. Here are a few establishments known for their excellent lunch specials:

- Café Loki: Located near Hallgrimskirkja Church, Café Loki is a cozy spot offering traditional Icelandic cuisine with a modern twist. Their Dagshérbergi often includes hearty Icelandic stews, freshly baked rye bread, and homemade desserts. Enjoy a taste of local flavors at an affordable price.
- Kaffi Vinyl: A popular vegan cafe in the heart of Reykjavik, Kaffi Vinyl offers creative and flavorful plant-based dishes for lunch. Their Dagshérbergi features a variety of vegan delights, from Buddha bowls to gourmet sandwiches, showcasing the diversity of vegan cuisine.
- Laundromat Café: Combining a laundromat and a cafe, Laundromat Café is a quirky and vibrant eatery known for its laid-back atmosphere and comfort food. Their Dagshérbergi menu often includes classic dishes like burgers, salads, and pasta, served in generous portions at reasonable prices.
- Hlemmur Mathöll: As Reykjavik's first food hall, Hlemmur Mathöll is a culinary hub offering a diverse range of dining options under one roof. Several vendors within the food hall offer daily specials featuring international cuisines, street food favorites, and fusion dishes, providing something for every palate.
- Cafe Babalú: Nestled in the city center, Cafe Babalú is a charming cafe known for its cozy ambiance and delicious homemade fare. Their Dagshérbergi menu changes daily and includes hearty soups, fresh salads, and flavorful sandwiches, all prepared with locally sourced ingredients.

Happy Hour Deals:

In addition to lunch specials, some restaurants and bars offer happy hour deals on drinks and appetizers during specific hours. This is a common practice in Reykjavik, and you can find establishments that provide discounts on alcoholic beverages and snacks.

Early Bird Offers:
Some restaurants may have early bird offers for dinner, but occasionally these promotions extend to lunch hours as well. Early bird deals typically feature reduced prices for those who dine during off-peak hours.

Lunch Buffets:
Some establishments, particularly those serving international cuisine or local Icelandic dishes, may offer lunch buffets. Buffets can provide a variety of options at a fixed price, allowing you to sample different dishes.

Local Cafés and Bakeries:
Local cafés and bakeries often have more affordable options for light lunches. You can find sandwiches, soups, and baked goods at reasonable prices, making them a great choice for a quick and budget-friendly meal.

Use delivery services on the cheap.
Take advantage of local offers on food delivery services. Most platforms including Uber Eats and Just Eat offer $10 off the first order in Iceland.

The Cheapest Supermarket in Iceland

Supermarkets in the Netherlands can vary a lot in price. There are many discount supermarkets and standard grocery stores, as well as ethnic markets.Discount supermarkets in Iceland include Lidl and Aldi. They are generally located in residential neighborhoods. However, you can find them in more out-of-town areas as well.
Other supermarket chains in the Netherlands include Marqt, Deen, and Hoogvliet. Ethnic grocery stores offer a wider selection of international foods and often sell for cheaper prices. You can get a 50 per cent discount around 5 pm at the Marqt supermarkets or ALBERT HEIJN on fresh produce.The cheaper the supermarket, the less discounts you will find, so check Marqt and at 5 pm. Some items are also marked down due to sell-by date after the lunchtime rush so its also worth to check in around 3 pm.

IKEA
Ikea offers free coffee (with a FAMILY CARD) in Reykjavik.

Cheapest supermarkets in Iceland

- **Bónus:** Bónus is known for offering lower prices compared to other supermarkets in Iceland. It's a popular choice for both locals and visitors looking to save on groceries.
- **Krónan:** Krónan is another supermarket chain in Iceland that generally offers competitive prices. It's worth checking out for affordable grocery shopping.
- **Netto:** Netto is a discount supermarket chain in Iceland that aims to provide cost-effective options for shoppers.
- **Aldi:** Aldi operates in Iceland and is known for its focus on affordability. While it might not have as many locations as some local chains, it's worth considering for budget-conscious shoppers.
-

Supermarkets often mark down prices for items nearing their expiry date. These may include perishable goods like meat, dairy, or bakery items. Be sure to check for discounted items in this section of the store.

Fruit picking

Iceland has a relatively short growing season, and due to its climate and geographical conditions, fruit cultivation is limited compared to some other countries. However, there are certain berries and fruits that can be found in the wild during the summer months. Here's a brief guide to some of the fruits you can find and pick in Iceland:

- **Berries:**
  - **Crowberries (Krækiber):** These dark purple to black berries are common in Iceland and can be found in heathlands and rocky areas. They are usually ready for picking from late summer to early autumn.
  - **Blueberries (Bláber):** Wild blueberries grow in various areas, especially in heathlands and forests. They are typically ripe in late summer.
  - **Bilberries (Aðalbláber):** Similar to blueberries, bilberries are also found in various regions and are ready for picking in late summer.
- **Arctic Thyme:**
  - While not a fruit, Arctic thyme is a herb that grows in Iceland and is often used for culinary purposes. You may find it while exploring the countryside.
- **Sea Buckthorn (Sandþúr):**
  - These orange berries grow on shrubs along the coast and are rich in vitamin C. They are usually ready for harvest in late summer and early autumn.
- **Rowan Berries (Reyniber):**
  - Rowan trees produce small red berries that are edible but are usually quite bitter. They can be found in various locations, including gardens and forests.

Iceland Food Culture

Icelandic food culture is deeply influenced by the island's geographical isolation and the surrounding North Atlantic Ocean. Fish and seafood feature prominently in Icelandic cuisine, reflecting the nation's reliance on the rich marine resources that surround it. Cod, haddock, salmon, and langoustines are staples, often prepared in traditional dishes that highlight the freshness and quality of these marine delights.

Lamb is another cornerstone of Icelandic food culture, renowned for its distinct flavor and tenderness. The country's open landscapes provide sheep with the opportunity to roam freely, contributing to the unique taste of Icelandic lamb. Dishes such as hangikjöt (smoked lamb) and kjötsúpa (meat soup) showcase the importance of lamb in local culinary traditions.

Dairy plays a vital role in Icelandic cuisine, with skyr standing out as a beloved product. Skyr, a thick and creamy yogurt, is a versatile ingredient used in various dishes and is often enjoyed with berries. Local cheeses and butter also contribute to the richness of Icelandic dairy offerings.

Harðfiskur, or dried fish, is a traditional Icelandic snack that has endured over time. Made by air-drying fish, typically cod or haddock, harðfiskur is appreciated for its nutritional value and is commonly consumed with butter.

While puffin and whale meat were once more prevalent in Icelandic diets, they are now considered delicacies and are available in specific restaurants. However, the consumption of these meats raises ethical and sustainability concerns, prompting careful consideration among locals and visitors alike.

Lastly, Iceland's innovative use of geothermal energy extends to its food culture. Some locals practice hot spring cooking, taking advantage of the country's natural geothermal resources to prepare food in a unique and sustainable way. This aspect of Icelandic food culture reflects the resourcefulness and connection to nature that defines the nation's culinary traditions.

Top dishes to Yry

- **Þorramatur:**
    - **History:** Þorramatur is a traditional Icelandic food usually consumed during the mid-winter festival called Þorrablót. It consists of various preserved and pickled foods such as hákarl (fermented shark), sviðasulta (head cheese), and hangikjöt (smoked lamb).
    - **Where to Try Cheaply:** Some local grocery stores or supermarkets may offer pre-packaged Þorramatur items at a lower cost than restaurants.
- **Plokkfiskur:**
    - **History:** Plokkfiskur is a fish stew made with white fish, potatoes, onions, and béchamel sauce. It's a comforting dish that has been a part of Icelandic cuisine for generations.

- **Where to Try Cheaply:** Local fish and chips shops or casual seafood restaurants are good places to find affordable plokkfiskur.
- **Fiskisúpa:**
  - **History:** Fiskisúpa is a fish soup made with various types of fish, vegetables, and sometimes cream. It's a popular and hearty dish, especially during the colder months.
  - **Where to Try Cheaply:** Look for local soup bars, seafood cafes, or fish markets that may offer affordable fish soup.
- **Hangikjöt:**
  - **History:** Hangikjöt is smoked lamb, traditionally prepared by smoking the meat over dried sheep dung. Today, it's often smoked using more modern methods.
  - **Where to Try Cheaply:** You can find hangikjöt in many supermarkets or delis at a lower price compared to restaurants. It's also a common ingredient in sandwiches.
- **Flatkaka:**
  - **History:** Flatkaka is a type of unleavened rye flatbread. It has been a staple in Icelandic households for centuries.
  - **Where to Try Cheaply:** Bakeries and grocery stores often sell flatkaka at reasonable prices. It's commonly used in traditional Icelandic breakfasts.
- **Kjötsúpa:**
  - **History:** Kjötsúpa is a traditional Icelandic meat soup made with lamb, root vegetables, and sometimes barley. It's a hearty and warming dish.
  - **Where to Try Cheaply:** Local cafes or diners may offer kjötsúpa at affordable prices, especially during lunch hours.
- **Skyr:**
  - **History:** Skyr is a traditional Icelandic dairy product, similar to yogurt but technically a type of cheese. It has been a part of Icelandic cuisine for over a thousand years.
  - **Where to Try Cheaply:** Skyr is widely available in supermarkets and convenience stores. It's a healthy and budget-friendly snack or breakfast option.

Desserts

Icelandic desserts often reflect the country's reliance on dairy products and the use of local ingredients. Here's a guide to some traditional Icelandic desserts, along with a bit of history and suggestions on where to try them inexpensively:

- **Skyr-Based Desserts:**
  - **History:** Skyr is a traditional Icelandic dairy product that has been a part of the cuisine for centuries. It is often used in various desserts, such as skyrkaka (Skyr cake) or skyrterta (Skyr tart).
  - **Where to Try Cheaply:** Skyr-based desserts can be found in bakeries, cafes, and supermarkets. They are usually more affordable than elaborate pastries.
- **Pönnukaka:**
  - **History:** Pönnukaka is a thin pancake, similar to a crepe, often served with sugar or jam. It's a popular dessert or snack in Iceland.
  - **Where to Try Cheaply:** Pancake houses, local cafes, and even some street food stalls may offer pönnukaka at reasonable prices.
- **Vatnssmári:**
  - **History:** Vatnssmári is a traditional Icelandic Christmas cake made with layers of cookies, cocoa, and sugar glaze.
  - **Where to Try Cheaply:** Some bakeries or dessert shops may offer vatnssmári, especially during the holiday season. Alternatively, you might find affordable variations in local supermarkets.
- **Kleina:**
  - **History:** Kleina is a deep-fried pastry that has been a part of Icelandic culture for generations. It's often flavored with cardamom and can be dusted with powdered sugar.
  - **Where to Try Cheaply:** Local bakeries or cafes may offer kleina at reasonable prices. It's a popular snack and is sometimes served with coffee.
- **Rjómaterta:**
  - **History:** Rjómaterta is a traditional Icelandic cream cake made with layers of sponge cake, whipped cream, and sometimes berries or jam.
  - **Where to Try Cheaply:** Some local bakeries or dessert shops may have affordable versions of rjómaterta. It's a classic Icelandic celebration cake.
- **Kókómjólk:**
  - **History:** Kókómjólk is a chocolate-flavored milk drink that has been a favorite among Icelanders for decades.
  - **Where to Try Cheaply:** You can find kókómjólk in supermarkets and convenience stores at affordable prices. It's a simple and beloved treat.
- **Hjónabandssæla:**
  - **History:** Hjónabandssæla, or "Happy Marriage Cake," is a traditional Icelandic cake filled with rhubarb jam and often topped with meringue.
  - **Where to Try Cheaply:** Look for local bakeries or cafes that may offer hjónabandssæla, especially during the summer months when rhubarb is in season.

20 must try foods and where to try

Iceland can be an expensive destination, but there are still ways to enjoy delicious and affordable meals. Here are 20 must-try cheap eats in Iceland and suggestions on where to find them:

- **Pylsur (Hot Dogs):**
  - **Where to Try:** Bæjarins Beztu Pylsur in Reykjavik is a famous hot dog stand and a local favorite.

Icelandic hotdogs, locally known as "pylsur," are a cherished delicacy celebrated for their distinctive flavor and condiment fusion. Bæjarins Beztu Pylsur, an iconic hotdog stand in Reykjavik renowned for serving some of the best hotdogs in Iceland. It is a must-visit destination for an authentic experience.

- **Fish and Chips:**
  - **Where to Try:** Icelandic Fish & Chips in Reykjavik offers sustainably sourced fish and a cozy atmosphere.
- **Flatkaka with Butter and Cheese:**
  - **Where to Try:** Visit local bakeries or supermarkets to pick up flatkaka and add your own butter and cheese.
- **Lamb Soup (Kjötsúpa):**
  - **Where to Try:** Hamborgarafabrikkan (The Hamburger Factory) in Reykjavik serves a hearty and reasonably priced lamb soup.
- **Skyr Parfait:**
  - **Where to Try:** Grab a Skyr parfait from any supermarket, or create your own by layering Skyr with fruits and granola.
- **Meat Soup (Kjötsúpa):**
  - **Where to Try:** Cafe Loki, located near Hallgrímskirkja in Reykjavik, offers a tasty and affordable kjötsúpa.
- **Kleina:**
  - **Where to Try:** Brauð & Co in Reykjavik is a popular bakery where you can find traditional Icelandic kleina.
- **Pönnukaka:**
  - **Where to Try:** Mokka Kaffi in Reykjavik is known for its pönnukaka, served with sugar and jam.
- **Fish Soup (Fiskisúpa):**
  - **Where to Try:** Sægreifinn (The Sea Baron) in Reykjavik's Old Harbor serves delicious fish soup at reasonable prices.
- **Baked Goods from Sandholt Bakery:**
  - **Where to Try:** Sandholt Bakery in Reykjavik offers a variety of delicious baked goods, including sandwiches and pastries.
- **Rúgbrauð Ice Cream Sandwich:**
  - **Where to Try:** Valdís Ice Cream Shop in Reykjavik lets you create your own ice cream sandwich with traditional rúgbrauð (rye bread).
- **Cheese and Skyr Platter:**

- **Where to Try:** Visit local grocery stores or markets to create your own cheese and Skyr platter.
- **Local Seafood Dishes at Reykjavik's Old Harbor:**
  - **Where to Try:** Explore the seafood restaurants in Reykjavik's Old Harbor for reasonably priced and fresh seafood.
- **Lopapeysa Soup:**
  - **Where to Try:** Visit local cafes or diners for a budget-friendly soup featuring lamb or ingredients inspired by the traditional Icelandic lopapeysa sweater.
- **Street Food at Hlemmur Mathöll:**
  - **Where to Try:** Hlemmur Mathöll, a food hall in Reykjavik, offers a variety of affordable street food options.
- **Bread and Butter Pudding:**
  - **Where to Try:** Cafés like Babalú in Reykjavik often serve delicious bread and butter pudding.
- **Local Crafted Ice Cream:**
  - **Where to Try:** Ice cream parlors like Ísbúð Vesturbæjar in Reykjavik offer locally crafted ice cream at reasonable prices.
- **Kleinur:**
  - **Where to Try:** Visit local bakeries or cafes to find kleinur, deep-fried pastries that are both delicious and affordable.
- **Rjómasulta (Sour Milk Dessert):**
  - **Where to Try:** Some traditional Icelandic restaurants may offer rjómasulta. Check out local menus for this treat.
- **Local Brewery Pubs:**
  - **Where to Try:** Check out local brewery pubs for affordable bites to accompany your craft beer experience.

Drinking

Iceland boasts a variety of local beer brands, each with its unique flavors. Here are a few local beer brands in Iceland along with a brief taste description.

- **Einstök Ölgerð:**
  - *Description:* Einstök is known for its craft beers, and its White Ale offers a refreshing taste with hints of coriander and orange peel.
  - *Supermarket Cost (approx.):* a bottle might cost around 500 to 800 ISK.
- **Gull:**
  - *Description:* Gull is a popular lager in Iceland, known for its crisp and light taste.
  - *Supermarket Cost (approx.):* A can or bottle might range from 400 to 600 ISK.
- **Víking Gylltur:**
  - *Description:* Víking Gylltur is a golden lager with a malty flavor and a slightly hoppy finish.
  - *Supermarket Cost (approx.):* Expect prices to be around 400 to 600 ISK.
- **Kaldi:**
  - *Description:* Kaldi is a microbrewery producing a range of beers. Their Pale Ale is characterized by a hoppy and fruity flavor.
  - *Supermarket Cost (approx.):* Prices can vary, but a bottle may be around 600 to 800 ISK.
- **Brío:**
  - *Description:* Brío is known for its unique brews, and their beers may include options like a pale ale or IPA.
  - *Supermarket Cost (approx.):* Prices may vary, with some specialty brews costing more.
- **Ölvisholt Brugghús:**
  - *Description:* Ölvisholt Brugghús produces a variety of craft beers, including the Lava Smoked Imperial Stout, known for its rich and complex flavors.
  - *Supermarket Cost (approx.):* Specialty beers might cost more, ranging from 800 to 1200 ISK.

Here's a guide to drinking cheaply in Iceland:

- **Buy Alcohol at Duty-Free Shops**: If you're arriving in Iceland by air, take advantage of duty-free shopping at the airport. You can purchase alcohol, including beer, wine, and spirits, at discounted prices compared to buying them at local shops or bars.
- **Visit Happy Hours**: Many bars and restaurants in Iceland offer happy hour specials, typically in the early evening. Look for establishments with discounted drink prices during these times to enjoy beer, cocktails, or wine at lower prices.
- **BYOB (Bring Your Own Bottle)**: Some restaurants allow customers to bring their own alcohol for a corkage fee. Consider bringing your own wine or spirits to enjoy with your meal to save money on expensive restaurant drink prices.
- **Shop at the State-run Liquor Stores**: In Iceland, alcohol sales are regulated by the government, and the state-run liquor stores, known as Vínbúðin, offer a wide

selection of alcoholic beverages. While prices may still be relatively high, shopping at these stores can be more affordable than buying drinks at bars or restaurants.

How to experience your first day in Iceland for under 50 dollars

Experiencing your first day in Iceland on a budget of under $50 will require some strategic planning and prioritization. Here's a suggested itinerary that allows you to explore Reykjavik and its surroundings while keeping costs down:

- **Breakfast:**
  - Start your day with an affordable breakfast. Consider purchasing some yogurt, skyr, or bread from a local supermarket. Many accommodations also offer complimentary breakfast.
- *Cost: $5 - $10*
- **Morning Sightseeing:**
  - Explore Reykjavik's city center on foot. Visit landmarks like Hallgrímskirkja (you can enter the church for free, but there's a small fee to go up the tower) and walk along the waterfront to see the Sun Voyager sculpture.
- *Cost: Free*
- **Lunch:**
  - Opt for a budget-friendly lunch at a local bakery or a hot dog stand. Bæjarins Beztu Pylsur, a famous hot dog stand, is a good choice for an affordable and iconic Icelandic meal.
- *Cost: $5 - $10*
- **Afternoon Activity:**
  - Spend the afternoon exploring one of Reykjavik's museums or art galleries. Some may have free admission or reduced prices during specific hours. The National Museum of Iceland and the Reykjavik Art Museum are worth considering.
- *Cost: $10 - $15*
- **Coffee Break:**
  - Enjoy a cup of coffee at a local café. Consider taking advantage of happy hour discounts if available.
- *Cost: $3 - $5*
- **Explore Reykjavik Street Art:**
  - Take a self-guided walking tour to discover Reykjavik's vibrant street art scene. It's a free and unique way to experience the city's creative spirit.
- *Cost: Free*
- **Dinner:**
  - Head to a budget-friendly restaurant, local diner, or even a food truck for dinner. Opt for a simple but delicious Icelandic meal.
- *Cost: $10 - $15*
- **Evening Stroll or Northern Lights Hunt:**
  - Depending on the season, take a leisurely evening stroll around the city or, if you're visiting during the Northern Lights season, consider joining a free guided Northern Lights walk. Check the forecast and aurora alerts.
- *Cost: Free*
- **Accommodation:**

- Choose budget accommodations such as hostels, guesthouses, or budget hotels for your first night. Booking in advance can help secure better prices.
  - *Cost: $20 - $25*

Remember to check for any free events, festivals, or local activities happening during your visit. Additionally, take advantage of the stunning natural scenery and landmarks that can be enjoyed at no cost. Iceland's outdoor beauty is often the most rewarding and budget-friendly aspect of the experience.

Itinerary for 3 days

Day 1: Reykjavik and Golden Circle

Morning:

- **Luxury Breakfast:**
- Start your day with a luxurious breakfast at a local café or bakery in Reykjavik. Opt for Icelandic delicacies like smoked salmon and Skyr parfait.

Late Morning to Afternoon:

2. **Explore Reykjavik:**

- Spend the late morning and early afternoon exploring Reykjavik's city center. Visit iconic landmarks like Hallgrímskirkja, take a stroll along the waterfront, and explore the shops and boutiques on Laugavegur Street.

Lunch:

3. **Gourmet Lunch:**

- Enjoy a gourmet lunch at a local restaurant, trying dishes with local ingredients like lamb and seafood.

Afternoon to Evening:

4. **Golden Circle Tour:**

- Take a self-guided or budget-friendly group tour of the Golden Circle. Visit Þingvellir National Park, Geysir Geothermal Area, and Gullfoss Waterfall.

Dinner:

5. **Fine Dining Dinner:**

- Choose a restaurant in Reykjavik for a fine dining experience. Some places offer early bird or prix fixe menus that can be more budget-friendly.

Day 2: South Coast and Waterfalls

Morning:

6. **Luxury Breakfast and Departure:**

- Start the day with a luxurious breakfast at your accommodation. Depart early for the South Coast.

Late Morning to Afternoon:

7. **Seljalandsfoss and Skógafoss:**

- Visit the stunning waterfalls of Seljałandsfoss and Skógafoss. Enjoy the natural beauty and take some leisurely walks around the areas.

Lunch:

8. Cozy Lunch Stop:

- Have lunch at a cozy café or restaurant along the South Coast. Savor local flavors with a view of the surrounding landscapes.

Afternoon to Evening:

9. Reynisfjara Black Sand Beach:

- Explore Reynisfjara Black Sand Beach, known for its dramatic basalt columns and powerful waves.

Dinner:

10. Seafood Feast:

- Indulge in a seafood feast at a restaurant in the Vik area. Try dishes like fresh Icelandic fish or langoustine.

Day 3: Glacier Lagoon and Relaxation

Morning to Afternoon:

11. Jökulsárlón Glacier Lagoon:

- Drive to Jökulsárlón Glacier Lagoon and enjoy the stunning scenery of floating icebergs. Take a boat tour if it fits your budget.

Lunch:

12. Picnic with a View:

- Pack a gourmet picnic with local cheeses, fruits, and snacks. Enjoy it with a view of the glacier lagoon.

Afternoon to Evening:

13. Relax in the Blue Lagoon:

- On your way back to Reykjavik, stop at the Blue Lagoon for a relaxing soak in the geothermal waters. Book tickets in advance for more budget-friendly rates.

Dinner:

14. Farewell Dinner in Reykjavik:

- Have a farewell dinner in Reykjavik at a restaurant with a cozy ambiance. Try Icelandic specialties like reindeer or arctic char.

Itinerary 7 Days

Day 1: Arrival in Reykjavik

- Arrive in Reykjavik, Iceland's capital city.
- Explore the city center, including landmarks like Hallgrímskirkja Church, Harpa Concert Hall, and the Sun Voyager sculpture.
- Visit the National Museum of Iceland to learn about the country's history and culture.
- Enjoy dinner at a local restaurant and experience Reykjavik's vibrant nightlife.

Day 2: Golden Circle Tour

- Take a guided tour or rent a car to explore the Golden Circle route.
- Visit Þingvellir National Park, where you can walk between the Eurasian and North American tectonic plates.
- See the erupting geysers at the Geysir Geothermal Area.
- Marvel at the majestic Gullfoss waterfall.
- Return to Reykjavik in the evening and relax.

Day 3: South Coast Adventure

- Drive along the South Coast, stopping at landmarks like Seljalandsfoss and Skogafoss waterfalls.
- Explore the black sand beaches of Reynisfjara and the basalt columns at Reynisdrangar.
- Visit the village of Vík and enjoy lunch at a local restaurant.
- Continue your journey eastward and spend the night in the town of Kirkjubæjarklaustur or Höfn.

Day 4: Glacier Lagoon and Diamond Beach

- Visit Jökulsárlón Glacier Lagoon, where you can see icebergs floating in the water.
- Explore nearby Diamond Beach, known for its ice chunks washed ashore.
- Take a boat tour of the glacier lagoon for a closer look at the ice formations.
- Head back west and spend the night in the town of Höfn or Skaftafell.

Day 5: Vatnajökull National Park

- Explore Vatnajökull National Park, home to Europe's largest glacier.
- Hike to Svartifoss waterfall and admire its unique basalt column formations.
- Take a guided glacier hike or ice cave tour for an unforgettable experience.
- Drive to the town of Egilsstaðir for the night, stopping at scenic viewpoints along the way.

Day 6: Lake Mývatn and Akureyri

- Explore the otherworldly landscapes of Lake Mývatn, including geothermal areas like Hverir and the pseudocraters at Skútustaðir.
- Visit the town of Akureyri, known as the "Capital of the North," and explore its charming streets and shops.
- Relax in the Mývatn Nature Baths or go whale watching from the nearby town of Húsavík.

- Spend the night in Akureyri or nearby accommodations.

Day 7: Return to Reykjavik

- Drive back to Reykjavik, stopping at any missed attractions or scenic viewpoints along the way.
- Return your rental car (if applicable) and spend your final day exploring Reykjavik.
- Visit any museums or galleries you missed earlier in the week.
- Enjoy a farewell dinner at a local restaurant and reflect on your incredible journey through Iceland.

Snapshot: How to have a $10,000 trip to Iceland on a $1,000 budget

Expense Category	$10,000 Trip Budget	$1,500 Budget Alternative
Flight	$1,500 (round trip)	$200 (off-peak, budget airline-Icelandair)
Accommodation	$3,000 (10 nights)	$300 (hostels, guesthouses and camping)
Transportation	$1,500 (car rental, gas)	$150 (public buses, shared rides)
Food	$1,500 (restaurants)	$300 (groceries, budget dining, street eats)
Activities/Excursions	$2,000 (tours, activities)	$100 (self-guided exploration, free attractions)
Miscellaneous/ Incidentals	LUXURY SPA day passes	$150 (limited spending)
Total	$10,000	$1,000

OUR SUPER CHEAP TIPS...

Here are our specific super cheap tips for enjoying a $5,000 trip to Iceland for just $300.

Cheapest route to Iceland from America

At the time of writing **Icelandair**are flying to Iceland direct from six US cities for around $150 return.

Icelandair: Iceland's national carrier, Icelandair, often provides direct flights to Reykjavik from several major cities in the United States, including New York, Boston, Seattle, and others.

When you fly transatlantic with Icelandair, you can choose to add a 1 to 7 day stopover in Iceland at no additional airfare

Delta Air Lines: Delta operates flights to Reykjavik from cities like Minneapolis and New York (JFK). They often have codeshare agreements with Icelandair.
American Airlines: American Airlines offers seasonal flights to Reykjavik from cities like Philadelphia and Chicago.
United Airlines: United Airlines may provide flights to Reykjavik from hubs such as Newark.

How to Find Super Cheap Flights to Iceland

Luck is just an illusion. Anyone can find incredible flight deals. If you can be flexible you can save huge amounts of money. In fact, the biggest tip I can give you for finding incredible flight deals is simple: find a flexible job. Don't despair if you can't do that theres still a lot you can do.

Book your flight to Iceland on a Tuesday or Wednesday

Tuesdays and Wednesdays are the cheapest days of the week to fly. You can take a flight to Iceland on a Tuesday or Wednesday for less than half the price you'd pay on a Thursday Friday, Saturday, Sunday or Monday.

Start with Google Flights (but NEVER book through them)

I conduct upwards of 50 flight searches a day for readers. I use google flights first when looking for flights. I put specific departure but broad destination (e.g Europe) and usually find amazing deals.

The great thing about Google Flights is you can search by class. You can pick a specific destination and it will tell you which time is cheapest in which class. Or you can put in dates and you can see which area is cheapest to travel to.

But be aware Google flights does not show the cheapest prices among the flight search engines but it does offer several advantages

1. You can see the cheapest dates for the next 8 weeks. Other search engines will blackout over 70% of the prices.
2. You can put in multiple airports to fly from. Just use a common to separate in the from input.
3. If you're flexible on where you're going Google flights can show you the cheapest destinations.
4. You can set-up price tracking, where Google will email you when prices rise or decline.

Once you have established the cheapest dates to fly go over to skyscanner.net and put those dates in. You will find sky scanner offers the cheapest flights.

Get Alerts when Prices to Iceland are Lowest

Google also has a nice feature which allows you to set up an alert to email you when prices to your destination are at their lowest. So if you don't have fixed dates this feature can save you a fortune.

Baggage add-ons

It may be cheaper and more convenient to send your luggage separately with a service like sendmybag.com Often the luggage sending fee is cheaper than what the airlines charge to check baggage. Visit Lugless.com or luggagefree.com in addition to sendmybag.com for a quotation.

Loading times

Anyone who has attempted to find a cheap flight will know the pain of excruciating long loading times. If you encounter this issue use google flights to find the cheapest dates and then go to skyscanner.net for the lowest price.

Always try to book direct with the airline

Once you have found the cheapest flight go direct to the airlines booking page. This is advantageous in the current covid cancellation climate, because if you need to change your flights or arrange a refund, its much easier to do so, than via a third party booking agent.

That said, sometimes the third party bookers offer cheaper deals than the airline, so you need to make the decision based on how likely you think it is that disruption will impede you making those flights.

More flight tricks and tips

www.secretflying.com/usa-deals offers a range of deals from the USA and other countries. For example you can pick-up a round trip flight non-stop from from the east coast to johannesburg for $350 return on this site

Scott's cheap flights, you can select your home airport and get emails on deals but you pay for an annual subscription. A free workaround is to download Hopper and set search alerts for trips/price drops.

Premium service of Scott's cheap flights.
They sometime have discounted business and first class but in my experience they are few and far between.

JGOOT.com has 5 times as many choices as Scott's cheap flights.

kiwi.com allows you to be able to do radius searches so you can find cheaper flights to general areas.

Finding Error Fares

Travel Pirates (www.travelpirates.com) is a gold-mine for finding error deals. Subscribe to their newsletter. I recently found a reader an airfare from Montreal-Brazil for a $200 round trip (mistake fare!). Of course these error fares are always certain dates, but if you can be flexible you can save a lot of money.

Things you can do that might reduce the fare to Iceland:--
· Use a VPN (if the booker knows you booked one-way, the return fare will go up)
· Buy your ticket in a different currency

If all else fails...

If you can't find a cheap flight for your dates I can find one for you. I do not charge for this nor do I send affiliate links. I'll send you a screenshot of the best options I find as airlines attach cookies to flight links. To use this free service please review this guide and send me a screenshot of your review - with your flight hacking request. I aim to reply to you within 12 hours. If it's an urgent request mark the email URGENT in the subject line and I will endeavour to reply ASAP.

How to Find CHEAP FIRST-CLASS Flights to Iceland

Upgrade at the airport
Airlines are extremely reluctant to advertise price drops in first or business class tickets so the best way to secure them is actually at the airport when airlines have no choice but to decrease prices

dramatically because otherwise they lose money. Ask about upgrading to business or first-class when you check-in. If you check-in online look around the airport for your airlines branded bidding system. KLM have terminals where you can bid on upgrades.

Use Air-miles

When it comes to accruing air-miles for American citizens **Chase Sapphire Reserve card** ranks top. If you put everything on there and pay it off immediately you will end up getting free flights all the time, aside from taxes.

Get 2-3 chase cards with sign up bonuses, you'll have 200k points in no time and can book with points on multiple airlines when transferring your points to them.

Please note, this is only applicable to those living in the USA. In the Bonus Section we have detailed the best air-mile credit cards for those living in the UK, Canada, Germany, Austria, Iceland and Australia.

Arriving

Iceland has two main international airports: Keflavík International Airport (KEF) and Reykjavík Airport (RKV). Keflavík International Airport is the primary gateway for international flights, while Reykjavík Airport primarily serves domestic flights. Here's how you can get from each airport to the nearest city, Reykjavík, as cheaply as possible:

1. Keflavík International Airport (KEF):
Options for transportation to Reykjavík:
- Public Bus (Strætó):
    - The most economical option is to take the public bus (Strætó) from Keflavík to Reykjavík.
    - The journey takes approximately 45-75 minutes.
    - Check the Strætó website for schedules and fares.
- Airport Shuttle Services:
    - Shared airport shuttle services are available, providing door-to-door transfers.
    - Prices can be more budget-friendly when booking shared shuttles in advance.
- Carpooling or Ride-Sharing:
    - Explore carpooling or ride-sharing options to share transportation costs with other travelers.
- Renting a Car:
    - If you're traveling in a group, renting a car can be cost-effective and allows for flexibility in exploring other parts of Iceland.

2. Reykjavík Airport (RKV):
Options for transportation to Reykjavík:
- Public Bus (Strætó):
    - The public bus (Strætó) also serves Reykjavík Airport, providing an affordable option for transportation to the city center.
    - Check the Strætó website for schedules and fares.
- Taxi and Ride-Sharing:
    - Taxis are available at the airport, but they can be more expensive than other options.
    - Ride-sharing services may also be available.
- Walking or Cycling:
    - Depending on your location in Reykjavík, walking or cycling may be feasible, especially if you have light luggage.

General Tips:
- Book in Advance:
    - Whether you choose public transportation or shuttle services, booking in advance can often lead to lower prices.
- Compare Options:
    - Compare prices and services for different transportation options to find the most cost-effective solution.
- Off-Peak Travel:
    - Traveling during off-peak hours or seasons may result in lower prices for transportation services.
- Check for Deals and Discounts:

- Look for deals or discounts on transportation services, especially when booking round-trip tickets or packages.
-

Note: Alcohol is EXTREMELY expensive in Iceland

In Iceland, duty-free alcohol is typically purchased at Keflavik International Airport, which is the main international gateway. There are several duty-free stores within the airport where you can buy alcohol before leaving or upon arrival. Keep in mind that duty-free stores are generally found in the departure area after security, and you'll need to present your boarding pass.

The duty-free stores at Keflavik Airport offer a variety of alcoholic beverages, including local Icelandic options and international brands. Prices are often more favorable than those in regular stores due to tax exemptions.

Saving money on Transport

There are no trains in Iceland. Buses are the only alternative to hiring a car. Here's a guide to help you navigate the Icelandic bus system:

Bus Pass	Cost	Pros	Cons
Reykjavik City Card	48 hours: $28	- Unlimited travel on Reykjavik's public buses. - Free admission to Reykjavik's thermal pools, museums, and attractions. - Discounts on various tours and activities.	- Limited to Reykjavik area only. - Validity limited to 48 hours.
Stræto Bus Passport	1 day: $15, 3 days: $30, 7 days: $40	- Unlimited travel on Stræto buses across Iceland. - Flexibility to choose from 1, 3, or 7-day options. - Access to both urban and rural areas.	- Not valid for other modes of transport (e.g., taxis, ferries). - Limited coverage for remote regions.
Iceland On Your Own Pass	1 day: $20, 2 days: $35, 3 days: $45	- Unlimited travel on Stræto buses across Iceland, including the Golden Circle route. - Discounts on various attractions, tours, and accommodations. - Validity options ranging from 1 to 3 days.	- More expensive compared to other options. - Limited coverage for remote areas.
Reykjavik Excursions City Card	24 hours: $35, 48 hours: $45, 72 hours: $55	- Unlimited travel on Reykjavik Excursions buses within the Reykjavik area. - Free admission to selected museums and attractions in Reykjavik. - Discounts on tours and activities operated by Reykjavik Excursions.	- Limited to Reykjavik area only. - Validity options may not suit all travelers' itineraries.
Stræto Travel Card	1 month: $100	- Unlimited travel on Stræto buses for an entire month, offering great value for long-term visitors or residents. - Access to both urban and rural areas across Iceland.	- Expensive for short-term visitors. - Not suitable for tourists with shorter stays.

See the best of Iceland by Bus

Using the Stræto bus system is a convenient way to get around Iceland, especially if you want to explore different regions beyond the capital city, Reykjavik. Here's a first-timers guide on how to navigate the Stræto bus system in Iceland:

1. Understand the Stræto Bus System:

Stræto operates the public bus system in Iceland. It connects major towns and cities, making it an excellent option for travelers looking to explore various regions. The buses are clean, comfortable, and equipped with amenities like free Wi-Fi.

2. Plan Your Route:

Use the Strætó journey planner on their website or mobile app to plan your route. Enter your departure point, destination, and preferred time, and the system will provide you with the available bus options.

3. Purchase Tickets:

Tickets for Strætó buses can be purchased in several ways:

- **Onboard:** You can buy tickets directly from the bus driver. Note that the driver only accepts cash in Icelandic króna (ISK), so be sure to have local currency on hand.
- **Online:** Purchase tickets in advance through the Strætó website or mobile app. This is particularly convenient if you want to secure your tickets and avoid cash transactions.
- **At Bus Stations:** Tickets are also available at larger bus stations, tourist information centers, or designated ticket sales points.

4. Check the Schedule:

Strætó bus schedules can vary based on the route and the season. Check the timetable for your specific route to ensure you're aware of departure times and any potential schedule changes.

5. Be Punctual:

Strætó buses generally adhere to their schedules, so make sure to be at the bus stop a little ahead of the scheduled departure time. Icelandic buses are known for their punctuality.

6. Bus Stops and Stations:

Identify the bus stops and stations for your journey. Major towns and cities will have designated bus stations, while smaller stops may be signposted. The Strætó app provides real-time information on bus locations and schedules.

7. Enjoy the Scenery:

Traveling by bus in Iceland offers the opportunity to enjoy the stunning landscapes. Sit back, relax, and take in the views as you journey through the country.

8. Explore Multiple Regions:

Strætó connects various regions, allowing you to explore beyond Reykjavik. Whether you want to visit the Golden Circle, the South Coast, or the East Fjords, Strætó can be a cost-effective and efficient means of transportation.

9. Plan Ahead for Remote Areas:

While Strætó covers many regions, some remote areas may not be easily accessible by public bus. For specific destinations off the beaten path, consider alternative transportation options.

10. Use the Strætó App:

Download the Strætó app for real-time bus tracking, schedules, and ticket purchases. The app provides a user-friendly interface, making it convenient for travelers.

Traveling around Iceland by public bus can be an economical and scenic way to see the country. However, it's important to note that the public bus network in Iceland is not as extensive as in some other countries, and services may be limited in certain areas. Additionally, schedules can vary based on the season. Here's a suggested itinerary focusing on places accessible by public bus:

Day 1: Reykjavik

- Start your journey in Reykjavik, Iceland's capital. Explore the city's landmarks, including Hallgrímskirkja, Harpa Concert Hall, and the vibrant streets of downtown.
- Visit museums like the National Museum of Iceland or the Reykjavik Art Museum.
- Overnight in Reykjavik.

Day 2: Golden Circle (Route 1 Bus)

- Take a bus from Reykjavik to the Golden Circle. The Golden Circle includes Thingvellir National Park, Geysir Geothermal Area, and Gullfoss Waterfall.
- Explore the historic and geological wonders of Thingvellir.
- Witness the erupting geysers at Geysir Geothermal Area.
- Admire the powerful Gullfoss Waterfall.
- Return to Reykjavik for the night.

Day 3: South Coast (Route 51 Bus)

- Catch a bus to the South Coast. Visit Seljalandsfoss and Skogafoss waterfalls.
- Explore the black sand beaches at Reynisfjara.
- Optionally, visit the Skogar Folk Museum or hike to the plane wreck at Sólheimasandur.
- Overnight in Vik or nearby.

Day 4: Vatnajökull National Park (Route 51 Bus)

- Take a bus to Vatnajökull National Park.
- Explore the scenic landscapes around Vatnajökull, Europe's largest glacier.
- Visit Svartifoss waterfall and the surrounding area.
- Consider a glacier hike or ice cave tour if available and within your budget.
- Overnight in the area.

Day 5: East Fjords (Route 51 Bus)

- Travel to the East Fjords by bus, enjoying the picturesque coastal views.
- Explore charming villages like Seydisfjordur, with its colorful houses and cultural attractions.
- Take in the stunning scenery along the fjords.
- Overnight in the East Fjords.

Day 6: Akureyri (Transfer to Route 56 Bus)

- Head to Akureyri, the capital of North Iceland, by bus.
- Explore Akureyri's botanical gardens, museums, and the iconic church.
- Optionally, take a dip in the geothermal pools at Akureyri's swimming complex.
- Overnight in Akureyri.

Day 7: Lake Myvatn (Route 62 Bus)

- Take a bus to Lake Myvatn, known for its geothermal features and diverse landscapes.
- Explore attractions like Húsavík (whale watching), Hverir geothermal area, and Dimmuborgir lava formations.
- Relax in the Myvatn Nature Baths.
- Overnight in the Lake Myvatn area.

Day 8: Return to Reykjavik

- Take a bus back to Reykjavik, enjoying the scenic landscapes along the way.
- Spend your last day in Reykjavik or explore any missed attractions.
- Overnight in Reykjavik.

Keep in mind that this itinerary is a general guide, and actual bus schedules and routes may vary. It's crucial to check the latest bus schedules, plan accordingly, and confirm overnight accommodations in advance. Additionally, consider that some remote locations might not be easily accessible by public bus, and you may need to arrange alternative transportation for certain activities or destinations.

Ride Share

In Iceland, there are a few rideshare apps available for travelers and locals alike:

- **Bolt**: Formerly known as Taxify, Bolt is a popular ridesharing app operating in Reykjavik and other urban areas in Iceland. It offers affordable rides with licensed drivers and allows users to book trips conveniently through the app.
- **Hreyfill**: Hreyfill is a taxi app that provides on-demand taxi services in Reykjavik and surrounding areas. While it's not a traditional rideshare app like Bolt or Uber, it offers similar convenience for booking taxi rides in the city.
- **Starfsbílar**: This app offers ridesharing services primarily for commuters and travelers between towns and cities in Iceland. It connects drivers with available seats in their vehicles to passengers heading in the same direction, providing a cost-effective transportation option for longer journeys.

Flying might be cheaper

Flying might sometimes be a more cost-effective and time-efficient option, especially if you are traveling between distant locations. However, it's essential to consider factors like travel time, convenience, and the overall experience when choosing between bus travel and flying in Iceland.

Here are routes, airlines and costs

Airline	Popular Routes	Cost (One	Pros	Cons
Icelandair	Reykjavik to Akureyri	$70 - $150	- Well-established airline with a wide network of routes within Iceland.	- Prices can vary depending on the time of booking and
	Reykjavik to Isafjordur	$80 - $160	- Offers comfortable flights with amenities such as free in-flight	- Limited number of flights per day.
	Reykjavik to Egilsstadir	$60 - $140	- Option to bundle flights with tours or accommodation for added savings.	- Baggage fees may apply for checked luggage.
	Reykjavik to Husavik	$80 - $170	- Provides connections to popular tourist destinations in northern Iceland.	- Limited flexibility in flight times.
	Reykjavik to Vestmannaeyjar	$50 - $120	- Offers seasonal flights to destinations such as Vestmannaeyjar.	- May not operate year-round, particularly to smaller
	Reykjavik to Akureyri	$70 - $150	- Well-established airline with a wide network of routes within Iceland.	- Prices can vary depending on the time of booking and
	Reykjavik to Isafjordur	$80 - $160	- Offers comfortable flights with amenities such as free in-flight	- Limited number of flights per day.
	Reykjavik to Egilsstadir	$60 - $140	- Option to bundle flights with tours or accommodation for added savings.	- Baggage fees may apply for checked luggage.
	Reykjavik to Husavik	$80 - $170	- Provides connections to popular tourist destinations in northern Iceland.	- Limited flexibility in flight times.
	Reykjavik to Vestmannaeyjar	$50 - $120	- Offers seasonal flights to destinations such as Vestmannaeyjar.	- May not operate year-round, particularly to smaller
PLAY	Reykjavik to Akureyri	$60 - $130	- New budget airline offering competitive prices on domestic routes.	- Limited routes and destinations compared to larger
	Reykjavik to Isafjordur	$70 - $150	- Modern fleet with a focus on customer service and comfort	- Limited flight frequency on some routes
	Reykjavik to Egilsstadir	$50 - $120	- No-frills approach helps keep ticket prices low.	- Limited amenities onboard compared to full-service
	Reykjavik to Husavik	$60 - $140	- Offers flexible booking options and transparent pricing.	- Additional fees may apply for services such as seat selection.
	Reykjavik to Vestmannaeyjar	$40 - $100	- Provides a budget-friendly option for travelers on a tight budget.	- Limited availability of flights to certain destinations.
Air Iceland Connect	Reykjavik to Akureyri	$80 - $160	- Regional airline offering flights to destinations across Iceland.	- Prices may be higher compared to budget carriers on
	Reykjavik to Isafjordur	$90 - $170	- Well-established network connecting Reykjavik with remote regions of	- Limited flight frequency on some routes.
	Reykjavik to Egilsstadir	$70 - $150	- Provides connections to smaller airports in Iceland.	- Limited availability of flights to certain destinations.
	Reykjavik to Husavik	$90 - $180	- Offers reliable service with a focus on safety and comfort.	- Limited amenities onboard compared to larger airlines.
	Reykjavik to Vestmannaeyjar	$60 - $130	- Options to add extras such as baggage and seat selection for added	- Limited flexibility in flight times.

Driving in Iceland

Iceland's stunning landscapes and diverse attractions make it an ideal destination for a road trip. However, driving in Iceland comes with its own set of considerations. Here are some tips for a smooth and budget-friendly road trip:

1. Renting a Car:

When renting a car, book in advance to secure the best rates. Compare prices from different rental companies and consider opting for a smaller, fuel-efficient car to save on rental and fuel costs.

2. Fuel Economy:

Choose a fuel-efficient vehicle to save on petrol expenses during your journey. Fill up your tank in larger towns where prices may be more competitive.

3. Plan Your Route:

Plan your route in advance to optimize your travel and minimize unnecessary driving. Iceland's attractions are spread out, so careful planning can help you make the most of your time and fuel.

4. Gas Stations:

Gas stations in rural areas can be sparse, so fill up whenever you have the opportunity, especially before venturing into remote regions. Some gas stations may only accept credit cards, so be prepared.

5. Pack Snacks:

Bring snacks and non-perishable food items for the road. This can save you from frequent stops at restaurants, which can be expensive in Iceland.

6. Camping and Accommodations:

Consider camping to save on accommodation costs. Iceland offers numerous campsites, and camping in designated areas is an economical way to experience the country's natural beauty.

7. Shop in Larger Towns:

Stock up on groceries and supplies in larger towns like Reykjavik, where prices may be more reasonable. This can help you avoid inflated costs in more remote locations.

8. Take Advantage of Hostels:

Opt for hostels or guesthouses, especially in smaller towns, for budget-friendly accommodations. Many hostels offer communal kitchens, allowing you to prepare your meals.

9. Pack Essentials:

Bring essentials like a reusable water bottle and a travel-friendly cooler. This can help you save on buying drinks and snacks on the road.

10. Be Mindful of Speed Limits:

Iceland's speed limits are strictly enforced, and fines can be hefty. Stick to the posted speed limits to avoid penalties and ensure your safety on the road.

11. Travel Insurance:

Consider comprehensive travel insurance that covers your rental car. This can save you from unexpected expenses in case of accidents or damages.

12. Check Road Conditions:

Stay informed about road conditions, especially during winter. Some roads may be impassable, and certain areas may require a four-wheel-drive vehicle. Check conditions on reliable websites before setting out.

13. Enjoy Free Attractions:

Many of Iceland's natural wonders are free to explore. Take advantage of hiking trails, waterfalls, and scenic viewpoints without spending a dime.

14. Toll roads

As of that time, there were only a few specific locations with tolls. It's important to note that road infrastructure and toll systems can change, so it's advisable to check for the latest information closer to your travel date.

- **Hvalfjörður Tunnel:**
    - The Hvalfjörður Tunnel, also known as the Hvalfjarðargöng, has a toll booth. It's a subsea tunnel that shortens the travel distance between Reykjavik and the western part of Iceland.
- **Vaðlaheiðargöng Tunnel:**
    - The Vaðlaheiðargöng Tunnel, located near Akureyri in North Iceland, is another tunnel with a toll.
- **Krýsuvíkurbjarg and Breiðdalsvík Tunnels:**

- There are also tolls on the Krýsuvíkurbjarg Tunnel (serving the Reykjanes Peninsula) and the Breiðdalsvík Tunnel (in the Eastfjords region).

Do you need a car?

Here's a detailed pros and cons chart for traveling around Iceland with a rented car:

Aspect	Pros	Cons
Flexibility	- Freedom to create your own itinerary and explore off-the-beaten-path locations.	- Unpredictable weather conditions may affect travel plans.
	- Ability to stop and admire landscapes at your own pace.	- Limited flexibility if you are on a tight schedule.
Scenic Drives	- Stunning landscapes throughout the country accessible by car.	- Some remote areas may have challenging or unpaved roads.
	- Opportunity to take scenic detours and explore hidden gems.	- Roads might be closed in winter, limiting access to some attractions.
Cost Efficiency	- Potentially cost-effective for groups, as car rental expenses are shared.	- Fuel and rental costs may be higher than other modes of transportation.
	- Savings on guided tours and public transportation.	- Parking fees in popular tourist areas can add up.
Autonomy	- Complete control over your schedule and pace of travel.	- Driving long distances can be tiring and time-consuming.
	- Ability to adapt plans on the go based on personal preferences.	- Finding parking in crowded tourist spots may be challenging.
Accessibility	- Access to remote areas and hidden natural wonders.	- Some attractions may be inaccessible by car, requiring alternative means.
	- Convenience of reaching attractions at your own convenience.	- Limited parking space in busy tourist areas.
Comfort and Storage	- Comfortable and private travel experience with personal space.	- Limited storage space in smaller rental cars, especially for larger groups.
	- Ability to carry luggage, camping gear, and supplies easily.	- Unfamiliarity with the type of car and driving conditions in Iceland.
Local Interaction	- Opportunity to interact with locals in rural areas.	- Language barrier may pose challenges in remote areas.
	- Chance to discover hidden local gems and authentic experiences.	- Limited exposure to local culture if staying mainly in tourist areas.
Weather Independence	- Shelter from unpredictable and harsh Icelandic weather.	- Risk of encountering challenging weather conditions, especially in winter.
	- Ability to stay warm and dry while exploring diverse landscapes.	- Need to be well-prepared for changing weather conditions.
Photography Opportunities	- Flexibility to stop and capture photos of landscapes and wildlife.	- Driving responsibilities may limit spontaneous photo opportunities.
	- Golden hours and sunset/sunrise photography at your own pace.	- Limited time for photography if following a tight schedule.

Renting a Campervan

Iceland's dramatic landscapes and diverse attractions make it an ideal destination for a campervan adventure. Here's a guide to help you rent a campervan in Iceland affordably:

1. Book in Advance:

Secure lower prices by booking your campervan in advance. Prices tend to increase as the travel date approaches, especially during peak seasons.

2. Compare Rental Companies:

Research and compare prices from various campervan rental companies. Look for reputable companies with positive reviews, and don't forget to consider customer feedback on their experiences.

Here are a few campervan rental companies and platforms that were known for offering a range of options, including budget-friendly choices:

- **Campervan Iceland:**
  - Website: Campervan Iceland
  - Offers a variety of campervans, including budget options.
  - Allows free mileage and includes basic insurance.
- **Happy Campers:**
  - Website: Happy Campers
  - Known for budget-friendly campervans with basic amenities.
  - Offers free extras like a gas stove, pots, pans, and more.
- **Go Campers:**
  - Website: Go Campers
  - Provides a range of campervans with different sizes and features.
  - Offers unlimited mileage and basic insurance.
- **Camper Van Iceland:**
  - Website: Camper Van Iceland
  - Offers budget-friendly campervans suitable for various group sizes.
  - Includes basic insurance and allows free mileage.
- **KúKú Campers:**
  - Website: KúKú Campers
  - Known for their colorful and distinctive campervans.
  - Provides budget-friendly options with basic amenities.
- **Motorhome Iceland:**
  - Website: Motorhome Iceland
  - Offers a range of campervans, including budget options.
  - Provides unlimited mileage and basic insurance.
- **Rent.is:**
  - Website: Rent.is
  - Features various campervan models, including budget-friendly choices.
  - Includes basic insurance, unlimited mileage, and extras.

3. Opt for Off-Peak Seasons:

Traveling during the off-peak seasons (shoulder seasons) can significantly reduce rental costs. Prices are generally lower, and you'll encounter fewer tourists, allowing for a more relaxed experience.

4. Choose a Smaller Campervan:

Selecting a smaller campervan can save you money on both rental and fuel costs. Compact campervans are often more fuel-efficient and may come with lower rental fees.

5. Bring Your Own Essentials:

To cut down on rental costs, bring your camping essentials such as sleeping bags, portable stoves, and cookware. Confirm with the rental company what is included in the rental package.

6. Be Flexible with Pick-Up and Drop-Off Locations:

Some rental companies may offer lower rates if you are flexible with pick-up and drop-off locations. Explore options in different cities to find the most budget-friendly deal.

7. Camp at Designated Sites:

Camping fees can add up, so take advantage of Iceland's numerous designated campsites. These sites often provide basic facilities, making them a cost-effective and scenic choice.

8. Utilize Free Camping Areas:

Iceland allows free camping in certain areas, but it's essential to know the rules and regulations. Many locations require self-contained vehicles, so check if your campervan meets the criteria.

9. Check for Discounts and Promotions:

Keep an eye out for discounts, promotions, or special offers from rental companies. Some may have seasonal sales or early booking discounts that can significantly lower your overall costs.

10. Read the Terms and Conditions:

Carefully read the terms and conditions of the rental agreement. Pay attention to mileage limits, insurance coverage, and any potential additional fees. Understanding the terms can help you avoid unexpected charges.

12. Travel with Friends:

Sharing the cost of the campervan rental with friends can make the overall expenses more manageable. Choose a campervan size that comfortably accommodates your group.

13. Budget for Fuel:

Fuel costs can be a significant portion of your expenses. Choose a fuel-efficient campervan, plan your routes efficiently, and fill up when in larger towns where prices may be more competitive.

Icelandic Regions

Iceland is divided into eight administrative regions. These regions serve as the highest level of administrative divisions in the country. The regions are:

- **Capital Region (Höfuðborgarsvæðið):** This region includes the capital city, Reykjavik, and its surrounding municipalities. It is the most populous region and the economic and cultural center of Iceland.
- **Southern Peninsula (Suðurnes):** Situated southwest of the Capital Region, this region includes the Reykjanes Peninsula and the town of Keflavík. It is known for its geothermal activity and proximity to the Keflavík International Airport.
- **Western Region (Vesturland):** This region is located in the western part of Iceland and includes towns such as Akranes and Borgarnes. It is known for its diverse landscapes, including fjords and coastal areas.
- **Westfjords (Vestfirðir):** The Westfjords is a large and remote region in the northwest of Iceland. It is characterized by its dramatic fjords, rugged coastline, and picturesque landscapes. Ísafjörður, mentioned in a previous response, is the largest town in this region.
- **Northwestern Region (Norðurland vestra):** This region is situated in the northwestern part of Iceland and includes towns such as Sauðárkrókur and Húnaflói. It is known for its agricultural activities and coastal beauty.
- **Northeastern Region (Norðurland eystra):** Located in the northeastern part of the country, this region includes towns like Akureyri, the second-largest urban area in Iceland. It is known for its fjords, mountains, and vibrant cultural scene.
- **Eastern Region (Austurland):** This region is in the eastern part of Iceland and includes towns such as Egilsstaðir. It is known for its diverse landscapes, including mountains, fjords, and the largest forested area in Iceland.
- **Southern Region (Suðurland):** Situated in the southern part of Iceland, this region includes towns like Selfoss. It is known for its agricultural activities, waterfalls, and proximity to popular tourist attractions such as the Golden Circle.

1. Reykjavik:

- *Overview:* Iceland's capital and largest city, known for its vibrant arts scene, modern architecture, and lively nightlife.
- *Highlights:* Hallgrímskirkja, Harpa Concert Hall, Reykjavik Old Harbour, and the iconic Sun Voyager sculpture.
- *Cultural Scene:* Museums, galleries, and festivals make it a cultural hub.

2. Akureyri:

- *Overview:* The largest town outside the capital, situated in northern Iceland.
- *Highlights:* Akureyri Botanical Garden, Akureyri Church, and nearby natural wonders like Goðafoss waterfall.
- *Cultural Scene:* Known for its music festivals and vibrant arts community.

3. Hafnarfjörður:

- *Overview:* A harbor town located just south of Reykjavik.

- *Highlights:* Hafnarfjörður Museum of Vikings, the Hafnarfjörður Free Church, and its charming old town.
- *Cultural Scene:* Rich in folklore and legends, often hosting cultural events.

4. Reykjanesbær (Keflavik):

- *Overview:* Located on the Reykjanes Peninsula, near Keflavik International Airport.
- *Highlights:* Viking World Museum, The Giantess in the Mountain, and the scenic Reykjanes coastline.
- *Cultural Scene:* Strong maritime influence and history tied to the U.S. military presence.

5. Selfoss:

- *Overview:* One of the larger towns in South Iceland, situated on the banks of the Ölfusá River.
- *Highlights:* Selfoss Church, the nearby hot spring area at Reykjadalur, and proximity to the Golden Circle attractions.
- *Cultural Scene:* Agricultural traditions and access to natural wonders.

6. Egilsstaðir:

- *Overview:* The largest town in East Iceland.
- *Highlights:* Seydisfjordur village, Hallormsstaður National Forest, and Lagarfljót lake.
- *Cultural Scene:* Gateway to the East Fjords, known for its natural beauty.

7. Ísafjörður:

- *Overview:* The largest town in the Westfjords, known for its picturesque setting.
- *Highlights:* Historic buildings, Westfjords Heritage Museum, and the nearby Hornstrandir Nature Reserve.
- *Cultural Scene:* Emphasis on maritime heritage and outdoor activities.

8. Vestmannaeyjar (Westman Islands):

- *Overview:* An archipelago off the south coast, with Heimaey being the only inhabited island.
- *Highlights:* Eldfell volcano, Stórhöfði peninsula for puffin watching, and the Eldheimar Museum.
- *Cultural Scene:* Rich in natural history, especially known for the 1973 volcanic eruption.

What is the interior of Iceland like?

The interior of Iceland, known as the Highlands, is sparsely populated and less visited compared to the coastal regions. The Highlands are characterized by vast expanses of uninhabited wilderness, rugged landscapes, glaciers, volcanoes, and geothermal areas. Due to its remote and challenging terrain, visitor access to the interior is limited, especially outside of the summer months when some Highland roads are temporarily accessible.

1. Volcanic Activity:

- The Highlands are geologically active, with numerous volcanoes, hot springs, and geysers. This area is part of the Mid-Atlantic Ridge, contributing to its dynamic geological features.

2. Glacial Rivers:

- Glacial rivers, formed by the melting ice from surrounding glaciers, cut through the Highlands. Crossing these rivers can be challenging, and some areas are accessible only by modified vehicles.

3. Glacial Lakes:

- Picturesque glacial lakes, such as Þórisvatn and Langisjór, dot the landscape, offering serene beauty amid the rugged terrain.

4. Rugged Mountains:

- Massive and rugged mountains, including the iconic Mount Herðubreið and the volcanic Askja caldera, dominate the skyline. The terrain is often desolate and marked by lava fields.

5. Fjallabak Nature Reserve:

- The Fjallabak region, part of the Highlands, is known for its colorful rhyolite mountains, hot springs, and hiking trails like the Laugavegur Trek.

6. Landmannalaugar:

- Famous for its colorful landscapes, hot springs, and diverse geological formations, Landmannalaugar is a popular destination in the Highlands.

7. Lack of Infrastructure:

- The interior has limited infrastructure, with very few paved roads. Many areas are accessible only by F-roads, which often require a 4x4 vehicle. Travelers should be well-prepared and informed about road conditions.

8. Unpredictable Weather:

- Weather conditions in the interior can be harsh and unpredictable, with sudden changes. Storms, high winds, and low temperatures are not uncommon.

9. Protected Wilderness:

- Much of the interior is a protected wilderness area, preserving its natural state. Travelers are encouraged to follow Leave No Trace principles and respect the fragile environment.

Exploring the interior of Iceland offers a unique adventure for those seeking remote and untouched landscapes, but it requires careful planning and adherence to safety guidelines due to its challenging conditions.

Write me a guide to visit the interior of Iceland on a budget

Reykjavik

The beating heart of Iceland where history, culture, and natural wonders converge in a city that thrives on contrasts. Reykjavik, the world's northernmost capital, may be small in size, but it boasts a rich history dating back to the first Norse settlers in the 9th century. Named "Smoky Bay" after the columns of steam rising from the hot springs in the area, Reykjavik has evolved from a humble Viking settlement into a vibrant and modern city.

Stepping onto the streets of Reykjavik is like entering a storybook where colorful houses line the winding streets, and the distinctive Hallgrímskirkja church towers over the cityscape. The spirit of the Vikings is palpable in the air, blending seamlessly with a contemporary, artistic vibe that characterizes this unique metropolis.

As you explore Reykjavik, keep in mind that this picturesque city comes with a reputation for being a bit on the expensive side. However, fear not, as we have some money-saving tips to ensure you can experience all the wonders without breaking the bank. Embrace the local culture by dining at cozy cafés and enjoying the affordable street food scene, where you can savor Icelandic specialties without denting your wallet.

To maximize your budget, consider exploring the city on foot or renting a bike, taking advantage of Reykjavik's compact layout. Take a dip in the city's public geothermal pools, such as Laugardalslaug, where you can relax like a local without spending a fortune. And, of course, don't forget to immerse yourself in the breathtaking natural beauty that surrounds Reykjavik, from the iconic Golden Circle to the mesmerizing Northern Lights.

Reykjavik invites you to delve into its captivating past, revel in its vibrant present, and discover the secrets to enjoying this enchanting city without breaking the bank. Get ready for an adventure that blends history, culture, and savvy budgeting in a way that only Reykjavik can offer.

1. Save on Accommodation:

- Opt for budget-friendly accommodations like hostels, guesthouses, or budget hotels. Look for options with shared facilities to save more.
- Consider staying in the capital's outskirts for lower prices, and use public transportation to get to the city center.

Budget Hotels:

Fosshotel Rauðará:
Price Range: $80 - $150 per night (Prices may vary based on room type and season)

Advantages:
Affordable hotel with basic amenities.
Central location, making it convenient for exploring the city.
On-site restaurant for added convenience.
Disadvantages:
Basic facilities; not suitable for those seeking luxury.
Limited on-site amenities compared to higher-end hotels.

OK Hotel:
Price Range: $70 - $120 per night (Prices may vary based on room type and season)

Advantages:
Budget-friendly option with clean and simple rooms.
Central location within walking distance to major attractions.
Helpful and friendly staff.
Disadvantages:
Limited on-site amenities.
Basic accommodations without luxurious features.

Guesthouses:

Grettisborg Apartments:
Price Range: $100 - $180 per night (Prices may vary based on apartment size and season)

Advantages:
Self-catering apartments for added flexibility.
Often more intimate and homely atmosphere.
Good option for longer stays.
Disadvantages:
Limited on-site services compared to hotels.
Check-in and assistance may not be available 24/7.

101 Guesthouse:
Price Range: $90 - $150 per night (Prices may vary based on room type and season)

Advantages:
Centrally located in the heart of Reykjavik.
Cozy and personalized guesthouse experience.
Often includes a traditional Icelandic breakfast.
Disadvantages:
Limited facilities compared to larger hotels.

May have fewer rooms, so availability could be an issue during peak seasons.

Hostels:

KEX Hostel:
Price Range: Dormitory beds from $30 per night, private rooms from $80 per night
Advantages:
Located in a historic building near the city center.
Social atmosphere with common areas and a bar.
Offers a variety of room types, including dorms and private rooms.
Disadvantages:
Shared facilities might not be suitable for everyone.
Noise levels may vary depending on the crowd.

Loft Hostel:
Price Range: Dormitory beds from $30 per night, private rooms from $100 per night
Advantages:
Centrally located with easy access to Reykjavik's attractions.
Stylish and modern design.
Rooftop terrace with great views.
Disadvantages:
Shared dormitory-style accommodation may not be suitable for everyone.
Limited private room options.

Galaxy Pod Hostel:
Price Range: Pod beds from $40 per night, private pod rooms from $90 per night
Advantages:
Unique pod-style beds for added privacy.
Modern and futuristic design.
Social common areas for interaction.
Disadvantages:
Pods might feel cramped for some guests.
Limited space for personal belongings.

Luxury Stay

Ion City Hotel:

Nestled in the vibrant city center of Reykjavik, Ion City Hotel offers a haven of contemporary luxury amidst the bustling streets of Iceland's capital. With its sleek Scandinavian design and sophisticated ambiance, the hotel exudes modern elegance, providing guests with a refined retreat in the heart of the city. Each meticulously designed room and suite showcases chic furnishings, minimalist decor, and panoramic views of Reykjavik's iconic skyline, creating a serene and stylish sanctuary for discerning travelers.

Day Pass Inclusions:

Indulge in a day of relaxation and pampering with Ion City Hotel's exclusive day pass, granting access to the hotel's array of luxury facilities. Guests can immerse themselves in tranquility at the hotel's spa, where a range of rejuvenating treatments and therapies await. From invigorating massages to soothing facials, the spa offers a holistic wellness experience designed to replenish mind, body, and soul. Afterward, unwind in the sauna, enveloping yourself in warmth and serenity as stress melts away.

Starting Price for Day Pass: $150 USD

Features:

- **Luxury Spa:** Access to the hotel's luxurious spa facilities, where guests can indulge in a variety of revitalizing treatments and therapies tailored to their needs. From massages to body scrubs, the spa offers an oasis of relaxation and rejuvenation.
- **Sauna:** Relax and unwind in the hotel's tranquil sauna, where the soothing heat promotes detoxification and stress relief. Whether seeking solace from the cold Icelandic weather or simply craving a moment of serenity, the sauna provides the perfect escape.
- **Fitness Center:** Stay active and energized during your visit with access to the hotel's state-of-the-art fitness center. Equipped with modern cardio and strength training equipment, the fitness center offers everything needed for a satisfying workout session.

Affordable Luxurious Accommodation in Reykjavik	Pros	Cons	Starting Prices
Galaxy Pod Hostel	- Unique pod-style accommodation - Privacy curtains and personal storage	- Limited space inside pods - Shared bathrooms may require wait times	From $50 per night for pod beds
Reykjavik Lights Hotel	- Contemporary design with Nordic influences - Comfortable rooms with	- Located slightly outside the city center - Limited on-site facilities	From $80 per night for standard rooms
Fosshotel Reykjavik	- Sleek and stylish decor - Convenient location near city attractions and	- Prices may fluctuate depending on demand - Limited on-site	From $100 per night for standard rooms

Getting around

- Bus Route 1: This route takes you on the "City Circle" tour, allowing you to see many of Reykjavik's main sights. As you embark on this journey, you'll pass by landmarks such as Hallgrímskirkja Church, Harpa Concert Hall, Reykjavik City Hall, and the Old Harbour. The bus will then loop back to BSI Bus Terminal, completing the circle.
- Bus Route 14: This route takes you to the western part of Reykjavik, passing by areas such as Laugardalur Park, the Reykjavik Botanical Gardens, and the Laugardalslaug thermal pool.
- Bus Route 12: This route heads towards the eastern part of Reykjavik, passing by residential neighborhoods and areas such as Ellidaárdalur Valley and Kringlan Shopping Mall.
- Bus Route 5: This route takes you to the southern part of Reykjavik, passing by the University of Iceland, the National Museum of Iceland, and the iconic Perlan building.

Guided Bus Route 1 Tour

As you embark on Bus Route 1 from the main stop at BSI Bus Terminal in Reykjavik, get ready for a captivating journey through the city's rich history and vibrant culture. Here's a detailed guide highlighting key sights and their historical significance:

- **Hallgrímskirkja Church**: Designed by architect Guðjón Samúelsson and completed in 1986, Hallgrímskirkja stands as a symbol of Icelandic national pride and Lutheran heritage. Marvel at its imposing facade inspired by Iceland's volcanic landscapes and be sure to notice the statue of Leif Erikson, the Norse explorer, located in front of the church.
- **Harpa Concert Hall**: As you pass by Harpa Concert Hall, take in its striking architecture, characterized by a geometric glass facade that reflects Iceland's natural surroundings. Built in 2011, Harpa has quickly become a cultural hub, hosting concerts, exhibitions, and events that celebrate Iceland's artistic talent.
- **Reykjavik City Hall**: Pause to admire Reykjavik City Hall, a modernist structure nestled on the shores of Tjörnin Pond. Built in 1992, it serves as the administrative center of the city and features an interactive model of Iceland, providing insights into its geography and history.
- **Old Harbour**: Delve into Reykjavik's maritime heritage as you pass through the Old Harbour district. Once a bustling hub for fishing and trade, it's now a vibrant waterfront area teeming with activity. Keep an eye out for the historic warehouses and fishing vessels that line the harbor, offering glimpses into Iceland's seafaring past.
- **Perlan (The Pearl)**: Ascend Öskjuhlíð Hill to reach Perlan, a distinctive landmark offering panoramic views of Reykjavik and beyond. Originally built as hot water storage tanks in the 1980s, Perlan now houses a museum, observation deck, and restaurant. Explore the exhibits that delve into Iceland's natural wonders and geological phenomena.
- **University of Iceland**: Pass by the University of Iceland, founded in 1911 as a center of higher education and research. Admire its historic campus, characterized

by elegant buildings and lush gardens. Take note of the University's role in shaping Iceland's intellectual and cultural landscape over the past century.

- **National Museum of Iceland**: Conclude your journey near the National Museum of Iceland, a treasure trove of artifacts and exhibits that trace Iceland's history from its settlement to the present day. Explore the galleries filled with Viking relics, medieval manuscripts, and ethnographic displays, gaining insight into Iceland's unique identity and cultural heritage.

Free tours

Free Tour	Pros	Cons	Tips Expected	How to Book
City Walk Reykjavik	- Led by knowledgeable local guides.	- Limited availability and group size may be large.	Yes	Book online through the City Walk Reykjavik website.
Reykjavik Free Walking Tour	- Covers major landmarks and attractions in Reykjavik.	- Tips are encouraged for the guides.	Yes	No need to book in advance; just show up at the meeting point at the scheduled time.
Walk the Streets of Reykjavik	- Provides insight into the city's history and culture.	- Not available daily; check schedule in advance.	Yes	Check the schedule on the Reykjavik City website and show up at the meeting point on time.
Reykjavik Pub Crawl	- Experience Reykjavik's nightlife with locals.	- Participants are expected to purchase drinks.	Yes	Sign up for the pub crawl at participating bars or online through various tour websites.
Reykjavik Street Art Tour	- Discover vibrant street art and murals around the city.	- Limited frequency; may not be available every day.	Yes	Check the schedule on the Reykjavik Street Art Tour website and book online in advance.
Reykjavik Food Walk	- Sample Icelandic cuisine and learn about local food culture.	- Food or beverage purchases may be required.	Yes	Reserve your spot online through the Reykjavik Food Walk website.

2. Best Eats:

- Try local street food and food trucks for a taste of Icelandic cuisine without the hefty restaurant bill.
- Visit local markets like the Grandi Mathöll or the Kolaportið Flea Market for affordable and delicious options.

Here's a list of 20 cheap eats in Reykjavik with tips on what to try:

- Bæjarins Beztu Pylsur:
  - **What to Eat:** Hot dogs with "everything" (eina með öllu).
- Noodle Station:
  - **What to Eat:** Icelandic-style noodle soup.
- Reykjavik Chips:
  - **What to Eat:** Hand-cut fries with various dipping sauces.
- The Soup Company:
  - **What to Eat:** Daily changing soup options with bread.
- Hlöllabátar:
  - **What to Eat:** Icelandic-style subs and sandwiches.
- Sandholt Bakery:
  - **What to Eat:** Freshly baked pastries and sandwiches.
- Bergsson Mathús:
  - **What to Eat:** Breakfast items, sandwiches, and salads.
- Krua Thai:
  - **What to Eat:** Affordable Thai dishes, like Pad Thai and curries.
- Sæta Svínið Gastropub:
  - **What to Eat:** Gourmet hot dogs and burgers.
- Glo:
  - **What to Eat:** Healthy and vegetarian options with a salad bar.
- Bergsson RE:
  - **What to Eat:** Breakfast menu, sandwiches, and coffee.
- 10-11 or Bonus Supermarkets:
  - **What to Eat:** Grab fresh and affordable snacks, sandwiches, and salads.
- Joylato:
  - **What to Eat:** Gelato and waffles.
- Kaffi Vinyl:
  - **What to Eat:** Vegan dishes, including burgers and brunch options.
- Fish and More:
  - **What to Eat:** Fish and chips, seafood soup.
- Núðluskálin:
  - **What to Eat:** Asian-inspired noodle dishes.
- Matstofan Café:
  - **What to Eat:** Pizza, sandwiches, and coffee.
- Serrano:
  - **What to Eat:** Burritos, quesadillas, and tacos.
- Brauð & Co:
  - **What to Eat:** Artisanal bread and pastries.
- Sushibarinn:
  - **What to Eat:** Affordable sushi options.

Tips:

3. Free and Low-Cost Attractions:

- **Harpa Concert Hall:**
  - Harpa is an iconic concert hall located on the waterfront. While some events may require tickets, Harpa occasionally hosts free concerts and performances, especially during special events or festivals.
- **Aurora Reykjavik:**
  - Aurora Reykjavik is a multimedia exhibition about the Northern Lights, but it also hosts live music events. Some of these events may be free, and they often feature local artists.
- **Gaukurinn:**
  - Gaukurinn is a popular bar in Reykjavik that hosts live music, including free gigs. Check their schedule for events featuring local bands and musicians.
- **Kex Hostel:**
  - Kex Hostel is known for its laid-back atmosphere and occasional live performances. They often feature local and international artists, and some events may be free.
- **Dillon Whiskey Bar:**
  - Dillon is a whiskey bar in Reykjavik that hosts live music, including rock and blues. Some nights may offer free entry for live performances.
- **Reykjavik Downtown Hostel:**
  - This hostel occasionally hosts free live music events, particularly during the summer months. Check their schedule or inquire about any upcoming performances.
- **Reykjavik Street Music:**
  - Reykjavik's streets come alive with street performers, especially during the summer. You can encounter musicians showcasing their talent in various locations around the city.
- **Ingolfstorg Square:**
  - Ingolfstorg Square in the city center is a gathering place where you might find street performers, including musicians, adding to the lively atmosphere.
- **Secret Solstice Festival (During the Midnight Sun):**
  - While not entirely free, the Secret Solstice Festival during the Midnight Sun period in June often has some free events and performances. It's worth checking the schedule for any open-air concerts or activities.
- **Bars and Cafés:**
  - Explore local bars and cafés, especially those with a focus on the arts and culture scene. Some establishments host free live music nights to create a cozy and entertaining atmosphere. There is tons of free live music in Reykjavik: Reykjavik, the capital of Iceland, has a vibrant music scene, and you can often find free live music performances at various venues. Here are some places where you might discover free live music in Reykjavik:

Tips for appreciating Icelandic traditional music

Icelandic traditional music has deep roots in the country's rich cultural heritage, drawing influences from Norse mythology, medieval poetry, and the unique natural landscapes of Iceland. Here are some aspects of traditional music in Icelandic culture:

- **Rímur:**
  - **Definition:** Rímur is a traditional form of Icelandic epic poetry, often sung or chanted. It dates back to the medieval period and is characterized by intricate rhyming patterns.
  - **Performance:** Rímur is typically performed with a melodic and rhythmic structure, accompanied by string instruments such as the langspil (a type of zither) or the fiðla (a fiddle).
- **Folk Songs (Þjóðlag):**
  - **Definition:** Þjóðlag refers to Icelandic folk songs that have been passed down through generations.
  - **Themes:** Folk songs often revolve around themes of love, nature, and historical events. They are characterized by simple melodies and are sometimes accompanied by traditional instruments like the langspil and Icelandic drums.
- **Rímur and Romance:**
  - **Romantic Themes:** Many rímur and folk songs explore themes of romance, often weaving tales of love, heartbreak, and the beauty of the Icelandic landscape.
  - **Nature Influences:** The natural environment, including mountains, rivers, and the sea, frequently serves as a backdrop for romantic narratives.
- **Traditional Instruments:**
  - **Langspil:** The langspil is a traditional Icelandic zither with one or two melody strings and several sympathetic strings. It's played with a bow or by plucking.
  - **Fiðla:** The fiðla is a traditional Icelandic fiddle that has been used in Icelandic folk music for centuries.
- **Huldufólk (Hidden People) and Folklore:**
  - **Connection to Folklore:** Icelandic traditional music often reflects the country's folklore, including stories of elves, trolls, and hidden people (huldufólk).
  - **Narrative Elements:** Some songs tell stories about encounters with supernatural beings or mythical creatures, adding a mystical element to the music.
- **Icelandic Christmas Music:**
  - **Yuletide Songs:** Traditional Icelandic Christmas music, often referred to as Jólasöngur, is an integral part of the holiday season. These songs blend festive melodies with themes of winter and celebration.
- **Modern Influences and Revival:**
  - **Contemporary Interpretations:** While preserving traditional forms, some Icelandic musicians and bands have incorporated traditional elements into modern compositions.

5. Nature on a Budget:

- Utilize free hiking trails such as those around Mount Esja, offering stunning views of Reykjavik.

6. Happy Hour Deals:

- Enjoy Iceland's nightlife during happy hours when drinks and food are significantly cheaper. Many bars and restaurants in Reykjavik offer happy hour specials.
- Lebowski Bar:

- Known for its laid-back atmosphere and themed after the movie "The Big Lebowski," Lebowski Bar often offers happy hour specials on drinks.
- B5 Bar:
  - B5 Bar is a stylish venue with a happy hour that usually includes discounted prices on selected drinks.
- Prikid:
  - Prikid, one of Reykjavik's oldest cafés, has a happy hour with reduced prices on beer and other beverages.
- Micro Bar:
  - A great spot for craft beer enthusiasts, Micro Bar may offer happy hour deals on its diverse selection of craft beers.
- Húrra:
  - Húrra is a popular bar and venue that occasionally offers happy hour specials on drinks.
- Kaldi Bar:
  - Kaldi Bar is associated with the Kaldi Brewery and often features happy hour deals on their craft beers.

7. Free Hot Springs:

- Experience the luxury of geothermal pools without the Blue Lagoon price tag. Visit the Secret Lagoon or the Reykjadalur Hot Springs for a relaxing soak without breaking the bank.

There are no free hot springs near Reykjavik accessible by bus. However, there are several hot springs within a reasonable distance from Reykjavik that you can visit by car or organized tour. Some popular options include:

- Reykjadalur Hot Springs: Located about a 45-minute drive from Reykjavik, Reykjadalur offers natural hot springs where you can bathe in warm geothermal water. To get there by bus, you can take a public bus to Hveragerdi and then hike to Reykjadalur from the town.
- Seljavallalaug: This historic outdoor swimming pool is fed by a natural hot spring and surrounded by scenic mountains. It's about a 2-hour drive from Reykjavik. While there's no direct bus route to Seljavallalaug, you can take a bus to the nearby town of Skogar and then hike to the pool.
- Hveragerdi Hot Springs: Hveragerdi is known for its geothermal activity, and you can find several hot springs in the area. It's about a 40-minute drive from Reykjavik. While there's no direct bus route to the hot springs, you can take a bus to Hveragerdi and then explore the area on foot.
- Landbrotalaug Hot Spring: This small, natural hot spring is located on the Snaefellsnes Peninsula, about a 2-hour drive from Reykjavik. While there's no direct bus route to Landbrotalaug, you can take a bus to nearby towns like Stykkisholmur and then arrange transportation to the hot spring.

8. Discount Cards:

- Invest in the Reykjavik City Card, which provides free entry to several museums and galleries, along with unlimited public transportation for a set period.

- **24-Hour Card:** Typically started at around 3,900 to 4,500 Icelandic króna (ISK).
- **48-Hour Card:** Generally ranged from 5,900 to 6,900 ISK.
- **72-Hour Card:** Typically began at around 7,900 to 8,900 ISK.

The amount you can save with the Reykjavik City Card depends on the attractions and activities you plan to visit during your stay in Reykjavik. The card offers free admission to many museums and attractions, free use of public transportation, and discounts on various services.

Here the museums you can enter with the card and there costs:

- **National Museum of Iceland:**
  - Adult: Around 2,000 ISK (Icelandic króna)
  - Children (6-17 years): Free
- **Reykjavik Art Museum - Hafnarhús:**
  - Adult: Around 2,000 ISK
  - Children (18 years and under): Free
- **Reykjavik Art Museum - Kjarvalsstaðir:**
  - Adult: Around 2,000 ISK
  - Children (18 years and under): Free
- **Reykjavik Art Museum - Ásmundarsafn:**
  - Adult: Around 1,600 ISK
  - Children (18 years and under): Free
- **The Settlement Exhibition:**
  - Adult: Around 1,700 ISK
  - Children (17 years and under): Free
- **The Reykjavik Maritime Museum:**
  - Adult: Around 1,700 ISK
  - Children (6-17 years): Free
- **Árbær Open Air Museum:**
  - Adult: Around 1,600 ISK
  - Children (17 years and under): Free
- **The Saga Museum:**
  - Adult: Around 2,200 ISK
  - Children (6-17 years): Around 900 ISK
- **The National Gallery of Iceland:**
  - Adult: Around 2,000 ISK
  - Children (18 years and under): Free
- **The Whales of Iceland Exhibition:**
  - Adult: Around 2,900 ISK
  - Children (7-15 years): Around 1,500 ISK
- **Reykjavik Zoo and Family Park:**
  - Adult: Around 1,800 ISK
  - Children (3-17 years): Around 800 ISK
- **The Icelandic Phallological Museum:**
  - Adult: Around 2,200 ISK
  - Children (13-17 years): Around 1,000 ISK

9. Local Transportation:

- Use the efficient and reasonably priced public transportation system. Consider purchasing a multi-day bus pass for added savings.
- Walk or rent a bike to explore Reykjavik, taking in the city's charm on a budget.

10. Off-Season Travel:

- Consider visiting during the off-season (fall or spring) when accommodation and tour prices tend to be lower, and you can still enjoy many attractions.

By combining these budget-friendly tips with the natural beauty and culture of Reykjavik and the Capital Region, you can have a luxurious experience without overspending.

Luxury for Less experiences Reykjavik

1. Enjoy the View from Hallgrímskirkja:

- Admire panoramic views of Reykjavik from the top of Hallgrímskirkja, Iceland's iconic church. Entrance to the church is free, but there's a small fee to access the tower.

2. Explore Harpa Concert Hall:

- Wander around the Harpa Concert Hall, a modern architectural masterpiece. While attending a concert can be pricey, exploring the building and its surroundings is free.

3. Take a Stroll in Reykjavik Botanical Garden:

- Experience tranquility in the Reykjavik Botanical Garden. Entrance is free, and it's a perfect place to relax among various plant species.

4. Visit Árbæjarsafn Open Air Museum:

- Immerse yourself in Icelandic history at Árbæjarsafn, an open-air museum showcasing traditional buildings and artifacts. Admission is affordable, and it provides a glimpse into the country's past.

5. Wander Around Tjörnin:

- Enjoy the serene beauty of Tjörnin, a small lake in central Reykjavik. It's a perfect spot for a leisurely walk, and you might encounter ducks and swans.

6. Attend a Free Concert at Harpa:

- Keep an eye out for free concerts or events at Harpa Concert Hall. Occasionally, they offer complimentary performances, allowing you to enjoy music without the expense.

7. Discover Street Art in Grafarvogur:

- Explore the street art in Grafarvogur, an area with vibrant murals that add a touch of urban luxury to the surroundings.

8. Relax at Nauthólsvík Geothermal Beach:

- Indulge in the luxury of a geothermal beach at Nauthólsvík. While there's a small fee for the hot tubs, the sandy beach is free to access.

9. Hike Mount Esja:

- Hike to the top of Mount Esja for breathtaking views of Reykjavik and the surrounding landscapes. The trail is free, and the sense of accomplishment is priceless.

10. Attend a Free Walking Tour:

- Join a free walking tour of Reykjavik to discover the city's history and hidden gems. It's an excellent way to get acquainted with the local culture.

11. Explore the Reykjavik Street Food Scene:

- Delight in the local street food scene. While some items may be indulgent, you can find affordable and delicious bites like Icelandic hot dogs.

12. Discover the Sun Voyager Sculpture:

- Marvel at the Sun Voyager sculpture on the waterfront. This modern art piece is free to appreciate and offers a picturesque view of the sea and mountains.

13. Soak in the Laugardalslaug Swimming Pool:

- Experience the local swimming culture at Laugardalslaug. It's an affordable geothermal swimming pool with hot tubs and saunas.

14. Picnic in Hljómskálagarður Park:

- Have a luxurious picnic in Hljómskálagarður Park, situated by Tjörnin. Enjoy the greenery and perhaps some live music if there's an event.

15. Visit Reykjavik Art Museum – Ásmundarsafn:

- Explore Ásmundarsafn, part of the Reykjavik Art Museum. While some exhibitions may have a fee, the outdoor sculptures and gardens are free to access.

16. Experience Icelandic Culture at Reykjavik City Library:

- Immerse yourself in Icelandic literature and culture at Reykjavik City Library. It's a peaceful space, and you might find free cultural events.

17. Discover the Reykjavik Maritime Museum:

- Learn about Iceland's maritime history at the Reykjavik Maritime Museum. While the entrance fee is modest, it offers an enriching experience.

18. Attend a Free Yoga Class in a Park:

- Join a free yoga class in one of Reykjavik's parks during the summer months. It's a luxurious way to connect with nature and locals.

19. Hike to Grotta Lighthouse:

- Take a scenic walk to Grotta Lighthouse during low tide. Enjoy the coastal views and the peaceful ambiance.

20. Explore Reykjavik's Old Harbor:

- Wander around Reykjavik's Old Harbor, where you can watch boats, enjoy the maritime atmosphere, and perhaps spot some seals. It's a simple yet luxurious way to experience the city's maritime charm.

21. City of Reykjavik Walking Tours:

The City of Reykjavik occasionally organizes free walking tours guided by volunteers. These tours often cover key landmarks and historical sites in Reykjavik. Check the official website of the City of Reykjavik or contact the tourist information center for details on upcoming tours.

RECAP

- **Use Public Transportation:** Opt for Reykjavik's efficient public bus system instead of taxis. Purchase a Reykjavik City Card for free bus rides and discounts on attractions. Estimated Savings: Varies depending on usage. Act: Purchase in advance or upon arrival.
- **Cook Your Meals:** Save money on dining out by preparing your meals. Shop at budget-friendly supermarkets like Bónus or Krónan and take advantage of hostel kitchens or accommodations with cooking facilities. Estimated Savings: 50% or more compared to dining out. Act: Plan meals and shop for groceries in advance.
- **Look for Free Attractions:** Explore Reykjavik's numerous free attractions, including landmarks like Hallgrímskirkja, Harpa Concert Hall, and the Sun Voyager sculpture. Visit museums on free entry days or enjoy outdoor activities such as walking tours or hiking trails. Estimated Savings: Up to 100% on attraction fees. Act: Check schedules and plan visits accordingly.
- **Take Advantage of Happy Hours:** Enjoy drinks at discounted prices during happy hours at local bars and pubs. Look for establishments offering deals on beer, wine, and cocktails, typically in the early evening or late afternoon. Estimated Savings: 20-50% off regular drink prices. Act: Research happy hour times and locations in advance.
- **Book Accommodations Wisely:** Consider staying in budget accommodations such as hostels, guesthouses, or Airbnbs. Look for accommodations with shared facilities or opt for dormitory-style rooms to save on costs. Booking in advance or during off-peak seasons can also result in lower rates. Estimated Savings: Up to 50% compared to hotels. Act: Book early for the best rates, especially during peak seasons.
- **Utilize Free Walking Tours:** Join free walking tours offered by local guides to explore Reykjavik's landmarks and learn about its history and culture. While these tours are technically free, tipping the guides at the end is customary. Estimated Savings: Up to 100% on tour fees. Act: Arrive at the meeting point on time; tipping is optional but appreciated.
- **Purchase the Reykjavik City Card:** Invest in the Reykjavik City Card for access to various attractions, museums, and thermal pools at discounted rates. The card also includes free bus transportation within Reykjavik and discounts on tours and activities. Estimated Savings: Varies depending on usage. Act: Purchase in advance or upon arrival.
- **Bring Your Reusable Water Bottle:** Avoid purchasing bottled water by bringing a reusable water bottle. Reykjavik has excellent tap water, so you can refill your bottle for free at public water fountains or restaurants. Estimated Savings: Up to 100% on bottled water purchases. Act: Bring a reusable water bottle from home.
- **Look for Discounted Tours and Activities:** Research and compare prices for tours and activities in Reykjavik. Look for discounted deals on tour websites, group booking discounts, or combo packages that offer savings when booking multiple activities together. Estimated Savings: Varies depending on the activity and deal. Act: Research and book in advance to secure the best deals.
- **Visit Tourist Information Centers:** Stop by tourist information centers in Reykjavik for free maps, brochures, and local advice on budget-friendly activities and dining options. They can provide valuable insights into saving money while exploring the city. Estimated Savings: Varies depending on recommendations. Act: Visit early in your trip for guidance on money-saving opportunities.

Exploring Þríhnúkagígur

The cheapest tour to Þríhnúkagígur volcano in Iceland typically starts around $400 USD per person. Exploring Þríhnúkagígur without a tour typically involves a bit of planning and organization, especially if you're opting for a DIY approach. Here's a guide to exploring Þríhnúkagígur from Reykjavik on your own:

- **Transportation**: Start by arranging transportation from Reykjavik to the base of the volcano. While there are no public transport options directly to Þríhnúkagígur, you can rent a car or join a group tour to get to the site.

- **Hiking**: Once you arrive at the base of the volcano, you'll need to hike to the summit. The hike is relatively challenging and can take around 1.5 to 2 hours, depending on your fitness level and the weather conditions. Make sure to wear sturdy hiking boots and dress in layers, as the weather in Iceland can be unpredictable.
- **Safety Precautions**: Before attempting the hike, check the weather forecast and trail conditions. It's essential to stay on designated paths and follow any posted signs or markers. Additionally, be mindful of your physical limitations and avoid hiking alone, if possible.
- **Magma Chamber**: Once you reach the summit of Þríhnúkagígur, you'll find the entrance to the magma chamber. Visiting the magma chamber of Þríhnúkagígur volcano requires joining a guided tour. Access to the magma chamber is restricted for safety reasons, and specialized equipment and knowledge are necessary to ensure a safe and informative experience for visitors. Therefore, it is not possible to explore the magma chamber without a tour. It's recommended to book a tour with a reputable operator that offers guided visits to Þríhnúkagígur volcano for a memorable and safe adventure.

Þríhnúkagígur stands as the singular location on Earth where visitors can descend into a dormant volcano and safely traverse its expansive lava chamber. There are descent-only options from $200. https://insidethevolcano.com/the-tour

Greater Reykjavik Towns

Welcome to Greater Reykjavik, a region of vibrant towns, rich cultural offerings, and stunning landscapes that captivate every traveler. Greater Reykjavik, also known as the Capital Region (Höfuðborgarsvæðið), encompasses Reykjavik and its surrounding municipalities. The towns and areas within Greater Reykjavik include:

- **Kópavogur:** A neighboring town to the south of Reykjavik, Kópavogur is the second most populous municipality in Iceland. It offers a mix of residential and commercial areas.
- **Hafnarfjörður:** Located to the southwest of Reykjavik, Hafnarfjörður is known for its picturesque harbor, historical sites, and folklore about hidden elves and dwarves.
- **Garðabær:** Situated to the southeast of Reykjavik, Garðabær is a residential suburb known for its affluent neighborhoods and green spaces.
- **Mosfellsbær:** To the northeast of Reykjavik, Mosfellsbær is a town surrounded by nature, offering easy access to outdoor activities and scenic landscapes.
- **Seltjarnarnes:** A peninsula to the west of Reykjavik, Seltjarnarnes is known for its coastal location and the Grotta lighthouse, offering beautiful views of the surrounding area.

These towns together form the Greater Reykjavik area, creating an interconnected urban region with shared services and infrastructure. The Capital Region is the most densely populated part of Iceland, housing a significant portion of the country's population and serving as the economic, cultural, and political center of Iceland.

Kópavogur

The second-largest city in Iceland and is part of the Reykjavik metropolitan area. While Kópavogur itself may not be as touristy as Reykjavik, it still offers various attractions and opportunities for a comfortable experience on a budget. Here's a guide with specifics and approximate prices:

Accommodation:

- **Hotel Smári:**
    - A modern hotel located in Kópavogur. Prices for standard rooms can start around $90 - $130 per night.

Dining:

- **Fjörukráin:**
    - A popular restaurant in Kópavogur offering Icelandic and international dishes. Prices for main courses are typically around $20 - $35.
- **Kópavogur Bakery (Kópavogsbakari):**
    - Enjoy Icelandic pastries and baked goods at local bakeries. Prices for coffee and treats are approximately $5 - $10.

Activities:

- **Árbæjarsafn Open Air Museum:**
    - Explore the Árbæjarsafn Open Air Museum in neighboring Reykjavik, showcasing Icelandic history. Entrance fees are around $10.
- **Geothermal Pools:**
    - Relax in one of the local geothermal swimming pools, such as Salalaug in Kópavogur. Entrance fees are usually affordable, around $8 - $12.

Nature and Outdoor Exploration:

- **Kópavogur Church and Surroundings:**
    - Visit Kópavogur Church and take a stroll around the nearby areas. Exploring the outdoors is often free.
- **Heiðmörk Nature Reserve:**
    - Head to Heiðmörk, a nature reserve near Kópavogur, for hiking and enjoying nature. Entrance is usually free.

Transportation:

- **Public Bus or Walk:**
    - Public buses connect Kópavogur to Reykjavik and other nearby areas. Prices for bus tickets are approximately $3 - $5.
- **Rent a Bike:**
    - Consider renting a bike for local exploration. Prices vary, but daily rentals can start around $15 - $20.

Shopping:

- **Kópavogur Shopping Malls:**
    - Explore local shopping malls for a mix of international and Icelandic brands. Prices vary, but there are options for different budgets.

Hafnarfjörður

Hafnarfjörður, located just south of Reykjavik, is known for its rich folklore, historical sites, and picturesque harbor. While luxury on a budget is a relative concept, I can provide you with some recommendations for enjoying a more comfortable experience in Hafnarfjörður without breaking the bank. Please note that prices are approximate and can vary based on the season, availability, and other factors.

Accommodation:

- **Hotel Viking:**
  - A charming hotel with a Viking-themed atmosphere. Prices for standard rooms may start around $100 - $150 per night. Check for seasonal promotions or special offers.
- **Lava Hostel:**
  - If you're looking for budget-friendly accommodation without sacrificing comfort, Lava Hostel offers dormitory beds and private rooms. Prices for dorm beds can start around $30 - $40 per night.

Dining:

- **Von Mathús:**
  - A local restaurant offering a mix of Icelandic and international cuisine. Prices for main courses can range from $15 - $30.
- **Gamla Vínhúsið:**
  - Located in a historic building, this restaurant serves seafood and traditional Icelandic dishes. Main course prices are typically around $20 - $35.

Activities:

- **Hafnarfjörður's Old Town (Gamla Hafnarborg):**
  - Explore the charming Old Town with its cobbled streets, colorful houses, and historical sites. Entrance to Hafnarborg, the local art museum, is usually around $8.
- **Harbor Walk and Boat Tour:**
  - Enjoy a leisurely walk along the harbor, and consider taking a boat tour to explore the surrounding coastline. Prices for boat tours can start around $30 - $50.

Coffee and Treats:

- **Pallett Kaffikompaní:**
  - A cozy café offering coffee, pastries, and light meals. Prices for coffee and pastries range from $5 - $10.
- **Brynja:**
  - Treat yourself to a famous Icelandic ice cream at Brynja. A cone with a couple of scoops is around $5 - $8.

Transportation:

- **Public Bus or Walk:**

- Hafnarfjörður is easily navigable on foot, and public buses connect the town to Reykjavik and other nearby areas. Prices for bus tickets are approximately $3 - $5.

Shopping:

- **Hafnarfjörður Flea Market:**
- Explore the local flea market for unique finds and souvenirs. Prices vary, but it's a great place for budget-friendly shopping.

Highlights:

- **Borganes Peninsula:** Hike or drive to enjoy breathtaking views of the surrounding landscapes.
- **Leirvogur Beach:** Relax on this peaceful beach with views of Mount Esja.
-

3. Visit the Hafnarfjörður Museum:

Explore the Hafnarfjörður Museum to learn about the town's history and folklore. Admission is typically around $8-10 per person.

4. Enjoy Local Cuisine in Downtown Hafnarfjörður:

Savor Icelandic cuisine in local eateries in downtown Hafnarfjörður. A meal at a mid-range restaurant can cost around $20-30 per person.

5. Attend the Viking Festival:

Check for local events, such as the Viking Festival, which occasionally takes place in Hafnarfjörður. Ticket prices may vary but can be around $20-30.

6. Relax at the Sundlaugin Hafnarfjarðar Pool:

Unwind at the Sundlaugin Hafnarfjarðar swimming pool. Entrance fees are typically affordable, ranging from $6-10.

7. Discover the Hafnarfjörður Parks:

Explore local parks like Hafnarfjörður Park and Hellisgerði Park. These green spaces offer a tranquil escape and are free to enter.

8. Attend the Hafnarfjörður Cultural Festival:

If your visit coincides, attend the Hafnarfjörður Cultural Festival, showcasing local arts and performances. Some events may have free admission.

9. Walk through the Lava Fields:

Take a walk through the surrounding lava fields, such as Hellisgerði Lava Park. This outdoor activity is free of charge.

10. Visit the Elves' Garden:

Explore the Elves' Garden, a unique attraction in Hafnarfjörður. Entrance is often free, and it's an interesting spot with small elf houses.

11. Enjoy a Coffee in Cafés:

Relax in local cafés, enjoying a cup of coffee and pastries. Prices for a coffee and a snack can range from $5-10.

12. Experience the Icelandic Wonders Museum:

Visit the Icelandic Wonders Museum, showcasing mystical and supernatural aspects of Icelandic folklore. Admission is around $15-20.

13. Capture the Sunset at Hafnarfjall Mountain:

Hike or drive to Hafnarfjall Mountain for a stunning sunset view over Hafnarfjörður. This outdoor experience is free.

14. Attend a Concert at the Hafnarfjörður Theatre:

Check for concerts or performances at the Hafnarfjörður Theatre. Ticket prices vary, but some events may offer affordable options.

15. Participate in Hiking Trails:

Explore nearby hiking trails, such as Hafnarfjörður's coastal path. Enjoying nature on foot is a budget-friendly activity.

16. Discover the Hafnarfjörður Art Gallery:

Explore the Hafnarfjörður Art Gallery, featuring local and international artworks. Admission prices are usually around $5-10.

17. Try Fish and Chips by the Harbor:

Indulge in a budget-friendly meal like fish and chips from local seafood stalls by the harbor. Prices can range from $10-15.

18. Attend Outdoor Concerts or Events:

Check for outdoor concerts or events happening in Hafnarfjörður's public spaces. Some outdoor performances may be free of charge.

19. Explore the Hellisgerði Park Labyrinth:

Wander through the labyrinth in Hellisgerði Park, an artistic feature that adds a unique touch to the park. This is a free and interesting activity.

20. Enjoy the Hafnarfjörður Botanical Garden:

Visit the Hafnarfjörður Botanical Garden, where you can enjoy a variety of plants. Entrance is typically free.

Garðabær

Garðabær is another municipality in the Reykjavik metropolitan area, known for its residential neighborhoods and proximity to the capital. While Garðabær is primarily residential, it offers a serene atmosphere and access to nearby attractions. Here's a guide for a budget-friendly yet comfortable experience in Garðabær:

Accommodation:

- **Garðabær Apartments:**
    - Look for apartments available for short-term rentals. Prices can vary, but you may find options starting around $100 - $150 per night.
- **Guesthouses:**
    - Explore guesthouses in Garðabær or neighboring areas for budget-friendly accommodation.

Dining:

- **Local Cafés:**
    - Visit local cafés for coffee and light meals. Prices for coffee and treats are approximately $5 - $10.
- **Supermarkets and Grocery Stores:**
    - Take advantage of local supermarkets for budget-friendly meals. You can buy groceries and prepare simple meals if you have access to a kitchen.

Activities:

- **Bessastaðir:**
    - Explore the area around Bessastaðir, the official residence of the President of Iceland. While entrance to the residence is restricted, you can enjoy the surrounding nature.
- **Hiking and Nature Walks:**
    - Garðabær and its surroundings offer opportunities for hiking and nature walks. Enjoy the serene environment and beautiful landscapes.

Nature and Outdoor Exploration:

- **Garðskagaviti Lighthouse:**
    - Visit Garðskagaviti Lighthouse for scenic views of the coastline. Exploring the area is typically free.
- **Álftanes Peninsula:**
    - Take a short drive to Álftanes Peninsula for a coastal walk and birdwatching. Enjoy the natural beauty without spending much.

Transportation:

- **Public Bus or Walk:**
    - Public buses connect Garðabær to Reykjavik and neighboring areas. Prices for bus tickets are approximately $3 - $5.
- **Rent a Bike:**
    - Consider renting a bike for local exploration. Prices vary, but daily rentals can start around $15 - $20.

Mosfellsbær

Mosfellsbær is a town located just northeast of Reykjavik, known for its beautiful landscapes, proximity to nature, and cultural attractions. While it's primarily a residential area, it offers a tranquil setting and opportunities for outdoor activities. Here's a guide for a budget-friendly yet comfortable experience in Mosfellsbær:

Accommodation:

- **Guesthouses or Homestays:**
    - Look for guesthouses or homestays in Mosfellsbær for a more personalized and budget-friendly accommodation experience. Prices can vary, but you may find options starting around $80 - $120 per night.
- **Budget Hotels in Reykjavik:**
    - If there are limited accommodation options in Mosfellsbær, consider staying in budget hotels in Reykjavik and exploring Mosfellsbær during the day. Prices for budget hotels can start around $70 - $120 per night.

Dining:

- **Local Cafés and Bakeries:**
    - Explore local cafés and bakeries for coffee, pastries, and light meals. Prices for coffee and treats are approximately $5 - $10.
- **Supermarkets and Local Markets:**
    - Visit supermarkets for budget-friendly meals or snacks. You can also explore local markets for fresh produce and local specialties.

Activities:

- **Álafoss Wool Store:**
    - Visit Álafoss, a historic wool store in Mosfellsbær. Explore the shop and surrounding area, which is often free.
- **Hiking in the Surrounding Nature:**
    - Mosfellsbær is surrounded by stunning nature. Consider hiking or walking trails in the area, such as those leading to Esja Mountain.

Nature and Outdoor Exploration:

- **Esja Mountain:**
    - Embark on a hike up Esja Mountain for panoramic views of the surroundings. Hiking is usually free, but be sure to check trail conditions.
- **Icelandic Lava Show:**
    - While not directly in Mosfellsbær, the Icelandic Lava Show in nearby Hafnarfjörður is a unique experience. Tickets are around $25.

Transportation:

- **Public Bus or Walk:**
    - Public buses connect Mosfellsbær to Reykjavik and other nearby areas. Prices for bus tickets are approximately $3 - $5.
- **Rent a Car:**
    - Consider renting a car for more flexibility in exploring the surrounding areas. Prices for car rentals can vary, so shop around for the best deals.

Shopping:

- **Álafoss Wool Store:**

- Explore Álafoss for Icelandic wool products and souvenirs. Prices vary based on your choices.

Additional Tips:

- **Off-Season Travel:**
- Consider visiting during the off-season for potential discounts on accommodation and a quieter experience.
- **Local Events:**
- Check for local events, festivals, or community activities that might offer free or low-cost entertainment.

Always check the latest prices, reviews, and any ongoing promotions before planning your trip. Mosfellsbær offers a serene environment and is an excellent choice for those who appreciate nature and want to experience Icelandic culture in a more relaxed setting.

Seltjarnarnes

Seltjarnarnes is a small town located on a peninsula just west of Reykjavik, Iceland. Known for its coastal beauty and proximity to the capital, it provides a tranquil environment with stunning views. While it is primarily residential, there are opportunities for a budget-friendly yet comfortable experience. Here's a guide for Seltjarnarnes:

Accommodation:

- **Guesthouses or Homestays:**
  - Explore guesthouses or homestays in Seltjarnarnes for a more intimate experience. Prices can vary, but you may find options starting around $80 - $120 per night.
- **Budget Hotels in Reykjavik:**
  - Consider staying in budget hotels in Reykjavik, as Seltjarnarnes is in close proximity. Prices for budget hotels can start around $70 - $120 per night.

Dining:

- **Local Cafés and Restaurants:**
  - Discover local cafés and restaurants for coffee, snacks, and light meals. Prices for coffee and treats are approximately $5 - $10.
- **Supermarkets and Local Markets:**
  - Utilize supermarkets for budget-friendly meals or snacks. Check out local markets for fresh produce and local specialties.

Activities:

- **Grótta Lighthouse:**
  - Visit Grótta Lighthouse, located on the northern tip of the peninsula. The area is known for birdwatching, and access to the lighthouse is usually free.
- **Coastal Walks:**

- Enjoy leisurely walks along the coastline. Seltjarnarnes offers beautiful views, especially during the midnight sun or Northern Lights.

Nature and Outdoor Exploration:

- **Sundlaug Seltjarnarness:**
    - Visit the local swimming pool, Sundlaug Seltjarnarness, for a relaxing experience. Entrance fees are typically affordable, around $8 - $12.
- **Seltjarnarnes Nature Reserve:**
    - Explore the Seltjarnarnes Nature Reserve for hiking and birdwatching. Entrance is usually free.

Transportation:

- **Public Bus or Walk:**
    - Public buses connect Seltjarnarnes to Reykjavik and other nearby areas. Prices for bus tickets are approximately $3 - $5.
- **Rent a Bike:**
    - Consider renting a bike for local exploration. Prices vary, but daily rentals can start around $15 - $20.

South Iceland

Welcome to South Iceland, a region of unparalleled natural beauty where glaciers, volcanoes, and lush landscapes create a mesmerizing tapestry of contrasts. As you embark on your journey through South Iceland, you'll find yourself immersed in a world shaped by both fire and ice, with a history as captivating as the landscapes themselves.

South Iceland is home to some of the country's most iconic landmarks, including the mighty Vatnajökull, Europe's largest glacier, and the spectacular Jökulsárlón glacial lagoon, where icebergs drift serenely against a backdrop of stunning mountain scenery. The region is also dotted with powerful waterfalls like Skógafoss and Seljalandsfoss, whose thunderous cascades echo the untamed spirit of this extraordinary land.

Beyond the natural wonders, South Iceland carries the echoes of its Viking past, with historical sites like Þingvellir National Park, where the ancient Icelandic Parliament, Alþingi, convened more than a millennium ago. Explore the black sand beaches of Reynisfjara, surrounded by dramatic basalt columns, and discover the folklore that weaves through the charming villages along the coast.

While South Iceland offers an awe-inspiring experience, it's worth noting that traveling in this region can also be budget-friendly with a few insider tips. Consider staying in guesthouses or cottages in smaller towns to experience local hospitality while saving on accommodation costs. Plan your meals by exploring local grocery stores and enjoying picnics against the backdrop of South Iceland's breathtaking scenery.

To make the most of your budget, take advantage of free natural attractions, such as hiking trails and hot springs, scattered throughout the region. Renting a car can also be a cost-effective way to explore, providing the flexibility to venture off the beaten path and discover hidden gems without the constraints of a tour schedule.

South Iceland invites you to embark on a journey where history and nature converge, where glaciers meet volcanoes, and where savvy travelers can revel in the enchantment of this extraordinary region without breaking the bank. Get ready for an adventure that unfolds like a saga, with every step revealing the magic that defines South Iceland

- **Vík í Mýrdal:**
  - Vík is a small coastal village known for its black sand beaches, particularly Reynisfjara Beach. The nearby basalt sea stacks, Reynisdrangar, and the Dyrhólaey peninsula are popular attractions.

Affordable Luxurious Accommodation in Vík	Pros	Cons	Starting Prices
Puffin Hostel Vík	- Budget-friendly accommodation - Convenient location near Vík's attractions	- Shared facilities may not suit all travelers - Basic amenities	From $30 per night for dorm beds
HI Vík Hostel	- Stunning views of Reynisdrangar sea stacks - Social atmosphere with communal	- Shared facilities can be crowded - Limited availability during peak season	From $40 per night for dorm beds
Guesthouse Carina	- Cozy and welcoming atmosphere - Close proximity to downtown Vík shops and restaurants	- Limited on-site amenities - Shared bathrooms may require wait times	From $70 per night for double rooms

Hotel Katla	- Modern and comfortable rooms - On-site restaurant serving local cuisine	- Prices may vary depending on room type and season - Limited availability during peak season	From $100 per night for standard rooms
Puffin Hotel Vík	- Central location in Vík - Stylish and contemporary design	- Higher price compared to other options - Limited availability during	From $120 per night for standard rooms

- **Selfoss:**
  - Selfoss is a town situated on the banks of the Ölfusá River. It serves as a gateway to the Golden Circle, a popular tourist route. Selfoss itself has a charming atmosphere with local shops and restaurants.
- **Hella:**
  - Hella is a town located along the southern ring road, making it a convenient stop for travelers exploring the region. It offers accommodation, services, and access to nearby attractions.
- **Hvolsvöllur:**
  - Hvolsvöllur is a town known for its proximity to natural wonders like waterfalls and glaciers. It's often a base for those exploring the southern part of the country.
- **Skógar:**
  - Skógar is a small village known for the iconic Skógafoss waterfall and the Skógar Folk Museum. The area offers hiking opportunities and stunning views of the coastline.
- **Vestmannaeyjar (Westman Islands):**
  - While not on the mainland, Vestmannaeyjar is an archipelago located off the southern coast of Iceland. The largest island, Heimaey, is known for its volcanic landscapes, puffin colonies, and the Eldfell volcano.
- **Grindavík:**
  - Grindavík is a coastal fishing town located near the Blue Lagoon geothermal spa. It's a popular stop for those

visiting the Blue Lagoon or exploring the Reykjanes Peninsula.

Keflavik

1. Affordable Accommodation:

- Opt for budget-friendly accommodations in Keflavik, such as guesthouses or hostels. Many options offer comfortable stays without the hefty price tag.

2. Explore the Keflavik Harbor:

- Take a leisurely stroll along the Keflavik Harbor, enjoying the views of the boats and the Atlantic Ocean. It's a peaceful and cost-free activity.

3. Visit the Viking World Museum:

- Explore the Viking World Museum to learn about Iceland's maritime history and Viking heritage. While there's an entrance fee, it provides an enriching experience.

4. Relax at the Geothermal Pools:

- Soak in the Keflavik geothermal pools. The local swimming pools offer a budget-friendly way to experience the relaxing benefits of geothermal waters.

5. Enjoy Local Cuisine in Downtown Keflavik:

- Savor Icelandic cuisine in local restaurants and cafes in downtown Keflavik. Opting for local establishments can provide a taste of luxury without breaking the bank.

6. Discover the Bridge Between Continents:

- Visit the Bridge Between Continents, a symbolic bridge connecting the North American and Eurasian tectonic plates. This natural wonder is free to explore.

7. Experience the Reykjanes Geopark:

- Explore the Reykjanes Geopark, known for its unique geological features. Discover bubbling hot springs, dramatic coastlines, and lava fields on a budget.

8. Walk around Keflavik Old Town:

- Wander through Keflavik's Old Town, where you'll find charming streets, historic buildings, and a laid-back atmosphere.

9. Hike to the Gunnuhver Hot Springs:

- Take a hike to the Gunnuhver Hot Springs in Reykjanes. Witness the powerful geothermal activity, including mud pools and steam vents.

10. Discover the Garðskagi Lighthouse:

- Visit the Garðskagi Lighthouse for stunning coastal views. The lighthouse and surrounding area offer a peaceful escape at no cost.

11. Birdwatching at Sandgerdi:

- Head to the Sandgerdi area for birdwatching. The coastal location is known for its diverse birdlife, providing a unique and budget-friendly nature experience.

12. Attend Local Events and Festivals:

- Check for local events and festivals happening in Keflavik during your visit. Many cultural and community events are often free to attend.

13. Explore the Reykjanes Art Museum:

- Visit the Reykjanes Art Museum to explore local and international art. The museum often features rotating exhibits and reasonable admission fees.

14. Discover the Grindavik Fishing Village:

- Explore the nearby fishing village of Grindavik, known for its authentic charm and proximity to the Blue Lagoon. Enjoy the local atmosphere without the high tourist prices.

15. Capture the Sunset at the Reykjanesviti Lighthouse:

- Experience a luxurious sunset at the Reykjanesviti Lighthouse. The views of the coastline and the setting sun create a memorable and cost-free experience.

16. Explore the Reykjanes Peninsula by Car:

- Rent a car and explore the Reykjanes Peninsula at your own pace. This allows you to discover hidden gems and breathtaking landscapes without the cost of guided tours.

17. Enjoy Scenic Drives:

- Take advantage of the scenic drives around Keflavik and the Reykjanes Peninsula. The diverse landscapes offer a luxurious experience without the luxury price tag.

18. Visit the Icelandic Museum of Rock 'n' Roll:

- Explore the Icelandic Museum of Rock 'n' Roll in Keflavik. The museum provides a fascinating journey through Iceland's musical history at an affordable entrance fee.

19. Relax at the Grindavik Hot Springs:

- Discover the Grindavik Hot Springs for a relaxing soak. While there may be a small fee, it's a more budget-friendly alternative to larger geothermal spas.

20. Capture the Northern Lights:

- If visiting during the winter months, venture outside of Keflavik to capture the Northern Lights. The dark skies of Reykjanes Peninsula provide a chance to witness this natural spectacle without added expenses.

The Jökulsárlón Glacier Lagoon

Jökulsárlón Glacier Lagoon is a relatively recent natural formation, born out of the retreat of Breiðamerkurjökull, a glacier stemming from the immense Vatnajökull ice cap. The lagoon began to form in the early 20th century as the glacier started receding rapidly, leaving behind a deepening depression which filled with meltwater. Over time, the lagoon expanded as more icebergs calved off the glacier and floated into the water, creating a surreal landscape of sparkling ice formations.

Since its formation, Jökulsárlón has become one of Iceland's most iconic attractions, drawing thousands of visitors each year. Initially, it was mainly frequented by researchers and photographers fascinated by its unique beauty. However, with the growth of Iceland's tourism industry, Jökulsárlón has gained widespread popularity among travelers seeking awe-inspiring natural wonders.

The lagoon's accessibility via the nearby Route 1, Iceland's ring road, has contributed to its increasing visitation. Tourists can easily reach Jökulsárlón by road, making it a must-see destination for those exploring the southeastern region of Iceland. Additionally, its appearance in several films and television shows, including the James Bond movie "Die Another Day" and the HBO series "Game of Thrones," has further boosted its fame and attracted more visitors.

Today, Jökulsárlón Glacier Lagoon remains a symbol of Iceland's dynamic natural landscape, serving as a testament to the ongoing effects of climate change while captivating visitors with its ethereal beauty and dramatic ice formations.

1. Travel Planning:

a. **Off-Peak Season:** Similar to the Northern Lights, visit during the off-peak season to avoid crowds and get better deals on accommodations and activities.

b. **Flexible Dates:** Be flexible with your travel dates to find the best prices on flights and accommodations.

2. Flights:

a. **Booking in Advance:** Look for deals on flights and book well in advance. Consider using budget airlines or package deals that include flights and accommodation.

b. **Airports:** Fly into Keflavík International Airport (KEF) and then consider taking a domestic flight or bus to Jökulsárlón to save on transportation costs.

3. Accommodation:

a. **Guesthouses and Cabins:** Opt for guesthouses or cabins in the nearby towns like Höfn or Kirkjubæjarklaustur. They offer cozy stays and are often more budget-friendly than hotels.

b. **Camping:** If you're adventurous, consider camping. Iceland has many designated campsites, and camping can be a cost-effective way to enjoy nature.

c. **Airbnb:** Explore Airbnb options for unique and potentially more affordable accommodations.

4. Transportation:

a. **Car Rental:** Renting a car is advisable for flexibility. Compare rental prices and book in advance for better deals.

b. **Bus Services:** If you're on a tighter budget, consider taking a bus. Several companies operate routes to and from Jökulsárlón.

5. Glacier Lagoon Tours:

a. **Boat Tours:** Take a boat tour to get up close to the glaciers. Look for group tours for better pricing and book in advance.

b. **Iceberg Beach Exploration:** Explore the Diamond Beach nearby, where icebergs from the lagoon wash ashore. This can be a self-guided and cost-free activity.

6. Luxury on a Budget:

a. **Picnic with a View:** Pack your own meals and enjoy a picnic with a stunning view of the glacier lagoon.

b. **Affordable Comfort:** Look for accommodations that provide a balance of comfort and affordability. Some guesthouses offer beautiful views and cozy atmospheres.

7. Clothing and Gear:

a. **Rent or Borrow Gear:** If you need specific gear for glacier exploration, consider renting or borrowing to save costs.

b. **Layering:** As Jökulsárlón can be cold, prioritize layering to stay warm. Bring your own thermal layers and a good waterproof jacket.

8. Enjoying the Experience:

a. **Free Activities:** Besides the boat tour, there are many free activities, like walking along the shores of the lagoon or exploring the nearby landscapes.

b. **Photography:** Capture the beauty of Jökulsárlón with your camera or smartphone. This is a cost-free way to create lasting memories.

Estimated Budget:

- **Accommodation:** $50 - $150 per night
- **Car Rental/Transportation:** $30 - $50 per day

- **Glacier Lagoon Boat Tour:** $50 - $100 per person
- **Meals:** $20 - $40 per day
- **Miscellaneous:** $100 - $200 (for activities, souvenirs, etc.)

Vík í Mýrdal

Vík í Mýrdal is a charming village on Iceland's South Coast, known for its stunning black sand beaches, dramatic cliffs, and proximity to iconic landmarks. While Iceland is generally known for being on the pricier side, there are ways to enjoy a touch of luxury on a budget in Vík. Here's a guide with specifics and approximate prices:

Accommodation:

- **Hotel Katla Hofdabrekka:**
  - A well-reviewed hotel in Vík with comfortable rooms.
  - **Approximate Price:** $120 - $200 per night (Prices may vary based on the season and room type).
- **Icelandair Hotel Vík:**
  - A modern hotel with stylish design and scenic views.
  - **Approximate Price:** $150 - $250 per night (Prices may vary based on the season and room type).

Dining:

- **Suður-Vík Restaurant:**
  - A cozy restaurant offering Icelandic cuisine with a focus on local ingredients.
  - **Approximate Price:** $20 - $40 per person for a meal (Prices may vary based on menu choices).
- **Halldórskaffi:**
  - A popular café and restaurant known for its homemade food and welcoming atmosphere.
  - **Approximate Price:** $15 - $30 per person for a meal (Prices may vary based on menu choices).

Attractions:

- **Reynisfjara Black Sand Beach:**
  - Explore the iconic black sand beach, Reynisfjara, and marvel at the basalt columns and Reynisdrangar sea stacks.
  - **Approximate Price:** Free (Parking may have a small fee).
- **Dyrhólaey:**
  - Visit the Dyrhólaey viewpoint for panoramic views of the surrounding area, including the black sand beach and sea cliffs.
  - **Approximate Price:** Free.

Tours and Activities:

- **Glacier Hiking Tour (from Vík):**
  - Join a glacier hiking tour, exploring nearby glaciers with an experienced guide.
  - **Approximate Price:** $100 - $150 per person.
- **Reynisfjara Beach ATV Tour:**
  - Experience an ATV tour on the black sand beaches and surrounding areas.
  - **Approximate Price:** $80 - $120 per person.

Transportation:

- **Car Rental:**
- Rent a car to explore the South Coast at your own pace and visit nearby attractions.
- **Approximate Price:** $50 - $100 per day (depending on the car type and rental company).

Additional Tips:

- **Book in Advance:** To secure the best prices on accommodations, tours, and car rentals, consider booking in advance, especially if you're visiting during the peak tourist season.
- **Grocery Stores:** If your accommodation has kitchen facilities, consider buying groceries from local stores to prepare some meals, saving on dining expenses.

Selfoss

Selfoss is a town in southern Iceland, situated on the banks of the Ölfusá River. It is the largest town in the Árborg municipality and serves as a regional center for services and commerce. Here's an overview of Selfoss:

Attractions and Points of Interest:

- **Ölfusá River:** The town is located on the banks of the Ölfusá River, which is one of Iceland's major rivers. It adds to the scenic beauty of the area and provides opportunities for riverside walks.
- **Selfoss Church (Tryggvaskáli):** The modern and distinctive church in Selfoss is often photographed for its unique architecture. It's a notable landmark in the town.
- **Selfoss Suspension Bridge:** This bridge spans the Ölfusá River and connects the town of Selfoss. It offers picturesque views of the river and surrounding landscapes.
- **Hotels and Accommodations:** Selfoss has a range of accommodations, including hotels and guesthouses, making it a convenient base for exploring nearby attractions.
- **Local Cuisine:** Explore local restaurants and cafes in Selfoss to try Icelandic cuisine. Some places may offer traditional dishes featuring local ingredients.
- **Cultural Events:** Check for any local events or festivals that might be taking place during your visit. Selfoss hosts various cultural events and celebrations throughout the year.

Affordable Luxurious Accommodation in Selfoss	Pros	Cons	Starting Prices
Selfoss Hostel	- Budget-friendly accommodation - Convenient location near Selfoss	- Shared facilities may not suit all travelers - Basic amenities	From $30 per night for dorm beds
Selfoss HI Hostel	- Cozy atmosphere with communal kitchen and lounge - Close	- Shared facilities can be crowded - Limited availability during peak season	From $40 per night for dorm beds

Guesthouse Garun	- Comfortable rooms with modern amenities - Welcoming and	- Limited on-site amenities - Shared bathrooms may require wait	From $70 per night for double rooms
Hotel Selfoss	- Modern and stylish design - On-site restaurant and bar	- Prices may vary depending on room type and season - Limited availability during peak season	From $100 per night for standard rooms
Vatnsholt Guesthouse	- Tranquil countryside setting - Spacious rooms with scenic views	- Requires transportation to reach downtown Selfoss - Limited dining options nearby	From $80 per night for double rooms

Activities in the Surrounding Area:

- **Golden Circle:** Selfoss is a good starting point for exploring the Golden Circle, which includes iconic attractions like Þingvellir National Park, Geysir Geothermal Area, and Gullfoss Waterfall.
- **Seljalandsfoss and Skogafoss Waterfalls:** These famous waterfalls are a short drive from Selfoss, offering breathtaking views and the opportunity to get up close to the cascading water.
- **Vatnajökull National Park:** Selfoss provides reasonable access to Vatnajökull National Park, where you can explore glaciers, ice caves, and unique geological formations.
- **Hiking and Nature Walks:** The surrounding countryside offers opportunities for hiking and nature walks. Check with local information centers for suggested trails and routes.

Transportation:

- **Car Rental:** Renting a car provides flexibility to explore the nearby attractions at your own pace. Several car rental companies operate in Selfoss.
- **Bus Services:** Strætó, the Icelandic public bus system, also serves Selfoss, connecting it to other towns and cities in the region. Check the Strætó website for bus schedules and routes.

Hella

Hella is a small town in southern Iceland, situated on the banks of the Ytri-Rangá River. It is located approximately 94 kilometers east of Reykjavik. Here's an overview of Hella:

Attractions and Points of Interest:

- **Ytri-Rangá River:** The town is situated along the Ytri-Rangá River, offering scenic views and opportunities for outdoor activities.
- **Hella's Geothermal Swimming Pool:** Visitors can enjoy relaxation and recreation at Hella's geothermally heated swimming pool. It's a common feature in Icelandic towns, providing a unique and refreshing experience.
- **Ferryhill:** A popular viewpoint in Hella, providing panoramic views of the surrounding landscapes, including the Hekla volcano.
- **Hella Horse Rental:** For those interested in Icelandic horse riding experiences, Hella offers opportunities to explore the countryside on horseback.
- **Hella Golf Course:** Golf enthusiasts can visit the Hella Golf Course to enjoy a round of golf amid the picturesque Icelandic scenery.

Activities in the Surrounding Area:

- **Þjórsárdalur Valley:** Located nearby, Þjórsárdalur Valley offers diverse landscapes, historical sites, and attractions like Hjálparfoss waterfall.
- **Hekla Volcano:** Hekla is one of Iceland's most active volcanoes, and its proximity to Hella makes it accessible for those interested in exploring the region's volcanic features.
- **Golden Circle:** Hella is a good starting point for those wanting to explore the Golden Circle, including attractions like Þingvellir National Park, Geysir Geothermal Area, and Gullfoss Waterfall.

Transportation:

- **Car Rental:** Renting a car provides the flexibility to explore the nearby attractions at your own pace. Several car rental companies operate in Hella.
- **Bus Services:** Strætó, the Icelandic public bus system, serves Hella, connecting it to other towns and cities in the region. Check the Strætó website for bus schedules and routes.

Hvolsvöllur

Hvolsvöllur is a small town in southern Iceland, situated along the Ring Road (Route 1) approximately 106 kilometers east of Reykjavik. Here's an overview of Hvolsvöllur:

Attractions and Points of Interest:

- **Lava Centre:** The Lava Centre in Hvolsvöllur is an interactive exhibition showcasing the geological forces that shape Iceland, including volcanic activity and earthquakes. It's an informative stop for those interested in the country's geological features.
- **Njál's Saga Centre:** This cultural center provides insights into Icelandic sagas, specifically the Njála (Njál's Saga), one of the most famous sagas in Icelandic literature.
- **Hvolsvöllur Swimming Pool:** Like many towns in Iceland, Hvolsvöllur has a geothermally heated swimming pool where visitors can relax and enjoy the warm waters.

Activities in the Surrounding Area:

- **Þórsmörk:** Hvolsvöllur is a gateway to Þórsmörk, a nature reserve known for its diverse landscapes, hiking trails, and stunning scenery. It's a popular destination for nature lovers and hikers.
- **Seljalandsfoss and Skogafoss Waterfalls:** These famous waterfalls are a short drive from Hvolsvöllur, offering spectacular views and the opportunity to get up close to the cascading water.
- **Eyjafjallajökull Visitor Centre:** Learn about the 2010 eruption of the Eyjafjallajökull volcano and its impact on air travel at the visitor center located near Hvolsvöllur.

Transportation:

- **Car Rental:** Renting a car provides the flexibility to explore the nearby attractions at your own pace. Several car rental companies operate in Hvolsvöllur.
- **Bus Services:** Strætó, the Icelandic public bus system, serves Hvolsvöllur, connecting it to other towns and cities in the region. Check the Strætó website for bus schedules and routes.

Skógar

Skógar, also known as Skogar, is a small village located along the southern coast of Iceland. It is situated at the southern end of the Eyjafjallajökull glacier and is known for its natural beauty, cultural attractions, and proximity to iconic landmarks. Here's an overview of Skógar:

Attractions and Points of Interest:

- **Skogafoss Waterfall:** One of Iceland's most famous waterfalls, Skogafoss is a powerful and picturesque cascade with a drop of approximately 60 meters. Visitors can walk close to the waterfall and even climb a staircase to get panoramic views from the top.
- **Skógar Museum (Skógasafn):** The Skógar Museum is an open-air folk museum that provides insights into Iceland's cultural heritage. It features historical buildings, artifacts, and exhibitions related to the country's rural life.
- **Skógar Church:** The village is home to a charming church, Skógar Church, which dates back to 1890. The church is known for its simple yet beautiful architecture.
- **Eyjafjallajökull Visitor Centre:** Learn about the eruption of the Eyjafjallajökull volcano in 2010 and its impact on the region. The visitor center offers multimedia exhibits and information about the volcanic activity.
- **Fimmvörðuháls Hiking Trail:** Skógar is a starting point for the Fimmvörðuháls hiking trail, a popular trek that takes you through diverse landscapes, including waterfalls, glaciers, and volcanic terrain. The trail connects Skógar to Þórsmörk.

Activities in the Surrounding Area:

- **Solheimajokull Glacier:** Explore the nearby Solheimajokull glacier, an outlet glacier from the larger Mýrdalsjökull glacier. Guided glacier hikes and ice climbing tours are available.
- **Dyrhólaey:** Visit the Dyrhólaey promontory, which offers breathtaking views of the surrounding coastline and is known for its iconic sea arch.
- **Reynisfjara Black Sand Beach:** A short drive from Skógar, Reynisfjara is a famous black sand beach with unique basalt columns and sea stacks.

Transportation:

- **Car Rental:** Renting a car provides flexibility to explore the nearby attractions at your own pace. Several car rental companies operate in the area.
- **Bus Services:** Strætó, the Icelandic public bus system, serves Skógar, connecting it to other towns and cities in the region. However, bus services to smaller villages may be less frequent.

Vestmannaeyjar (Westman Islands):

Vestmannaeyjar, commonly known as the Westman Islands, is a group of islands located off the south coast of Iceland. Visiting Vestmannaeyjar provides a unique opportunity to explore a volcanic archipelago with a rich history and diverse natural beauty. The combination of geological wonders, birdwatching, and the resilience of the local community makes the Westman Islands a fascinating destination in Iceland.

Main Island:

The largest and only inhabited island in the archipelago is called Heimaey. This is where the majority of the population resides, and it's the center of economic and cultural activities in the Westman Islands.

Attractions and Points of Interest:

- **Eldfell Volcano:** In 1973, a volcanic eruption on Heimaey led to the formation of Eldfell, a volcanic cone. Visitors can hike to the top of Eldfell for panoramic views of the island and surrounding ocean.
- **Pompeii of the North (Pompeii Norðursins):** During the 1973 eruption, a part of Heimaey was buried under lava and ash. The Pompeii of the North is an area where houses have been excavated, providing a unique glimpse into the impact of volcanic activity on a community.
- **Vestmannaeyjar Aquarium and Natural History Museum:** Learn about the marine life around the Westman Islands and the geological history of the area at the local aquarium and natural history museum.
- **Stórhöfði:** The southern tip of Heimaey, Stórhöfði, is a birdwatcher's paradise. It's home to various seabirds, including puffins, fulmars, and guillemots.
- **Eldheimar Volcano Museum:** This museum provides comprehensive information about the 1973 eruption, featuring interactive exhibits and artifacts. It's located at the foot of Eldfell.

Activities in the Surrounding Area:

- **Boat Tours:** Explore the waters around the Westman Islands on a boat tour. These tours often include opportunities to spot wildlife, including whales and seabirds.
- **Puffin Watching:** The Westman Islands are known for their puffin colonies. Take a boat tour to see these charming seabirds in their natural habitat.
- **Outdoor Activities:** Heimaey offers opportunities for outdoor activities such as hiking, golf, and exploring the unique landscapes shaped by volcanic activity.

Transportation:

- **Ferry:** You can reach Vestmannaeyjar by ferry from the mainland, specifically from the town of Þorlákshöfn. The ferry journey provides scenic views of the coastline and takes about 30-40 minutes.
- **Air Travel:** There is also a small airport on Heimaey with domestic flights

- connecting the Westman Islands to Reykjavik and other locations in Iceland.

Luxury for less in South Iceland

1. Witness the Power of Seljalandsfoss:

- Marvel at the majestic Seljalandsfoss waterfall. The unique feature here is the walking path that takes you behind the cascading water. Admission is free.

2. Explore Skogafoss and its Surroundings:

- Discover the iconic Skogafoss waterfall and climb the staircase for a panoramic view. Hiking along the Skogar River offers additional breathtaking scenery.

3. Hike to the Plane Wreck at Sólheimasandur:

- Embark on a captivating hike to the DC-3 plane wreck on Sólheimasandur. The scenery is surreal, and the experience is entirely cost-free.

4. Visit the Black Sand Beach at Reynisfjara:

- Take a leisurely stroll on Reynisfjara, a black sand beach with basalt columns and stunning sea stacks. The powerful waves crashing against the shore create a luxurious natural spectacle.

5. Explore the Fjaðrárgljúfur Canyon:

- Wander through the Fjaðrárgljúfur Canyon, a serene and picturesque gorge. The entrance is free, and you can enjoy the tranquility of the surroundings.

6. Discover the Hidden Gem of Gljúfrabúi:

- Seek out the hidden waterfall Gljúfrabúi, partially concealed within a cavern. It's a magical spot and offers a unique experience.

7. Soak in the Seljavallalaug Hot Spring:

- Enjoy a relaxing soak in Seljavallalaug, one of Iceland's oldest outdoor swimming pools. The hot spring is set against a stunning mountain backdrop.

8. Explore the Vík Church:

- Visit the charming Vík Church, a red-roofed chapel that stands against the backdrop of Reynisdrangar sea stacks.

9. Marvel at the Icebergs of Jökulsárlón Glacier Lagoon:

- Witness the floating icebergs at Jökulsárlón Glacier Lagoon. While boat tours have a cost, simply walking along the shore and admiring the ice formations is free.

10. Discover Diamond Beach:

- Adjacent to Jökulsárlón, Diamond Beach is known for its icebergs that wash ashore, resembling glistening diamonds against the black sand.

11. Hike to Svartifoss in Skaftafell:

- Take a trek to Svartifoss in Skaftafell National Park. The waterfall is framed by basalt columns, creating a picturesque and almost ethereal atmosphere.

12. Explore the Fjallsárlón Glacier Lagoon:

- Experience the serenity of Fjallsárlón, a smaller but equally captivating glacier lagoon. It's a less crowded alternative to Jökulsárlón.

13. Visit the Lighthouse at Dyrhólaey:

- Enjoy panoramic views from the Dyrhólaey viewpoint and visit the historic lighthouse. The cliffs offer stunning vistas of the surrounding coastline.

14. Hike to the Hot River at Reykjadalur:

- Trek to Reykjadalur and indulge in a natural hot river bath. The hike is free, and the reward is a luxurious soak in the warm geothermal waters.

15. Explore the Lava Fields of Eldhraun:

- Wander through the moss-covered lava fields of Eldhraun, created during a historical eruption. The unique landscape feels otherworldly.

16. Discover the Stakkholtsgjá Canyon:

- Venture into Stakkholtsgjá Canyon, a peaceful and enchanting location. The narrow gorge is surrounded by towering cliffs.

17. Experience the Gullfoss Canyon:

- Witness the power of Gullfoss, a magnificent two-tiered waterfall. The canyon adds a dramatic touch to this natural wonder.

18. Visit the Geysir Geothermal Area:

- Explore the Geysir Geothermal Area and witness the Strokkur geyser erupting at regular intervals. Entry is free, and the geothermal activity is a wonder to behold.

19. Hike to the Crater of Kerið:

- Hike to the volcanic crater of Kerið, where a striking blue lake contrasts with the red volcanic slopes. A small fee is required for entry.

20. Enjoy the Silence at Sólheimajökull Glacier:

- Admire the tranquil beauty of Sólheimajökull Glacier. While guided glacier tours are available, you can also appreciate the glacier's majesty from a distance without a cost.

These budget-friendly activities in South Iceland allow you to immerse yourself in the region's natural wonders, offering a sense of luxury without the need for extravagant spending.

North Iceland

A land of untamed wilderness, geothermal wonders, and cultural treasures that beckon you to explore a region shaped by the forces of nature. As you venture into North Iceland, you'll discover a captivating blend of history, folklore, and breathtaking landscapes that define this unique corner of the world.

This northern expanse is home to the mighty Goðafoss, the "Waterfall of the Gods," where history and myth intertwine. Legend has it that in the year 1000, chieftains threw their pagan idols into the falls, marking the symbolic acceptance of Christianity in Iceland. The region's rich history extends to Akureyri, the "Capital of the North," where charming streets, colorful houses, and cultural gems invite you to step back in time.

The geothermal activity in North Iceland is on full display at Lake Mývatn, surrounded by otherworldly landscapes of bubbling mud pots and steam vents. Dettifoss, Europe's most powerful waterfall, thunders in the Vatnajökull National Park, showcasing the raw power of nature in this remote and pristine region.

To navigate North Iceland on a budget, consider staying in guesthouses or budget-friendly accommodations, often run by friendly locals eager to share their stories. Explore the region's culinary scene by sampling local specialties at affordable cafes and restaurants, where you can savor traditional Icelandic dishes without straining your wallet.

North Iceland offers an abundance of free or low-cost attractions, from hiking trails through volcanic landscapes to relaxing in natural hot springs scattered throughout the region. Renting a car provides the freedom to explore the hidden gems of the North at your own pace, allowing you to uncover the secrets of this enchanting land without the constraints of a guided tour.

So, get ready to embark on a journey through North Iceland, where history echoes in every waterfall, and nature paints a canvas of wonder. Whether you're captivated by folklore or drawn to the untamed beauty of the Arctic landscapes, North Iceland welcomes you to an adventure that seamlessly blends history, culture, and budget-friendly exploration.

North Iceland is known for its stunning landscapes, geothermal wonders, and vibrant communities. While the region is less densely populated than the south, there are several towns and villages that attract visitors with their unique charm and proximity to natural attractions. Here are some of the most visited towns and villages in North Iceland:

Akureyri, often referred to as the "Capital of the North," stands as the largest town in North Iceland. Visitors to Akureyri can explore attractions such as the Akureyri Church, the Akureyri Art Museum, and the botanical garden. Serving as a hub for exploring the surrounding area, Akureyri is renowned for its lively cultural scene.

Húsavík, known as the whale-watching capital of Iceland, is a picturesque town nestled on the shores of Skjálfandi Bay. Tourists flock to Húsavík for whale-watching tours, offering glimpses of various whale species including humpback and minke whales. Notable attractions in Húsavík include the Húsavík Whale Museum and the iconic wooden Húsavíkurkirkja church.

Affordable Luxurious Accommodation in	Pros	Cons	Starting Prices
Húsavík Hostel	- Budget-friendly accommodation - Convenient location near Húsavík attractions	- Shared facilities may not suit all travelers - Basic amenities	From $30 per night for dorm beds
Húsavík Cape Hotel	- Cozy atmosphere with views of Skjálfandi Bay - Close proximity to downtown Húsavík	- Shared facilities can be crowded - Limited availability during peak season	From $50 per night for dorm beds
Fosshotel Húsavík	- Modern and comfortable rooms - On-site restaurant serving local cuisine	- Prices may vary depending on room type and season - Limited availability during peak season	From $100 per night for standard rooms
Húsavík Cape Guesthouse	- Charming guesthouse with personalized service - Peaceful location with views	- Limited on-site amenities - Shared bathrooms may require wait times	From $80 per night for double rooms
Guesthouse Húsavík	- Welcoming atmosphere with attentive staff - Convenient location near attractions	- Prices may vary depending on room type and season - Limited availability during peak season	From $70 per night for double rooms

These affordable accom

Myvatn (Mývatn) encompasses a region rather than a town, housing small villages like Reykjahlíð. It is celebrated for its stunning Lake Mývatn, geothermal areas, and diverse birdlife. Travelers can explore attractions like the Hverir geothermal area, Grjótagjá cave, and the Myvatn Nature Baths.

Dalvík, situated on the Eyjafjörður fjord, is steeped in fishing heritage and offers various outdoor activities. Winter brings opportunities for skiing, while summer attracts visitors for whale watching. The town hosts the annual Fiskidagurinn mikli (The Great Fish Day) festival.

Siglufjörður, nestled in a narrow fjord, captivates visitors with its scenic beauty and historic charm. The Herring Era Museum sheds light on the town's history during the herring industry boom. Today, Siglufjörður thrives as a cultural hub, hosting music festivals and art events.

Húsafell, situated in the western part of North Iceland, is enveloped by glaciers and hot springs. It serves as a gateway for exploring Langjökull glacier and nearby waterfalls, offering a serene retreat amidst nature with hiking and relaxation opportunities.

Ólafsfjörður, a small fishing town cradled in a fjord encircled by mountains, is famed for outdoor activities like hiking and skiing. With a cultural center and events such as the French Days festival, Ólafsfjörður exudes a vibrant atmosphere.

Sauðárkrókur, the largest town in Skagafjörður, is renowned for its agricultural and equestrian pursuits. Visitors can partake in horse riding and explore the scenic countryside, immersing themselves in the region's rich horse breeding tradition.

Akureyri

Akureyri, the "Capital of the North" and the vibrant heart of Iceland's second-largest urban area. Nestled on the shores of Eyjafjörður, surrounded by snow-capped mountains, Akureyri offers a charming blend of culture, history, and natural beauty that beckons travelers to explore the northern reaches of this captivating island.

Founded in 1778, Akureyri has evolved from a modest trading post into a lively town known for its warm atmosphere and cultural offerings. The town's iconic Akureyri Church, standing proudly on a hill overlooking the fjord, is a symbol of the community's resilience and spirit.

Akureyri's streets are adorned with vibrant houses, boutique shops, and inviting cafes, creating a welcoming atmosphere for both locals and visitors alike. The Akureyri Art Museum and the Nonni House provide insight into the region's artistic heritage and literary contributions.

Nature enthusiasts will find plenty to explore in the surrounding area. The nearby Hlíðarfjall ski resort offers winter sports enthusiasts a playground of snowy slopes, while the Botanical Garden showcases a surprising variety of plants, thriving despite the northern climate.

To make the most of your time and budget in Akureyri, consider strolling through the town's charming streets, where local markets and eateries provide a taste of Icelandic culture without breaking the bank. Opt for accommodations in guesthouses or cozy inns, where you can experience the warmth of local hospitality.

Akureyri invites you to embrace the slower pace of northern life, where the scenic beauty of the fjord, the warmth of the locals, and the cultural offerings create an inviting tapestry for an unforgettable experience. Whether you're seeking adventure on the slopes or a peaceful retreat surrounded by natural wonders, Akureyri welcomes you with open arms to discover the unique charm of Iceland's northern gem.

1. Affordable Accommodation:

- **North Star Apartments**: These guesthouse apartments provide self-catering accommodation with private bathrooms and kitchenettes. They are situated within walking distance of Akureyri's main attractions. Prices for a studio apartment start at around 12,000 ISK per night.

Affordable Luxurious Accommodation in Akureyri	Pros	Cons	Starting Prices
Akureyri H.I. Hostel	- Stunning views of Eyjafjörður fjord - Social atmosphere with communal	- Shared facilities may not suit all travelers - Limited availability during	From $35 per night for dorm beds
Akureyri Backpackers	- Cozy and welcoming atmosphere - Close proximity to downtown shops and	- Shared facilities can be crowded - Limited space in dormitory rooms	From $40 per night for dorm beds
Sæluhús Apartments	- Modern and well-equipped apartments - Private kitchenette and bathroom	- Limited on-site amenities - Prices may vary depending on apartment size and season	From $70 per night for studio apartments
Skjaldarvik Guesthouse	- Peaceful countryside setting - Charming wooden cottages with mountain	- Requires transportation to reach Akureyri city center - Limited dining options nearby	From $80 per night for double rooms

Hotel Kea	- Central location in downtown Akureyri - Elegant and comfortable rooms with	- Higher price compared to other options - Limited availability during peak season	From $100 per night for standard rooms

2. Explore the Akureyri Botanical Garden:

- Take a leisurely stroll in the Akureyri Botanical Garden, a tranquil oasis showcasing various plant species. Admission is usually free or at a nominal cost.

3. Visit Akureyri Church:

- Explore the iconic Akureyri Church, also known as Akureyrarkirkja. The church offers stunning views of the town and Eyjafjörður fjord and is a perfect spot for budget-friendly sightseeing.

4. Enjoy Akureyri Public Pool:

- Experience the luxury of Icelandic geothermal pools without breaking the bank. Akureyri Public Pool offers hot tubs, a sauna, and a relaxing atmosphere at an affordable entrance fee.

5. Walk Along the Akureyri Waterfront:

- Take a scenic walk along the Akureyri waterfront. Enjoy the views of the fjord, mountains, and colorful houses, providing a luxurious feeling without any cost.

6. Visit the Akureyri Art Museum:

- Explore the Akureyri Art Museum, featuring local and international artworks. The museum often has affordable admission fees and provides a cultural experience.

7. Savor Local Cuisine at Affordable Eateries:

- Indulge in local cuisine at affordable eateries and cafes. Akureyri has charming restaurants that offer delicious Icelandic dishes without the high-end price tag.

8. Discover the Christmas Garden:

- If visiting during the winter season, explore the Christmas Garden in Akureyri. The festive lights create a magical atmosphere, and wandering around is a cost-free winter luxury.

9. Attend Free Local Events:

- Check for free local events and festivals happening during your visit. Akureyri often hosts cultural events and concerts that may offer a taste of luxury without additional expenses.

10. Hike to Kjarnaskógur Forest:

- Enjoy the outdoors by hiking in Kjarnaskógur Forest, located just outside Akureyri. The trails are free, and the forest provides a serene escape into nature.

11. Visit the Akureyri Museum:

- Explore the Akureyri Museum, offering insights into the town's history and culture. Admission fees are generally reasonable, providing an enriching experience.

12. Relax in Hof Cultural Center:

- Spend some time in the Hof Cultural Center, a modern venue hosting various events. The architecture itself is worth admiring, and there may be free exhibitions or performances.

13. Experience the Fjord Cruise:

- Opt for an affordable fjord cruise to explore Eyjafjörður from a different perspective. Prices are often reasonable, and the scenic views are luxurious.

14. Hike to Sulur Mountain:

- For panoramic views of Akureyri and the surrounding area, hike to the top of Sulur Mountain. The hike is free, and the vistas are spectacular.

15. Explore Old Town Akureyri:

- Wander through the charming Old Town of Akureyri, where you can admire historic buildings, boutique shops, and local cafes with character.

Akureyri Luxury for less

1. Visit Goðafoss Waterfall:

- Marvel at Goðafoss, the "Waterfall of the Gods." The waterfall is easily accessible from the road, and the views are both grand and serene.

3. Relax in the Mývatn Nature Baths:

- Enjoy the geothermal luxury of Mývatn Nature Baths at a fraction of the cost of the Blue Lagoon. The views of the surrounding landscapes are equally stunning.

4. Discover the Town of Húsavík:

- Stroll through the charming town of Húsavík, known for its whale-watching tours. The harbor and seaside views provide a tranquil atmosphere.

5. Hike to Hljóðaklettar:

- Explore the unique rock formations of Hljóðaklettar in Ásbyrgi Canyon. The hiking trails are free, and the surreal landscapes are captivating.

6. Experience the Power of Dettifoss:

- Witness the sheer power of Dettifoss, one of Europe's most powerful waterfalls. The viewing platforms are easily accessible without an entrance fee.

7. Explore Lake Mývatn:

- Discover the beauty of Lake Mývatn, known for its diverse birdlife. Take a leisurely walk along the shore and enjoy the scenic surroundings.

8. Visit the Herring Era Museum in Siglufjörður:

- Explore the Herring Era Museum in Siglufjörður, showcasing the town's rich history. The museum provides insights into Iceland's fishing heritage.

9. Hike to the Hverir Geothermal Area:

- Experience the otherworldly landscapes of Hverir, a geothermal area near Lake Mývatn. Witness bubbling mud pots and steaming vents for free.

10. Explore the Troll Peninsula:

- Drive along the scenic Troll Peninsula, known for its dramatic fjords and picturesque coastal landscapes. The journey itself feels like a luxury.

11. Discover the Hofsós Infinity Pool:

- Take a dip in the infinity pool at Hofsós, offering breathtaking views of Skagafjörður. The pool has a small fee but provides a luxurious experience.

12. Hike to the Waterfall of Aldeyjarfoss:

- Hike to Aldeyjarfoss, a stunning waterfall surrounded by basalt columns. The journey through the rugged terrain adds to the sense of adventure.

13. Visit the Arctic Botanical Gardens in Akureyri:

- Explore the Arctic Botanical Gardens in Akureyri, highlighting plants from the Arctic and subarctic regions. The gardens are free to enter.

14. Experience the Puffin Colony in Húsavík:

- Take a stroll along the cliffs in Húsavík to witness puffins nesting during the breeding season. It's a delightful and cost-free nature experience.

15. Hike to the Krafla Caldera:

- Trek to the Krafla Caldera, a volcanic crater with a surreal landscape. The hiking trails offer panoramic views of the surrounding geothermal areas.

16. Visit the Akureyri Art Museum:

- Explore the Akureyri Art Museum, featuring local and international artworks. Admission is affordable, and it provides insight into the local art scene.

17. Relax at Húsavík's Hot Springs:

- Soak in the geothermal hot springs in Húsavík. Some hot springs are free, providing a relaxing and rejuvenating experience.

18. Explore the Vatnsnes Peninsula:

- Drive around the Vatnsnes Peninsula to spot seals along the coast. The scenic landscapes and wildlife encounters make it a memorable journey.

19. Visit the Akureyri Church:

- Admire the architecture of Akureyri Church. The church offers a peaceful atmosphere and stunning views of the surrounding mountains.

20. Experience the Christmas Garden in Akureyri:

- During the winter season, visit the Christmas Garden in Akureyri, where festive lights create a magical atmosphere. It's a charming and cost-free winter experience.

These budget-friendly activities in North Iceland allow you to immerse yourself in the region's natural wonders, cultural gems, and unique landscapes without breaking the bank.

East Iceland

a land of serene fjords, charming fishing villages, and a rich tapestry of culture and nature that invites you to slow down and savor the tranquility of this hidden gem. As you journey through East Iceland, you'll discover a region characterized by its remote beauty, where the landscapes unfold like a well-guarded secret waiting to be revealed.

Framed by the majestic Eastern Fjords, this part of Iceland offers a unique blend of tradition and natural wonders. The town of Seyðisfjörður, nestled at the end of a picturesque fjord, captivates visitors with its colorful houses and vibrant arts scene. Explore the history of East Iceland at Petra's Stone Collection, a fascinating museum displaying an extensive collection of Icelandic minerals and stones.

Nature takes center stage in East Iceland, with the imposing Vatnajökull Glacier extending its icy fingers into the region. Hike through the tranquil wilderness of East Iceland, where remote valleys and hidden waterfalls provide a sense of solitude and connection with nature.

For those looking to make the most of their budget in East Iceland, consider staying in guesthouses or charming farm accommodations that offer an authentic experience of Icelandic hospitality. Explore local markets and eateries, where you can savor fresh seafood and regional specialties without breaking the bank.

East Iceland beckons travelers to embrace the slow pace of life, where you can unwind in natural hot springs, stroll along serene fjords, and immerse yourself in the local culture. Renting a car provides the flexibility to explore the off-the-beaten-path treasures of East Iceland, from scenic coastal drives to encounters with friendly locals in quaint villages.

So, get ready to venture into the tranquil embrace of East Iceland, where fjords, folklore, and the timeless beauty of nature converge. In this remote and enchanting corner of the country, your journey becomes a poetic exploration of tradition and tranquility, offering a unique perspective on the soul-stirring landscapes of Iceland.

East Iceland is renowned for its serene landscapes, picturesque fjords, and quaint coastal villages, offering travelers a tranquil retreat amidst nature's splendor. Here are some notable towns and attractions in East Iceland:

Egilsstaðir stands as the largest town in East Iceland, serving as a bustling hub for services and activities. Surrounded by majestic mountains, Egilsstaðir beckons outdoor enthusiasts with opportunities for hiking and fishing. Nearby attractions include the Hallormsstaðaskógur forest, Iceland's largest forest, and the serene Lagarfljót lake.

Seyðisfjörður charms visitors with its quaint coastal setting adorned with colorful wooden houses and a vibrant arts community. Notable for hosting the weekly ferry connection to Denmark and the Faroe Islands during the summer, Seyðisfjörður also offers hiking trails, cascading waterfalls, and cultural events.

Nestled in a picturesque fjord, Fáskrúðsfjörður boasts a rich French heritage and historic architecture. The town's museum pays homage to the French fishermen who once operated there, while its scenic surroundings provide ample opportunities for hiking and birdwatching.

Seyðisfjörður enchants with its idyllic location in a deep fjord, featuring historic architecture highlighted by the iconic blue church. Visitors can explore hiking trails, indulge in birdwatching, and unwind in nearby hot springs, immersing themselves in the tranquility of the area.

Djúpivogur, a quaint fishing village steeped in Viking history, is celebrated for its abundant birdlife, making it a paradise for birdwatchers. The village is adorned with the Eggin í Gleðivík sculpture project, showcasing 34 eggs representing local bird species.

Vatnajökull National Park - East encompasses awe-inspiring glaciers like Vatnajökull and diverse landscapes ripe for exploration. Adventurers can partake in glacier hiking, ice caving, and remote wilderness expeditions, marveling at the park's natural wonders.

Hengifoss and Litlanesfoss captivate visitors with their natural beauty and unique features. Hengifoss, one of Iceland's tallest waterfalls, boasts distinctive red layers of clay, while Litlanesfoss showcases impressive basalt columns, offering breathtaking vistas and rewarding hiking experiences.

Stöðvarfjörður exudes tranquility, nestled in a serene fjord landscape embraced by mountains and sea. The village is renowned for its thriving arts scene and the Petra Stone Collection, a fascinating private collection of minerals and stones. Visitors can enjoy hiking and bask in the peaceful coastal ambiance.

East Iceland promises a tranquil and remote experience, inviting travelers to explore scenic fjords, uncover charming coastal towns, and immerse themselves in the region's unique culture and natural allure.

Exploring East Iceland offers a unique blend of fjords, charming fishing villages, and remote wilderness. Here are 20 budget-friendly activities that provide a touch of luxury in East Iceland:

1. Discover Seydisfjordur's Colorful Charm:

- Explore the picturesque village of Seydisfjordur with its colorful houses, art installations, and serene fjord views.

2. Hike to Hengifoss:

- Embark on a scenic hike to Hengifoss, one of Iceland's tallest waterfalls. The journey through the striking landscape adds to the allure.

3. Visit Petra's Stone Collection:

- Explore Petra's Stone Collection in Stöðvarfjörður, a unique museum showcasing a vast array of minerals and stones. Admission is affordable.

4. Enjoy a Stroll in Egilsstaðir:

- Take a leisurely stroll in Egilsstaðir, the largest town in East Iceland, along the banks of Lake Lagarfljót.

5. **Experience the Vök Baths:**

- Relax in the Vök Baths in Urriðavatn, a floating geothermal hot spring. While there's an admission fee, it's more budget-friendly compared to other hot springs.

6. **Explore the Papey Island Nature Reserve:**

- Take a ferry to Papey Island, a nature reserve with diverse birdlife and a tranquil atmosphere. The ferry fee is reasonable.

7. **Witness the Scenic Drive through the East Fjords:**

- Enjoy a scenic drive along the winding roads of the East Fjords, revealing stunning coastal views, charming villages, and picturesque landscapes.

8. **Discover the Wilderness in Borgarfjörður Eystri:**

- Explore the wilderness of Borgarfjörður Eystri, known for its hiking trails, puffin colonies, and untouched natural beauty.

9. **Visit the East Iceland Heritage Museum:**

- Gain insights into the region's history at the East Iceland Heritage Museum in Egilsstaðir. The museum offers a glimpse into local traditions and customs.

10. **Relax at Seydisfjordur's Geothermal Pools:**

- Unwind in Seydisfjordur's geothermal pools, offering a soothing and budget-friendly alternative to larger spa facilities.

11. **Hike to Gufufoss:**

- Hike to Gufufoss, a hidden gem waterfall near Seydisfjordur. The trail is free, and the secluded setting adds to the sense of discovery.

12. **Explore the Remote Village of Neskaupstaður:**

- Visit Neskaupstaður, a remote fishing village with a tranquil harbor and opportunities for coastal walks.

13. **Marvel at the Scenery in Stöðvarfjörður:**

- Enjoy the scenic views in Stöðvarfjörður, known for its fjord landscape and the artistic influences of the LungA Art Festival.

14. **Attend Seydisfjordur's Arts Festival:**

- If timing aligns, attend the Seydisfjordur Arts Festival, where local and international artists showcase their work in a creative and cultural atmosphere.

15. **Photograph the Scenic Lagarfljót Lake:**

- Capture the beauty of Lagarfljót Lake, reputedly home to the mythical Lagarfljót Worm. The lake's tranquility is a serene experience.

16. **Hike to Fardagafoss:**

- Take a short hike to Fardagafoss, a hidden waterfall near Egilsstaðir. The journey is rewarding, and the secluded location adds to its charm.

17. **Explore Petra's Stone Collection in Stöðvarfjörður:**

- Marvel at Petra's Stone Collection in Stöðvarfjörður, a remarkable display of minerals and stones collected by Petra Sveinsdóttir over the years.

18. Visit the Wilderness Center in Egilsstaðir:

- Explore the Wilderness Center near Egilsstaðir, offering a glimpse into Iceland's past with traditional turf houses and interactive exhibits.

19. Stroll Along the Seydisfjordur Harbor:

- Take a leisurely stroll along Seydisfjordur's harbor, lined with colorful houses and offering serene views of the fjord.

20. Enjoy Local Cuisine in East Iceland:

- Savor local cuisine in the region's cafes and restaurants. While dining out can be a bit pricey in Iceland, exploring local eateries can provide a taste of luxury on a budget.

These budget-friendly activities in East Iceland allow you to immerse yourself in the region's natural wonders, cultural richness, and off-the-beaten-path charm without exceeding your budget.

West Iceland

A region where folklore dances with powerful waterfalls, historic sites whisper tales of the past, and the stunning landscapes unfold like chapters in a storybook. As you embark on your journey through West Iceland, you'll encounter a perfect blend of nature and culture, offering a captivating narrative of Iceland's rich heritage.

One of the highlights of West Iceland is the mesmerizing Snæfellsnes Peninsula, often referred to as "Iceland in Miniature." This compact region boasts diverse landscapes, from the iconic Snæfellsjökull glacier to the rugged coastal cliffs of Arnarstapi, each telling a unique tale of geological wonders.

In Borgarnes, delve into Icelandic history at the Settlement Center, where exhibitions and interactive displays bring to life the sagas and stories of the early settlers. The historical significance continues at the enchanting Hraunfossar waterfalls, where rivulets of clear spring water cascade through lava fields, creating a truly magical spectacle.

To make the most of your budget in West Iceland, consider exploring the region on foot or by renting a bicycle, allowing you to meander through charming villages and coastal trails at a leisurely pace. Savor local cuisine at farm-to-table restaurants and seafood markets, where you can taste the flavors of the region without exceeding your budget.

West Iceland invites you to discover the natural wonders of the region, from the thundering beauty of the Glymur waterfall, Iceland's highest, to the relaxing warmth of the Deildartunguhver hot springs. Opt for budget-friendly accommodations in guesthouses or cozy cottages, often nestled in picturesque settings, providing a comfortable base for your exploration.

West Iceland is a region characterized by diverse landscapes, including lava fields, glaciers, hot springs, and coastal areas. Here are some notable towns and attractions in West Iceland:

Borgarnes:
Located on a peninsula along the shores of Borgarfjörður, Borgarnes is a historic town.

The Settlement Center provides insights into the Icelandic sagas and settlement history.

Nearby attractions include the Hraunfossar and Barnafoss waterfalls.

Akranes:
A town on the west coast known for its lighthouses and maritime history.

Akranesviti lighthouse offers panoramic views of the area.

The Akranes Folk Museum showcases local cultural heritage.

Snæfellsnes Peninsula:
Often referred to as "Iceland in Miniature," Snæfellsnes is a diverse region with a variety of landscapes.

Snæfellsjökull National Park features the iconic Snæfellsjökull volcano and glacier.

The town of Stykkishólmur is a charming fishing town with colorful houses and a picturesque harbor.

Hvalfjörður (Whale Fjord):
A scenic fjord known for its dramatic landscapes and hiking trails.

Glymur, one of Iceland's highest waterfalls, is located in the Hvalfjörður area.

The Hvalfjörður Tunnel provides a convenient route through the fjord.

Húsafell:
A tranquil area surrounded by glaciers, hot springs, and lava fields.

The Húsafell Stone Garden features a collection of stones from around Iceland.

A starting point for exploring the Langjökull glacier and the man-made ice cave at Into the Glacier.

Deildartunguhver:
The most powerful hot spring in Europe, known for its high water flow and geothermal activity.

Nearby attractions include the Hraunfossar and Barnafoss waterfalls.

Glymur:
Located in Hvalfjörður, Glymur is the second-highest waterfall in Iceland.

A popular hiking destination with scenic views of the surrounding landscapes.

Bifröst:
Home to Bifröst University, this small town is situated near the Grábrók volcano.

Offers opportunities for hiking and exploring the unique geological features of the area.

Glymur Waterfall

Exploring Glymur Waterfall in Iceland offers another fantastic natural wonder. Here's a detailed guide on how to experience Glymur Waterfall in a combination of luxury and budget style:

1. Travel Planning:

a. **Off-Peak Season:** Visit during the off-peak season (spring or fall) to avoid crowds and secure better prices on accommodations and activities.

b. **Flexible Dates:** Be flexible with your travel dates to find the best deals on flights and accommodations.

2. Flights:

a. **Booking in Advance:** Look for flight deals and book in advance. Consider budget airlines or travel packages that include flights and accommodation.

b. **Airports:** Fly into Keflavík International Airport (KEF) and then use local transportation to get to Glymur.

3. Accommodation:

a. **Guesthouses or Cabins:** Opt for guesthouses or cabins in nearby towns like Akranes or Reykholt. These options can be more affordable than hotels.

b. **Camping:** For a budget-friendly and adventurous option, consider camping at designated campsites near Glymur.

c. **Airbnb:** Explore Airbnb options for unique stays, potentially offering a local touch at a reasonable price.

4. Transportation:

a. **Car Rental:** Renting a car gives you flexibility. Compare prices and book in advance for better deals.

b. **Public Transportation:** If you're on a budget, consider using buses or a combination of buses and local transportation.

5. Glymur Hiking Tour:

a. **Self-Guided Hike:** Glymur Waterfall is accessible through a hiking trail. Consider a self-guided hike to save on tour costs.

Luxury for less in West Iceland

1. **Explore the Snæfellsnes Peninsula:**

   * Discover the Snæfellsnes Peninsula with its dramatic cliffs, charming fishing villages, and the iconic Snæfellsjökull volcano.
2. **Visit Kirkjufell and Kirkjufellsfoss:**

   * Marvel at Kirkjufell, the most photographed mountain in Iceland, and nearby Kirkjufellsfoss waterfall. Enjoy the scenery for free.
3. **Hike around Glymur:**

   * Embark on a hike to Glymur, Iceland's second-highest waterfall. The trail takes you through a canyon and offers stunning views.
4. **Relax at the Hraunfossar and Barnafoss Waterfalls:**

   * Explore Hraunfossar, a series of waterfalls streaming out of a lava field, and nearby Barnafoss waterfall. Admission is free.
5. **Soak in the Reykholt Thermal Pools:**

   * Enjoy a relaxing soak in the Reykholt Thermal Pools, a less crowded alternative to more famous geothermal spots.
6. **Visit the Settlement Center in Borgarnes:**

   * Explore the Settlement Center in Borgarnes, showcasing the history of Iceland's settlement era. The museum offers affordable entry fees.
7. **Walk through Eiríksstaðir Viking Longhouse:**

   * Visit Eiríksstaðir, a reconstructed Viking longhouse. The site provides insights into Viking history, and admission is budget-friendly.
8. **Hike in Snæfellsjökull National Park:**

   * Explore Snæfellsjökull National Park with its diverse landscapes, including lava fields, glaciers, and coastal cliffs.
9. **Discover Hvalfjörður Fjord:**

   * Drive around Hvalfjörður Fjord, known for its scenic beauty. Take a leisurely walk or hike in the surrounding hills for panoramic views.
10. **Visit Deildartunguhver Hot Springs:**

    * Witness the powerful Deildartunguhver Hot Springs, the largest thermal spring in Europe. Observation is free, and it's an impressive natural spectacle.
11. **Walk through the Grábrók Crater:**

    * Hike up the Grábrók Crater for panoramic views of the surrounding lava fields and lakes. The short walk is free and rewarding.
12. **Explore the West Iceland Heritage Museum:**

- Visit the West Iceland Heritage Museum in Borgarnes. The museum provides insights into the local history and culture at an affordable entry fee.

13. Discover the Húsafell Stone Arches:

- Explore the Húsafell Stone Arches, unique rock formations in the Húsafell area. The hike is free, and the natural sculptures are captivating.

14. Relax at Krauma Geothermal Baths:

- Enjoy the Krauma Geothermal Baths in Reykholt, featuring natural hot springs and cold glacial water. While there's an admission fee, it's more affordable than larger geothermal spas.

15. Visit the Icelandic Settlement Centre in Borgarnes:

- Explore the Icelandic Settlement Centre in Borgarnes, providing interactive exhibits on Iceland's settlement history at a reasonable cost.

16. Hike to the Hot River in Reykjadalur:

- Trek to the Reykjadalur Hot River, a geothermally heated river where you can bathe for free while surrounded by stunning landscapes.

17. Experience the Rauðfeldsgjá Gorge:

- Discover the Rauðfeldsgjá Gorge on the Snæfellsnes Peninsula, a hidden gem with a narrow canyon leading to a beautiful waterfall.

18. Visit the Akranes Lighthouse:

- Explore the Akranes Lighthouse for panoramic views of the coastline and the neighboring town. It's a serene and cost-free experience.

19. Discover Borgarnes:

- Stroll through the town of Borgarnes, enjoy its local charm, and walk along the waterfront for scenic views.

20. Witness the Búðir Black Church:

- Visit the iconic Búðir Black Church, set against a backdrop of lava fields and mountains. The church and its surroundings provide a picturesque setting.

These budget-friendly activities in West Iceland offer a taste of the region's natural beauty, history, and geothermal wonders without straining your wallet.

Ísafjörður

Ísafjörður is a picturesque town located in the Westfjords region of Iceland. It is the largest town in the Westfjords and serves as the regional center for commerce, culture, and services. Here are some interesting historical highlights and features of Ísafjörður:

1. Affordable Accommodation:

- Choose budget-friendly accommodations like guesthouses or hostels in Ísafjörður. Prices can vary, but you may find options starting around $60-80 per night.

2. Explore the Ísafjarðarbær Harbor:

- Take a leisurely stroll around the Ísafjarðarbær Harbor, enjoying the views of the fjord and surrounding mountains. This activity is free of charge.

3. Visit the Westfjords Heritage Museum:

- Explore the Westfjords Heritage Museum in Ísafjörður to learn about the region's history and culture. Admission is typically around $8-10 per person.

4. Hike in the Surrounding Mountains:

- Embark on a hike in the surrounding mountains for breathtaking views of Ísafjörður and the adjacent fjords. Many hiking trails are free to access.

5. Enjoy Local Cuisine in Downtown Ísafjörður:

- Savor Icelandic cuisine in local restaurants and cafes in downtown Ísafjörður. A meal at a mid-range restaurant can cost around $20-30 per person.

6. Attend Cultural Events:

- Check for local cultural events or festivals happening in Ísafjörður during your visit. Some events may offer free admission.

7. Relax at the Ísafjörður Swimming Pool:

- Unwind at the Ísafjörður swimming pool. Entrance fees are typically affordable, ranging from $6-10.

8. Walk around the Old Town:

- Wander through Ísafjörður's Old Town, where you'll find charming streets, historic buildings, and a cozy atmosphere. Exploring the town on foot is free.

9. Visit the Maritime Museum:

- Explore the Maritime Museum in Ísafjörður, featuring exhibits on the region's maritime history. Admission is usually around $8-10.

10. Capture the Sunset at the Ísafjörður Viewpoint:

- Hike or drive to the Ísafjörður viewpoint for a stunning sunset view over the town and the fjord. This outdoor experience is free.

11. Attend Outdoor Concerts or Performances:

- Check for outdoor concerts or performances happening in Ísafjörður's public spaces. Some events may be free of charge.

12. Explore the Bolungarvík Village:

- Take a day trip to the nearby Bolungarvík village, known for its authentic charm and proximity to Ísafjörður. Enjoy the local atmosphere without high tourist prices.

13. Experience the Westfjords Nature Center:

- Visit the Westfjords Nature Center in Ísafjörður. The center offers interactive exhibits on the region's unique flora and fauna, with admission typically around $5-8.

14. Walk along the Seashore:

- Enjoy a leisurely walk along the seashore in Ísafjörður, offering scenic views of the fjord and surrounding mountains. This activity is free.

15. Explore the Ski Museum:

- Discover the Ski Museum in Ísafjörður, showcasing the history of skiing in Iceland. Admission is usually around $5-8.

16. Visit the Library of Water:

- Explore the Library of Water in Ísafjörður, featuring artist Roni Horn's installations. Admission is typically free.

17. Attend a Photography Exhibition:

- Check for photography exhibitions in Ísafjörður's art galleries. Some exhibitions may offer free entry.

18. Try Local Bakeries:

- Indulge in budget-friendly treats from local bakeries in Ísafjörður. Prices for pastries and coffee can range from $5-10.

19. Discover the Vigur Island:

- Take a boat trip to Vigur Island, known for its birdlife and natural beauty. While the boat trip has a cost, exploring the island itself is free.

20. Join a Free Walking Tour:

- Participate in a free walking tour of Ísafjörður to learn about its history and landmarks. Local guides often offer insights into the town's culture.

More General Tips for Iceland Whale Watching

Whale watching is a popular activity in Iceland, and while most organized tours come with a high cost, there are a few ways you might be able to experience it more affordably or even for free:

- **Shore Watching:**
    - **Location:** Some areas in Iceland, like the Snaefellsnes Peninsula, offer opportunities to spot whales from the shore. Find a high vantage point or visit coastal areas known for whale sightings.
    - **Binoculars:** Bring binoculars for a closer look. This method is entirely free, and you can enjoy the natural beauty of the coastline while increasing your chances of spotting whales.
- **DIY Boat Tours:**
    - **Renting a Boat:** If you're in a group, consider renting a small boat and exploring coastal areas on your own. This can be more cost-effective when divided among several people.
    - **Small Fishing Tours:** In some fishing communities, you might find smaller, locally operated fishing boats that offer more affordable tours that could include whale watching.
- **Off-Peak Season Discounts:**
    - **Timing:** Visit during the off-peak season when tour operators may offer discounted rates. Typically, this is from September to April.
- **Discount Websites:**
    - **Tour Aggregators:** Use travel websites or tour aggregators to find discounted whale watching tours. Some platforms offer last-minute deals or promotions that can significantly reduce the cost.
- **Volunteer Opportunities:**
    - **Research Programs: Marine and Freshwater Research Institute** (MFRI), which conducts scientific research and offers opportunities for volunteers to participate in whale watching expeditions. While not entirely free, this could provide a unique experience at a lower cost.

Truly hidden gems in Iceland

- **Hraunfossar and Barnafoss**: Tucked away in the lava fields of western Iceland, these waterfalls are a hidden gem due to their unique setting. While not directly accessible by bus, you can rent a car from Reykjavik and drive along Route 1 (the Ring Road) to reach them. The journey takes about 1.5 to 2 hours.
- **Rauðisandur Beach**: With its remote location and stunning golden-red sand, Rauðisandur Beach is a hidden treasure. Drive along Route 60 from Patreksfjörður to reach the beach. The road is unpaved, so drive carefully, especially in adverse weather conditions.
- **Glymur Waterfall**: Iceland's second-highest waterfall, Glymur, is tucked away in Hvalfjörður, making it a hidden gem for those willing to hike to its breathtaking viewpoint. Take Route 47 from Reykjavik towards Hvalfjörður, then follow signs for the Glymur trailhead, where you can start the hike to the waterfall.
- **Drangshlíðarvík Cove**: Accessible only by a scenic hike from the road near Drangshlíð, this secluded black sand beach is surrounded by towering cliffs, adding to its hidden gem status. Check tide conditions before visiting, as the cove may be inaccessible at high tide.
- **Gjáin Valley**: Nestled in the highlands, Gjáin Valley is a hidden oasis with lush greenery and cascading waterfalls. While not directly accessible by bus, you can drive to Gjáin Valley from Þjóðvegur (Route 32) and then hike to reach the oasis, adding to its allure as a hidden gem.
- **Borgarfjörður Eystri**: Known for its puffin colonies and picturesque setting, Borgarfjörður Eystri is a hidden gem in the Eastfjords. Located off the beaten path, you can drive to Borgarfjörður Eystri from Route 94, immersing yourself in its remote beauty.
- **Hengifoss**: Majestic and surrounded by vibrant basalt columns, Hengifoss is a hidden gem waterfall in East Iceland. Drive to Hengifoss from Egilsstaðir along Route 931, then embark on a moderate hike to reach the waterfall, enhancing its status as a hidden treasure.
- **Laugarvellir Hot Springs**: Nestled in the central highlands, Laugarvellir Hot Springs offer a tranquil retreat in nature. Accessible only by a 4x4 vehicle due to rough terrain, the journey adds to the allure of this hidden gem. Follow F26 from Route 1 to reach the hot springs area.
- **Djúpavogshreppur Hot Pots**: Perched on the coastline with serene ocean views, Djúpavogshreppur Hot Pots offer a secluded relaxation spot. Accessible by car along Route 1 in the Eastfjords, their remote location adds to their appeal as a hidden gem.
- **Westfjords - Dynjandi Waterfall**: Cascading gracefully in a remote fjord, Dynjandi Waterfall is a hidden gem in the rugged Westfjords. Explore the region by car to discover this and other hidden treasures along scenic routes like Route 60, enhancing the sense of adventure and exploration.

Free Hot Springs in Iceland

Iceland is known for its numerous hot springs, some of which are free to access. Here's a detailed list of free hot springs, along with information on how to get to each via public transport:

1. Reykjadalur Hot Springs:

- **Location:** South Iceland, near Hveragerði.
  - **How to Get There:**
  - Take a bus from Reykjavik to Hveragerði.
  - From Hveragerði, follow the well-marked trail to Reykjadalur. It's about a 1.5 to 2-hour hike.

2. Landmannalaugar Hot Springs:

- **Location:** Fjallabak Nature Reserve, Highlands.
  - **How to Get There:**
  - Take a bus from Reykjavik to Landmannalaugar during the summer months.
  - The journey involves river crossings and challenging terrain, so it's recommended to join a guided tour or use the scheduled buses provided by tour operators.

3. Seljavallalaug:

- **Location:** South Iceland, near Skogafoss.
  - **How to Get There:**
  - Take a bus from Reykjavik to Skogar.
  - From Skogar, it's a roughly 5 km hike to Seljavallalaug. The pool is nestled in a beautiful valley.

4. Hrunalaug:

- **Location:** West Iceland, near Flúðir.
  - **How to Get There:**
  - Take a bus from Reykjavik to Flúðir.
  - Hrunalaug is a short drive from Flúðir. You may need to walk a bit, so consider hitchhiking or renting a bike.

5. Grettislaug:

- **Location:** North Iceland, near Saudarkrokur.
  - **How to Get There:**
  - Take a bus from Reykjavik to Saudarkrokur.
  - Grettislaug is a short distance from Saudarkrokur, and you may need to arrange local transport or hitchhike.

6. Strútslaug:

- **Location:** East Iceland, near Seydisfjordur.
  - **How to Get There:**
  - Take a bus from Reykjavik to Seydisfjordur.
  - Strútslaug is about a 20-minute drive from Seydisfjordur. Consider local transport or hitchhiking.

7. Krossneslaug:

- **Location:** Westfjords, near Sudavik.
  - **How to Get There:**
    - Take a bus from Reykjavik to Isafjordur.
    - From Isafjordur, arrange local transport or hitchhike to Sudavik and then to Krossneslaug.

8. Kerlingarfjöll Geothermal Area:

- **Location:** Central Highlands.
  - **How to Get There:**
    - There are no direct public transport options. Consider joining a guided tour or renting a car to reach this remote location.

Important Tips:

- Many of these hot springs are located in remote areas with limited or no public transport. Consider renting a car or joining guided tours for better access.
- Always check weather conditions and accessibility, especially in winter when roads might be closed.
- Respect local rules and nature. Practice Leave No Trace principles and avoid using soap in the hot springs.

Staying safe at hot springs in Iceland

hese geothermal areas pose unique risks. Here's a detailed guide on how to ensure your safety:

- **Follow Designated Paths:**
  - Stick to designated paths and trails to avoid fragile ground. Straying from established routes can lead to unstable terrain and potential hazards.
- **Observe Warning Signs:**
  - Pay attention to warning signs and information boards provided by local authorities. They often contain essential safety guidelines specific to each hot spring area.
- **Check Weather Conditions:**
  - Be aware of weather conditions, as they can change rapidly in Iceland. Unfavorable weather may impact visibility and increase the risk of accidents.
- **Wear Appropriate Footwear:**
  - Wear sturdy and slip-resistant footwear suitable for the terrain. Some areas may have uneven surfaces, and proper footwear can prevent slips and falls.
- **Test Water Temperature:**
  - Before entering a hot spring, test the water temperature cautiously. Geothermal areas can have varying temperatures, and some pools may be too hot for safe bathing.
- **Avoid Unstable Ground:**
  - Steer clear of areas with visibly unstable or thin ground. The surface might be fragile, and stepping on it could lead to injury or immersion in hot water.
- **Supervise Children:**

- Keep a close eye on children, and ensure they stay within safe areas. Hot springs may have unpredictable conditions, and supervision is crucial for their safety.
- **No Running or Diving:**
  - Avoid running or diving into hot springs. The ground might be slippery, and sudden movements can lead to accidents or injuries.
- **Stay Hydrated:**
  - Hot springs can be dehydrating. Bring water with you and stay hydrated, especially if you're spending an extended period in geothermal areas.
- **Respect Wildlife and Vegetation:**
  - Stay on designated paths to protect the fragile vegetation and prevent disturbing local wildlife. Respecting the environment is crucial for preserving these natural wonders.
- **Emergency Contacts:**
  - Carry emergency contact information and be aware of the nearest medical facilities. In case of an emergency, quick access to help is vital.
- **Check Local Guidelines:**
  - Research and follow any specific guidelines provided by local authorities for each hot spring location. Different areas may have unique safety considerations.
- **Pack Essentials:**
  - Bring essentials like a first aid kit, a cell phone for emergencies, and extra clothing. Being prepared enhances your ability to address unforeseen situations.
- **Inform Someone:**
  - Let someone know your plans, including your intended route and expected return time. In case of delays or emergencies, this information is crucial.

By adhering to these guidelines, you can enjoy the beauty of Iceland's hot springs while minimizing the risks associated with these geothermal areas. Always prioritize safety and respect the unique natural environment.

Where to see puffins and seals

Best Places to See Puffins and Seals in Iceland:

Puffins:

- **Dyrhólaey:**
  - Located on the southern coast, Dyrhólaey is a sea stack and headland where puffins nest during the summer months.
- **Látrabjarg:**
  - In the Westfjords, Látrabjarg is Europe's westernmost point and a major bird cliff. Puffins nest here in large numbers.
- **Ingólfshöfði:**
  - This isolated headland in the southeast is a nesting site for puffins. Guided tours are available to reach the area.
- **Papey Island:**
  - Take a boat tour to Papey Island off the east coast, where puffins inhabit the cliffs.
- **Grímsey Island:**
  - Located in the Arctic Circle, Grímsey is known for its puffin colonies. It's accessible by ferry or flight.
- **Hornstrandir Nature Reserve:**
  - In the remote Westfjords, Hornstrandir is a pristine area where puffins can be observed in their natural habitat.

Seals:

- **Jökulsárlón Glacier Lagoon:**
  - Along the southern coast, Jökulsárlón is not only famous for icebergs but also for seals that often swim near the floating ice.
- **Vatnsnes Peninsula:**
  - The Vatnsnes Peninsula in the northwest is known as "Seal Peninsula." Hike along the coast to spot seals, especially near Hvítserkur rock.
- **Þorlákshöfn Harbor:**
  - Close to Reykjavik, Þorlákshöfn Harbor is a great place to see seals. Binoculars are handy for observing them from a distance.
- **Seljalandsfoss Waterfall:**
  - Besides the stunning waterfall, Seljalandsfoss, located on the southern coast, is known for having seals in the nearby estuary.
- **Reykhólar:**
  - In the Westfjords, Reykhólar is a coastal area where you can often spot seals swimming close to the shore.
- **Húnaflói Bay:**
  - This bay in northern Iceland is frequented by seals. Tours are available for seal watching in the area.

Snorkeling in Iceland

Snorkeling in Iceland offers a captivating adventure amidst breathtaking natural landscapes. Here are some essential tips to make the most of your experience:

Choosing the right season is key, with the summer months (June to August) being the most popular due to milder water temperatures. Consider bringing your own travel snorkel gear for a cost-free adventure.

One of the top snorkeling spots in Iceland is the Silfra Fissure in Þingvellir National Park, renowned for its crystal-clear glacial water and visibility. Booking a guided snorkeling tour with a reputable operator is advisable, as they provide necessary equipment like drysuits, hoods, gloves, and fins, ensuring your safety and enhancing your experience.

Prepare for the unique sensation of snorkeling in a dry suit, which keeps you warm in the chilly water while allowing you to float effortlessly on the surface. Basic swimming skills are typically sufficient, but inform your guide if you're not a confident swimmer.

The Silfra snorkeling route usually covers four main sections: Silfra Big Crack, Silfra Hall, Silfra Cathedral, and Silfra Lagoon, each offering mesmerizing geological formations and vibrant colors.

Underwater visibility at Silfra is exceptional, often exceeding 100 meters, providing an unparalleled opportunity to witness the stunning underwater world.

Be mindful of the chilly water temperatures, which range from 2–4°C (36–39°F). However, the drysuit provides insulation, making the experience surprisingly comfortable.

Ensure you're in good health before embarking on the snorkeling adventure, and inform the tour operator of any medical conditions. Pregnant women are generally advised not to snorkel in Silfra.

Capture the beauty of your snorkeling journey with underwater photography. Some tour operators offer photography services, or you can bring your waterproof camera to document the experience.

Consider the extended daylight hours during the Icelandic summer, providing ample time for snorkeling excursions. Some operators even offer combo tours, combining snorkeling with other activities like caving or the Golden Circle tour.

Pack dry clothes to change into after snorkeling, along with warm layers to stay cozy in the Icelandic climate.

Due to its popularity, it's advisable to book your snorkeling tour in advance, especially during peak tourist seasons. Snorkeling in Silfra promises an

unforgettable and awe-inspiring exploration of Iceland's underwater wonders.
Snorkeling in Silfra Fissure without a tour is generally not recommended for several reasons:

- **Safety Concerns**: Silfra Fissure is located within Þingvellir National Park and is part of the UNESCO World Heritage Site. Snorkeling there requires proper equipment and knowledge of the area's conditions, such as water temperature and currents, to ensure your safety.
- **Legal Restrictions**: Snorkeling in Silfra Fissure may be subject to regulations set by Þingvellir National Park authorities. It's essential to comply with these regulations to avoid fines or legal issues.
- **Guidance and Equipment**: Tours typically provide necessary snorkeling equipment, such as drysuits and snorkels, along with guidance from experienced instructors who are familiar with the fissure's unique characteristics.

Understanding Icelanders

They are tough as nails, but with a heart of gold. Icelanders are known for their resilience, and that's not just because of the wild weather they deal with. They've got this fierce independence streak running through them, like they're determined to carve out their own path no matter what.

But here's the twist: while they're all about doing their own thing, they've also got this amazing sense of community. Seriously, you'll see it everywhere, from the smallest villages to the bustling city streets. It's like they've mastered the art of balancing rugged individualism with good old-fashioned neighborly vibes.

And let's talk about their love for nature. I mean, have you seen Iceland's landscapes? It's like Mother Nature went all out with her paintbrush. So, it's no surprise that Icelanders are super big on protecting the environment. They've got this deep-seated respect for the land and a real commitment to keeping it pristine for generations to come.

But hey, they're not all serious business. Icelanders know how to kick back and have a good time too. Whether it's getting lost in a book from one of their legendary authors or jamming out to some Icelandic tunes, they definitely know how to enjoy life.

And let's not forget their knack for finding practical solutions to just about anything. I mean, when you live on an island in the middle of the North Atlantic, you learn to be resourceful real quick. So, yeah, your average Icelander might be tough, independent, and fiercely protective of their environment, but they've also got a soft spot for community, culture, and a good old-fashioned adventure.

Useful Icelandic phrases with English pronunciation

- Hello - Halló (HAH-loh)
- Good morning - Góðan dag (GO-than dahg)
- Good afternoon - Góðan daginn (GO-than dahyinn)
- Good evening - Gott kvöld (got kvelt)
- Good night - Góða nótt (GO-tha noht)
- How are you? - Hvernig hefur þú það? (KVER-nik hev-ur thoo thahd)
- I'm fine, thank you - Ég er góð/ góður, þakka þér fyrir (Yehg air goth/ goth-ur, thak-ah thayr feer-eer)
- What is your name? - Hvað heitir þú? (Kvath hay-teer thoo?)
- My name is... - Ég heiti... (Yehg hay-tee...)
- Nice to meet you - Gaman að kynnast þér (Gah-man ath kin-nast thayr)
- Please - Vinsamlegast (Veen-sam-le-gast)
- Thank you - Þakka þér fyrir (Thak-ah thayr feer-eer)
- You're welcome - Ekkert að þakka (Ehk-kert ath thak-ah)
- Yes - Já (Yow)
- No - Nei (Nay)
- Excuse me - Afsakið (Af-sa-kith)
- I'm sorry - Því miður (Thvee meth-ur)
- Goodbye - Bless (bles)
- See you later - Sjáumst síðar (Syaumst see-thar)
- What time is it? - Hvað er klukkan? (Kvath air kluk-kahn?)
- Where is the bathroom? - Hvar er salernið? (Kvar air sah-lair-nith?)
- I need help - Ég þarf aðstoð (Yehg tharf ath-stoth)
- Excuse me, where is...? - Afsakið, hvar er...? (Af-sa-kith, kvar air...?)
- Can you help me? - Getur þú hjálpað mér? (Get-ur thoo hyowl-path mayr?)
- I don't understand - Ég skil það ekki (Yehg skil thahd ehk-ki)
- Please speak more slowly - Vinsamlegast talaðu hægar (Veen-sam-le-gast tal-athu hie-gar)
- How much does it cost? - Hversu mikið kostar það? (Kver-soo mik-ith kohs-tar thahd?)

The Icelandic language developed from Old Norse, which was spoken by the Norse settlers who arrived in Iceland in the 9th century. These settlers came primarily from Norway but also from other Scandinavian regions. Over time, Old Norse evolved into the modern Icelandic language through various influences and developments.

One significant factor in the preservation of the Icelandic language is its relative isolation from other languages. Iceland's geographical location, coupled with its sparse population and limited contact with outside cultures for much of its history, contributed to the preservation of linguistic traditions.

Additionally, the Icelandic language underwent linguistic changes and developments internally. These changes included phonetic shifts, grammatical modifications, and the adoption of new vocabulary from Old Norse manuscripts, literature, and religious texts.

During the medieval period, Icelandic literature flourished, particularly with the writing of the Icelandic sagas. These literary works played a crucial role in shaping and standardizing the language. The Icelandic sagas, along with the Icelandic Bible translations and other religious texts, helped establish a literary tradition that further solidified the language's structure and vocabulary.

In the 16th century, the Icelandic language faced challenges due to foreign influence, particularly from Danish, which was the dominant language of administration and education in Iceland under Danish rule. However, efforts to preserve and promote the Icelandic language intensified in the 19th and 20th centuries, leading to its official recognition and widespread use in various domains, including education, government, and literature.

Today, Icelandic remains one of the most well-preserved Germanic languages, maintaining many features of Old Norse and serving as a symbol of Iceland's cultural identity and heritage.

Thing's worth spending money on in Iceland because you can't experience it elsewhere

Unique Experiences in Iceland	Why Worth Spending Money	Starting Prices
Ice Cave Exploration	Opportunity to venture inside natural ice formations created by glaciers, providing a mesmerizing and otherworldly experience found only in Iceland	From $150 for guided tours
Snorkeling in Silfra Fissure	Dive between tectonic plates in crystal-clear glacial waters, offering a once-in-a-lifetime opportunity to snorkel in one of the world's clearest freshwater fissures	From $100 for guided tours
Horseback Riding on Icelandic Horses	Ride gentle and sturdy Icelandic horses through stunning landscapes, experiencing the unique tölt gait and deep connection between horse and rider	From $50 for guided tours
Whale Watching in Husavik	Encounter majestic whales in their natural habitat, with Husavik renowned as one of the best places in the world for whale watching due to its rich marine ecosystem	From $80 for guided tours
Midnight Sun and Northern Lights Tours	Witness the ethereal glow of the midnight sun in summer or the dancing colors of the northern lights in winter, showcasing Iceland's unique celestial phenomena	Varies based on tour duration

Top 20 Experiences

1. **Witness the Northern Lights** - Free if you can spot them from a dark spot outside the city, or opt for a self-guided tour.
2. **Explore the Golden Circle** - Drive yourself to save on tour costs or join a budget-friendly group tour.
3. **Relax in the Blue Lagoon** - Book in advance for cheaper rates or visit during off-peak hours.
4. **Visit the Glacier Lagoon, Jökulsárlón** - Visit independently to avoid tour fees, but consider car rental costs.
5. **Hike on a Glacier** - Look for discounted rates during the offseason or opt for shorter hikes to save money.
6. **Discover the Ice Caves** - Consider self-guided tours or group discounts to reduce costs.
7. **Explore the Inside of a Volcano** - Book tours directly with local operators for potential discounts.
8. **Go Whale Watching** - Look for deals online or visit lesser-known spots for cheaper tours.
9. **Visit the Black Sand Beaches of Reynisfjara** - Visit independently and explore at your own pace.
10. **Explore the Highlands** - Camp or hike independently to avoid pricey tours.
11. **Discover Waterfalls like Seljalandsfoss and Skógafoss** - Free to visit, just pay for transport if needed.
12. **Tour the Snæfellsnes Peninsula** - Share costs with friends or book budget accommodations in the area.
13. **Visit Puffins in the Westman Islands** - Visit during nesting season for the best chances of sightings.
14. **Explore the Westfjords** - Hitchhike or camp to cut down on transportation and accommodation costs.
15. **Dive or Snorkel in Silfra Fissure** - Book with local operators directly to avoid booking fees.
16. **Explore Reykjavik's Vibrant Culture** - Join free walking tours or visit museums during discounted hours.
17. **Go Horseback Riding** - Look for group discounts or shorter rides to save money.

18. **Visit Historic Sites like Thingvellir National Park** - Free to visit on your own, just pay for transport.
19. **Relax in Natural Hot Springs** - Seek out lesser-known hot springs for free or visit during the offseason.
20. **Experience the Midnight Sun** - Free to experience, just plan your activities around the extended daylight hours.

Recap: $10,000 trip to Iceland on a $1,000 budget

Transportation:

Item	Cost	Hacks/ Tips
Flights	$1,000	
- Book flights well in advance to get the best deals.		
- Use flight comparison websites and set price alerts.		
- Be flexible with your travel dates for cheaper options.		

I Rental Car I $400 I

I - Book the car in advance for the best rates.

I - Consider renting from local, budget-friendly companies.

I - Opt for a fuel-efficient car to save on gas costs.

I - Share the rental with travel companions.

Accommodation:

Item	Cost	Hacks/ Tips
Hostels/ Budget Hotels	$300	
- Stay in guesthouses, hostels, mountain huts or Uni dorms and get day passes to five-star spa's/ hotels		
- Consider guesthouses or Airbnb for local experiences.		
- Look for last-minute deals or discounts.		

Food:

Item	Cost	Hacks/ Tips
Groceries	$200	
- Street eats, groceries and cook meals.		
- Take advantage of local markets for fresh produce.		
- Pack snacks for day trips to avoid buying expensive food at attractions. A hot dog can run you $30!		

Activities:

Item	Cost	Hacks/ Tips
Sightseeing and Tours	$600	

- Prioritize free activities and natural wonders.		
- Look for discounted tour packages online.		
- Explore self-guided tours with maps and apps.		

I Entrance Fees I $100 I

I - Check if any attractions offer discounted tickets online.

I - Look for combination tickets for multiple attractions.

I - Take advantage of student or group discounts if applicable.

Miscellaneous:

Item	Cost	Hacks/ Tips
SIM Card/ Data	$20	
- Purchase a local SIM card for data on the go.		
- Use Wi-Fi at accommodations and public places.		

I Souvenirs/ Gifts I $150 I

I - Set a budget for souvenirs and stick to it.

I - Consider buying from local markets for unique items.

I Miscellaneous Expenses I $200 I

I - Account for unexpected costs and emergencies.

I - Carry a reusable water bottle and snacks to save on impulse purchases.

Total Estimated Cost: $1,000

Common complaints

Common Complaints	Solutions
High Cost of Living	- Budget and plan accordingly before your trip. - Look for budget-friendly accommodations, eateries, and activities. - Take advantage of free attractions and outdoor activities.
Unpredictable Weather	- Check weather forecasts regularly and dress in layers for changing conditions. - Be flexible with your itinerary and have indoor backup plans in case of inclement weather. - Embrace the Icelandic saying: "If you don't like the weather, just wait five minutes."
Crowded Tourist Spots	- Visit popular attractions during off-peak hours, early mornings, or late afternoons to avoid crowds. - Explore lesser-known destinations to experience Iceland's beauty away from the crowds. - Consider booking guided tours with smaller groups or off-the-beaten-path excursions.
Limited Dining Options	- Research and explore local eateries, food trucks, and markets for affordable dining options. - Consider self-catering with groceries from supermarkets or convenience stores. - Opt for lunch specials or happy hour deals at restaurants to save on dining expenses.
Expensive Activities	- Look for free or budget-friendly activities such as hiking, exploring natural landscapes, and visiting public museums and galleries. - Use discount passes or combo deals for attractions to save on admission fees. - Take advantage of seasonal discounts or special offers available for tours and activities.
Language Barrier	- Learn some basic Icelandic phrases or use translation apps to communicate with locals. - Most Icelanders speak English fluently, so don't hesitate to ask for help or directions if needed. - Utilize tourist information centers or online resources for assistance with language-related issues.
Limited Public Transportation	- Rent a car for flexibility and convenience in exploring Iceland's remote areas. - Use local buses, shuttle services, or rideshare apps in urban areas where public transportation is available. - Join guided tours or excursions that include transportation to attractions if public transit options are limited.

Money Mistakes to Avoid

Money Mistake	Solution
Not considering camping	With wild camping being completely free, you can save $100 a night on accommodation in Iceland, doing some camping in the shoulder season.
Not getting a sales tax refund on purchases	Solution: If you are not a permanent resident of Iceland, and you spend 6000 ISK or more on goods that you are bringing out of the country within 3 months of purchase, you can obtain a refund for VAT when leaving Iceland from Keflavik airport. Check out Keflavik Airport's tax refund page. Iceland offers a Value-Added Tax (VAT) refund for non-residents who make qualifying purchases and are leaving the country within three months of the purchase date.
Overlooking Hidden Fees	Solution: Be aware of potential fees for credit card transactions and ATM withdrawals. Choose credit cards with no foreign transaction fees and use ATMs associated with your bank to minimize additional charges.
Ignoring the High Cost of Dining Out	Solution: Balance your meals by occasionally opting for budget-friendly options like grocery stores or local markets. Splurge on dining experiences sparingly to keep overall costs in check.
Underestimating Transportation Costs	Solution: Research transportation options, including rental cars, public buses, or tours. Consider purchasing travel passes for multiple attractions to save money on individual tickets.
Not Utilizing Discounts or Coupons	Solution: Look for discounts on tours, activities, and attractions. Use apps, websites, or local tourism offices to find coupons and special promotions that can significantly reduce costs.
Overlooking Free or Low-Cost Activities	Solution: Take advantage of Iceland's natural beauty with activities like hiking, exploring waterfalls, or relaxing in natural hot springs. Many outdoor experiences come with no or minimal costs.
Disregarding Accommodation Alternatives	Solution: Explore budget-friendly accommodation options, such as guesthouses, hostels, or vacation rentals. Booking in advance can also secure better rates, especially during peak tourist seasons.
Ignoring the Weather's Impact on Plans	Solution: Check the weather forecast and plan activities accordingly. Weather-related cancellations or changes can lead to additional costs, so be prepared and flexible with your itinerary.
Neglecting Travel Insurance	Solution: Invest in comprehensive travel insurance to cover unexpected expenses, such as medical emergencies, trip cancellations, or lost belongings. It provides financial protection in unforeseen circumstances.
Using Foreign Currency for Small Purchases	Solution: While credit cards are widely accepted, use local currency for small purchases to avoid unfavorable exchange rates or unnecessary fees. Withdraw cash in advance to cover daily expenses.
Failing to Monitor Mobile Roaming Charges	Solution: Turn off data roaming and use local Wi-Fi to avoid expensive mobile data charges. Alternatively, consider purchasing a local SIM card for cost-effective internet access during your stay.
Not Taking Advantage of Duty-Free	Solution: Purchase duty-free items at the airport upon arrival or departure to save money on alcohol, souvenirs, and other goods. Check duty-free allowances to maximize savings.

ICELAND's Most Interesting History

Viking History

The Viking history of Iceland is a captivating saga that unfolds against the backdrop of the North Atlantic Ocean. From the initial Norse explorations to the establishment of the Icelandic Commonwealth, this narrative is a testament to the resilience, exploration, and cultural legacy of the Viking settlers.

1. Viking Exploration and Settlement:

In the late 9th century, Norse seafarers, often referred to as Vikings, set their sights on unexplored lands westward. Led by figures like Ingólfur Arnarson and his wife, Hallveig Fróðadóttir, the first Viking settlers arrived in Iceland around 874 AD. The harsh yet bountiful landscape presented both challenges and opportunities, leading to the establishment of one of the world's first parliamentary systems.

2. Alþingi - The Icelandic Parliament:

In 930 AD, the Alþingi, or Althing, was established in Þingvellir, marking the birth of what is considered the world's oldest parliament. The Althing served as a legislative and judicial assembly, where disputes were settled, laws were enacted, and communities convened annually. This democratic institution reflected the Vikings' commitment to self-governance and the rule of law.

3. The Sagas - Epics of Icelandic Culture:

The sagas, epic narratives of prose and poetry, emerged as a distinctive literary form during the Viking Age in Iceland. Composed between the 12th and 14th centuries, these sagas chronicled the lives, exploits, and conflicts of Viking heroes and heroines. Notable sagas include the "Njála Saga," the "Saga of the Icelanders," and the "Egil's Saga."

4. The Conversion to Christianity:

The Vikings in Iceland practiced the Old Norse religion, worshipping a pantheon of gods such as Odin, Thor, and Freyja. However, in the early 11th century, Iceland officially converted to Christianity, marking a significant shift in religious practices. The conversion was not without tensions, and echoes of the old beliefs persisted in folklore and traditions.

5. Viking Exploration and Leif Erikson:

Viking exploration extended beyond Iceland, and Leif Erikson, the son of Erik the Red, is often credited with leading the first known European expedition to North America around the year 1000 AD, nearly 500 years before Columbus. The settlement, known as Vinland, is believed to be located in areas like present-day Newfoundland.

6. Decline and Integration:

Over time, the Icelandic Commonwealth faced internal conflicts, external threats, and economic challenges. In 1262, Iceland entered into a union with Norway, followed by integration into the Kalmar Union with Denmark in the 14th century. This marked the end of Iceland's independent governance.

7. Modern Resurgence of Viking Heritage:

While Iceland lost its political autonomy, its Viking heritage endured. In the 19th and 20th centuries, there was a resurgence of interest in Icelandic sagas, folklore, and the Norse language. Today, Iceland proudly embraces its Viking legacy, with cultural festivals, Viking reenactments, and a continued connection to the ancient stories that shaped its identity.

Hldufólk History

The belief in elves and hidden people, commonly known as "huldufólk" in Icelandic folklore, is deeply ingrained in the cultural fabric of Iceland. This rich tradition dates back centuries, and while it might seem whimsical to outsiders, it holds a special place in the hearts and minds of many Icelanders. This intricate and enchanting history unfolds against the backdrop of Iceland's mystical landscapes and a society deeply connected to nature.

Historical Roots:

The roots of the belief in elves and hidden people can be traced to Iceland's medieval folklore and sagas. In these ancient tales, supernatural beings inhabited the landscape, living in rocks, hills, and secluded places. The respect for nature and a keen awareness of the mysterious forces that shaped the Icelandic environment led to the coexistence of humans and the hidden folk in the collective imagination.

The Hidden People in Icelandic Society:

Icelanders traditionally regarded the hidden people as an integral part of their society. They were seen as elusive beings with their own communities, living parallel lives to humans. The hidden folk were believed to possess magical powers, and encounters with them were both feared and revered.

Characteristics of Elves and Hidden People:

- **Appearance:** Descriptions of elves and hidden people vary, but they are often portrayed as ethereal beings, similar in appearance to humans but possessing an otherworldly beauty.
- **Clothing:** The hidden people were said to wear clothing in the style of the time when they first appeared to humans, contributing to the perception of an ancient and timeless existence.
- **Dwellings:** Elves were believed to reside in rocks, hills, or mounds. The distinctive Icelandic landscape, with its numerous rocks and hidden spots, fueled the imagination and strengthened the belief in these hidden communities.

Encounters and Interactions:

Stories abound of encounters between humans and the hidden people. Icelanders spoke of respecting certain rocks and locations believed to be inhabited by elves, avoiding interference with their dwellings. Disturbing an elf's habitat was thought to bring misfortune, and Icelanders took great care to navigate landscapes with a deep understanding of the hidden folk's territories.

Cultural Impact:

The belief in elves and hidden people continues to influence Icelandic culture. Roads have been rerouted to avoid disrupting their habitats, and construction plans have been altered to accommodate the hidden folk. Many Icelanders, even in modern times, approach these beliefs with a blend of reverence and practicality, acknowledging the importance of respecting the unseen inhabitants of their land.

Contemporary Perspectives:

While Iceland has become more modernized, the belief in elves and hidden people endures. Surveys have indicated that a significant portion of the population does not dismiss the existence of these beings outright. The enchantment of Icelandic folklore remains woven into the nation's identity, blending seamlessly with its commitment to environmental conservation and a deep connection to the natural world.

Iceland's history during World War II

Iceland's history during World War II is characterized by its strategic importance in the North Atlantic and its unique geopolitical position. Here's an overview of Iceland's role and experiences during the war:

1. Danish Occupation and German Invasion:

- **Pre-War Situation:** In 1918, Iceland had become a sovereign state in a personal union with Denmark. However, Denmark was occupied by Germany in 1940.
- **British Occupation:** Concerned about potential German control of Iceland, the United Kingdom invaded and occupied Iceland in May 1940. The move was initially welcomed by the Icelandic government, which sought to maintain its neutrality.

2. The United States Takes Over:

- **U.S. Presence:** In 1941, as the United States entered the war, it took over the defense of Iceland from the British. This marked the beginning of a significant American military presence in the country.
- **Strategic Importance:** Iceland's location in the North Atlantic made it a crucial strategic outpost for both monitoring German submarine activity and facilitating the Allied convoys.

3. The Invasion Fear and Neutrality:

- **German Threat:** There were concerns of a potential German invasion, leading to the construction of defensive installations and the establishment of military bases.
- **Maintaining Neutrality:** Despite the military presence, Iceland maintained its formal neutrality throughout the war. The Icelandic government, however, cooperated with the Allies for its defense.

4. Economic and Social Impact:

- **Economic Boost:** The war had a significant impact on Iceland's economy, providing a boost due to the Allied military presence. The construction of military infrastructure and the demand for local goods stimulated economic activity.
- **Social Changes:** The influx of foreign troops brought about social changes, including cultural exchanges and the introduction of new goods and ideas.

5. Post-War Changes and Independence:

- **Strategic Withdrawal:** After the war, the U.S. gradually reduced its military presence in Iceland, and the last American forces left in 1947.
- **Move Towards Independence:** Iceland's experience during World War II, combined with post-war geopolitical changes, contributed to the country's move towards full independence. In 1944, Iceland became a fully sovereign republic, severing its ties with Denmark.

6. Legacy and Remembrance:

- **Cold War Era:** Iceland's strategic importance persisted during the Cold War, leading to its membership in NATO (North Atlantic Treaty Organization) in 1949.
- **Base for U.S. Forces:** Keflavik Air Base continued to serve as a NATO base for the U.S. military during the Cold War.

7. War Memorials and Reminders:

- **Monuments:** Iceland has several monuments and memorials dedicated to the war, including those honoring the Allied forces and commemorating the Icelandic sailors who lost their lives in the conflict.
- **Cultural Impact:** World War II and its aftermath left a lasting impact on Icelandic culture, influencing literature, arts, and national identity.

Iceland's role in World War II reflects its journey from a Danish-ruled territory to a fully independent and neutral nation, with its experiences during the war shaping its modern identity and global relationships.

The secret to saving HUGE amounts of money when travelling to Iceland is...

Your mindset. Money is an emotional topic, if you associate words like cheapskate, Miser (and its £9.50 to go into Charles Dickens London house, oh the Irony) with being thrifty when traveling you are likely to say 'F-it' and spend your money needlessly because you associate pain with saving money. You pay now for an immediate reward. Our brains are prehistoric; they focus on surviving day to day. Travel companies and hotels know this and put trillions into making you believe you will be happier when you spend on their products or services. Our poor brains are up against outdated programming and an onslaught of advertisements bombarding us with the message: spending money on travel equals PLEASURE. To correct this carefully lodged propaganda in your frontal cortex, you need to imagine your future self.

Saving money does not make you a cheapskate. It makes you smart. How do people get rich? They invest their money. They don't go out and earn it; they let their money earn more money. So every time you want to spend money, imagine this: while you travel, your money is working for you, not you for money. While you sleep, the money, you've invested is going up and up. That's a pleasure a pricey entrance fee can't give you. Thinking about putting your money to work for you tricks your brain into believing you are not withholding pleasure from yourself, you are saving your money to invest so you can go to even more amazing places. You are thus turning thrifty travel into a pleasure fueled sport.

When you've got money invested - If you want to splash your cash on a first-class airplane seat - you can. I can't tell you how to invest your money, only that you should. Saving $20 on taxis doesn't seem like much, but over time you could save upwards of $15,000 a year, which is a deposit for a house which you can rent on Airbnb to finance more travel. Your brain making money looks like your brain on cocaine, so tell yourself saving money is making money.

Scientists have proved that imagining your future self is the easiest way to associate pleasure with saving money. You can download FaceApp — which will give you a picture of what you will look like older and grayer, or you can take a deep breath just before spending money and ask yourself if you will regret the purchase later.

The easiest ways to waste money traveling are:

Getting a taxi. The solution to this is to always download the google map before you go. Many taxi drivers will drive you around for 15 minutes when the place you were trying to get to is a 5-minute walk… remember while not getting an overpriced taxi to tell yourself, 'I am saving money to free myself for more travel.'
Spending money on overpriced food when hungry. The solution: carry snacks. A banana and an apple will cost you, in most places, less than a dollar.

Spending on entrance fees to top-rated attractions. If you really want to do it, spend the money happily. If you're conflicted, sleep on it. I don't regret spending $200 on a sky dive over the Great Barrier Reef; I regret going to the top of the shard on a cloudy day in Iceland for $60. Only you can know, but make sure it's your decision and not the marketing directors at said top-rated attraction.

Telling yourself 'you only have the chance to see/eat/experience it now'. While this might be true, make sure YOU WANT to spend the money. Money spent is money you can't invest, and often you can have the same experience for much less.

You can experience luxurious travel on a small budget, which will trick your brain into thinking you're already a high-roller, which will mean you'll be more likely to act like one and invest your money. Stay in five-star hotels for $5 by booking on the day of your stay on booking.com to enjoy last-minute deals. You can go to fancy restaurants using daily deal sites. Ask your airline about last-minute upgrades to first-class or business. I paid $100 extra on a $179 ticket to Cuba from Germany to be bumped to Business Class. When you ask, it will surprise you what you can get both at hotels and airlines.

Travel, as the saying goes, is the only thing you spend money on that makes you richer. You can easily waste money, making it difficult to enjoy that metaphysical wealth. The biggest money saving secret is to turn bargain hunting into a pleasurable activity, not an annoyance. Budgeting consciously can be fun, don't feel disappointed because you don't spend the $60 to go into an attraction. Feel good because soon that $60 will soon earn money for you. Meaning, you'll have the time and money to enjoy more metaphysical wealth while your bank balance increases.

So there it is. You can save a small fortune by being strategic with your trip planning. We've arranged everything in the guide to offer the best bang for your buck. Which means we took the view that if it's not an excellent investment for your money, we wouldn't include it. Why would a guide called 'Super Cheap' include lots of overpriced attractions? That said, if you think we've missed something or have unanswered questions, ping me an email: philgtang@gmail.com I'm on central Europe time and usually reply within 8 hours of getting your mail. We like to think of our guide books as evolving organisms helping our readers travel better cheaper. We use reader questions via email to update this book year round so you'll be helping other readers and yourself.

Don't put your dreams off!

Time is a currency you never get back and travel is its greatest return on investment. Plus, now you know you can visit Iceland for a fraction of the price most would have you believe.

Thank you for reading

Dear **Lovely Reader,**

If you have found this book useful, please consider writing a quick review on Online Retailers.

One person from every 1000 readers leaves a review on Online Retailers. It would mean more than you could ever know if you were one of our 1 in 1000 people to take the time to write a brief review.

Thank you so much for reading again and for spending your time and investing your trips future in Super Cheap Insider Guides.

One last note, please don't listen to anyone who says 'Oh no, you can't visit Iceland on a budget'. Unlike you, they didn't have this book. You can do ANYWHERE on a budget with the right insider advice and planning. Sure, learning to travel to Iceland on a budget that doesn't compromise on anything or drastically compromise on safety or comfort levels is a skill, but this guide has done the detective work for you. Now it is time for you to put the advice into action.

Phil and the Super Cheap Insider Guides Team

P.S If you need any more super cheap tips we'd love to hear from you e-mail me at philgtang@gmail.com, we have a lot of contacts in every region, so if there's a specific bargain you're hunting we can help you find it.

DISCOVER YOUR NEXT VACATION

☑ **LUXURY ON A BUDGET APPROACH**
☑ **CHOOSE FROM 107 DESTINATIONS**
☑ **EACH BOOK PACKED WITH REAL-TIME LOCAL TIPS**

All are available in Paperback and e-book on Online Retailers:
https://www.Online Retailers.com/dp/B09C2DHQG5

Several are available as audiobooks. You can watch excerpts of ALL for FREE on YouTube: https://youtube.com/channel/UCxo9YV8-M9P1cFosU-Gjnqg

COUNTRY GUIDES

Super Cheap AUSTRALIA
Super Cheap CANADA
Super Cheap DENMARK
Super Cheap FINLAND
Super Cheap FRANCE
Super Cheap GERMANY
Super Cheap Iceland
Super Cheap ITALY
Super Cheap IRELAND
Super Cheap JAPAN
Super Cheap LUXEMBOURG
Super Cheap MALDIVES 2024
Super Cheap NEW ZEALAND
Super Cheap NORWAY
Super Cheap SPAIN
Super Cheap SWITZERLAND

MORE GUIDES

Super Cheap ADELAIDE 2024
Super Cheap ALASKA 2024
Super Cheap AUSTIN 2024
Super Cheap BANGKOK 2024
Super Cheap BARCELONA 2024
Super Cheap BELFAST 2024
Super Cheap BERMUDA 2024
Super Cheap BORA BORA 2024
Super Cheap Great Barrier Reef 2024
Super Cheap CAMBRIDGE 2024
Super Cheap CANCUN 2024
Super Cheap CHIANG MAI 2024
Super Cheap CHICAGO 2024
Super Cheap DOHA 2024

Super Cheap DUBAI 2024
Super Cheap DUBLIN 2024
Super Cheap EDINBURGH 2024
Super Cheap GALWAY 2024
Super Cheap LAS VEGAS 2024
Super Cheap LIMA 2024
Super Cheap LISBON 2024
Super Cheap MALAGA 2024
Super Cheap Machu Pichu 2024
Super Cheap MIAMI 2024
Super Cheap Milan 2024
Super Cheap NASHVILLE 2024
Super Cheap NEW ORLEANS 2024
Super Cheap NEW YORK 2024
Super Cheap PARIS 2024
Super Cheap SEYCHELLES 2024
Super Cheap SINGAPORE 2024
Super Cheap ST LUCIA 2024
Super Cheap TORONTO 2024
Super Cheap TURKS AND CAICOS 2024
Super Cheap VENICE 2024
Super Cheap VIENNA 2024
Super Cheap YOSEMITE 2024
Super Cheap ZURICH 2024
Super Cheap ZANZIBAR 2024

Bonus Travel Hacks

I've included these bonus travel hacks to help you plan and enjoy your trip to Iceland cheaply, joyfully, and smoothly. Perhaps they will even inspire you to start or renew a passion for long-term travel.

Common pitfalls when it comes to allocating money to <u>your</u> <u>desires</u> while traveling

Beware of Malleable mental accounting

Let's say you budgeted spending only $30 per day in Iceland but then you say well if I was at home I'd be spending $30 on food as an everyday purchase so you add another $30 to your budget. Don't fall into that trap as the likelihood is you still have expenses at home even if its just the cost of keeping your freezer going.

Beware of impulse purchases in Iceland

Restaurants that you haven't researched and just idle into can sometimes turn out to be great, but more often, they turn out to suck, especially if they are near tourist attractions. Make yourself a travel itinerary including where you'll eat breakfast and lunch. Dinner is always more expensive, so the meal best to enjoy at home or as a takeaway. This book is full of incredible cheap eats. All you have to do is plan to go to them.

Social media and FOMO (Fear of Missing Out)

'The pull of seeing acquaintances spend money on travel can often be a more powerful motivator to spend more while traveling than seeing an advertisement.' Beware of what you allow to influence you and go back to the question, what's the best money I can spend today?

Now-or-never sales strategies

One reason tourists are targeted by salespeople is the success of the now-or-never strategy. If you don't spend the money now… your never get the opportunity again. Rarely is this true.

Instead of spending your money on something you might not actually desire, take five minutes. Ask yourself, do I really want this? And return to the answer in five minutes. Your body will either say an absolute yes with a warm, excited feeling or a no with a weak, obscure feeling.

Unexpected costs

> **"Holding on to anger is like grasping a hot coal with the intent of throwing it at someone else; you only hurt yourself." The Buddha.**

One downside to traveling is unexpected costs. When these spring up from airlines, accommodation providers, tours and on and on, they feel like a punch in the gut. During the pandemic my earnings fell to 20% of what they are normally. No one was traveling, no one was buying travel guides. My accountant out of nowhere significantly raised his fee for the year despite the fact there was a lot less money to count. I was so angry I consulted a lawyer who told me you will spend more taking him to court than you will paying his bill. I had to get myself into a good feeling place before I paid his bill, so I googled how to feel good paying someone who has scammed you.

The answer: Write down that you will receive 10 times the amount you are paying from an unexpected source. I did that. Four months later, the accountant wrote to me. He had applied for a COVID subsidy for me and I would receive… you guessed it almost exactly 10 times his fee.

Make of that what you want. I don't wish to get embroiled in a conversation about what many term 'woo-woo', but the result of my writing that I would receive 10 times the amount made me feel much, much better when paying him. And ultimately, that was a gift in itself. So next time some airline or train operator or hotel/ Airbnb sticks you with an unexpected fee, immediately write that you will receive 10 times the amount you are paying from an unexpected source. Rise your vibe and skip the added price of feeling angry.

Hack your allocations for your Iceland Trip

"The best trick for saving is to eliminate the decision to save." Perry Wright of Duke University.

Put the money you plan to spend in Iceland on a pre-paid card in the local currency. This cuts out two problems - not knowing how much you've spent and totally avoiding expensive currency conversion fees.

You could even create separate spaces. This much for transportation, this for tours/ entertainment, accommodation and food. We are reluctant to spend money that is pre-assigned to categories or uses.

Write that you want to enjoy a $3,000 trip for $500 to your Iceland trip. Countless research shows when you put goals in writing, you have a higher chance of following through.

Spend all the money you want to on buying experiences in Iceland

"Experiences are like good relatives that stay for a while and then leave. Objects are like relatives who move in and stay past their welcome." Daniel Gilbert, psychologist from Harvard University.

Economic and psychological research shows we are happier buying brief experiences on vacation rather than buying stuff to wear so give yourself freedom to spend on experiences knowing that the value you get back is many many times over.

Make saving money a game

There's one day a year where all the thrift shops where me and my family live sell everything there for a $1. My wife and I hold a contest where we take $5 and buy an entire outfit for each other. Whoever's outfit is liked more wins. We also look online to see whose outfit would have cost more to buy new. This year, my wife even snagged me an Armani coat for $1. I liked the coat when she showed it to me, but when I found out it was $500 new; I liked it and wore it a lot more.

Quadruple your money

Every-time you want to spend money, imagine it quadrupled. So the $10 you want to spend is actually $40. Now imagine that what you want to buy is four times the price. Do you still want it? If yes, go enjoy. If not, you've just saved yourself money, know you can choose to invest it in a way that quadruples or allocate it to something you really want to give you a greater return.

Understand what having unlimited amounts of money to spend in Iceland actually looks like

Let's look at what it would be like to have unlimited amounts of money to spend on your trip to Iceland.

Isolation

You take a private jet to your private Iceland hotel. There you are lavished with the best food, drink, and entertainment. Spending vast amounts of money on vacation equals being isolated.

If you're on your honeymoon and you want to be alone with your Amore, this is wonderful, but it can be equally wonderful to make new friends. Know this a study 'carried out by Brigham Young University, Utah found that while obesity increased risk of death by 30%, loneliness increased it by half.'

Comfort

Money can buy you late check outs of five-star hotels and priority boarding on airlines, all of which add up to comfort. But as this book has shown you, saving money in Iceland doesn't minimize comfort, that's just a lie travel agencies littered with glossy brochures want you to believe.

You can do late-check outs for free with the right credit cards and priority boarding can be purchased with a lot of airlines from $4. If you want to go big with first-class or business, flights offset your own travel costs by renting your own home or you can upgrade at the airport often for a fraction of what you would have paid booking a business flight online.

MORE TIPS TO FIND CHEAP FLIGHTS

"The use of travelling is to regulate imagination by reality, and instead of thinking how things may be, to see them as they are." Samuel Jackson

If you're working full-time, you can save yourself a lot of money by requesting your time off from work starting in the middle of the week. Tuesdays and Wednesdays are the cheapest days to fly. You can save thousands just by adjusting your time off.

The simplest secret to booking cheap flights is open parameters. Let's say you want to fly from Chicago to Paris. You enter the USA in from and select Iceland under to. You may find flights from New York City to Paris for $70. Then you just need to find a cheap flight to NYC. Make sure you calculate full costs, including if you need airport accommodation and of course getting to and from airports, **but in nearly every instance open parameters will save you at least half the cost of the flight.**

If you're not sure about where you want to go, use open parameters to show you the cheapest destinations from your city. Start with skyscanner.net they include the low-cost airlines that others like Kayak leave out. Google Flights can also show you cheap destinations. To see these leave the WHERE TO section blank. Open parameters can also show you the cheapest dates to fly. If you're flexible, you can save up to 80% of the flight cost. Always check the weather at your destination before you book. Sometimes a $400 flight will be $20, because it's monsoon season. But hey, if you like the rain, why not?

ALWAYS USE A PRIVATE BROWSER TO BOOK FLIGHTS

Skyscanner and other sites track your IP address and put prices up and down based on what they determine your strength of conviction to buy. e.g. if you've booked one-way and are looking for the return, these sites will jack the prices up by in most cases 50%. Incognito browsing pays.

Use a VPN such as Hola to book your flight from your destination

Install Hola, change your destination to the country you are flying to. The location from which a ticket is booked can affect the price significantly as algorithms consider local buying power.

Choose the right time to buy your ticket.

Choose the right time to buy your ticket, as purchasing tickets on a Sunday has been proven to be cheaper. If you can only book during the week, try to do it on a Tuesday.

Mistake fares

Email alerts from individual carriers are where you can find the best 'mistake fares". This is where a computer error has resulted in an airline offering the wrong fare. In my experience, it's best to sign up to individual carriers email lists, but if you ARE lazy Secret Flying puts together a daily roster of mistake fares. Visit https://www.secretflying.com/errorfare/ to see if there're any errors that can benefit you.

Fly late for cheaper prices

Red-eye flights, the ones that leave later in the day, are typically cheaper and less crowded, so aim to book that flight if possible. You will also get through the airport much quicker at the end of the day. Just make sure there's ground transport available for when you land. You don't want to save $50 on the airfare and spend it on a taxi to your accommodation.

Use this APP for same day flights

If your plans are flexible, use 'Get The Flight Out' (http://www.gtfoflights.com/) a fare tracker Hopper that shows you same-day deeply discounted flights. This is best for long-haul flights with major carriers. You can often find a British Airways round-trip from JFK Airport to Heathrow for $300. If you booked this in advance, you'd pay at least double.

Take an empty water bottle with you

Airport prices on food and drinks are sky high. It disgusts me to see some airports charging $10 for a bottle of water. ALWAYS take an empty water bottle with you. It's relatively unknown, but most airports have drinking water fountains past the security check. Just type in your airport name to wateratairports.com to locate the fountain. Then once you've passed security (because they don't allow you to take 100ml or more of liquids) you can freely refill your bottle with water.

Round-the-World (RTW) Tickets

It is always cheaper to book your flights using a DIY approach. First, you may decide you want to stay longer in one country, and a RTW will charge you a hefty fee for changing your flight. Secondly, it all depends on where and when you travel and as we have discussed, there are many ways to ensure you pay way less than $1,500 for a year of flights. If you're travelling long-haul, the best strategy is to buy a return ticket, say New York, to Bangkok and then take cheap flights or transport around Asia and even to Australia and beyond.

Cut your costs to and from airports

Don't you hate it when getting to and from the airport is more expensive than your flight! And this is true in so many cities, especially European ones. For some reason, Google often shows the most expensive options. Use Omio to compare the cheapest transport options and save on airport transfer costs.

Car sharing instead of taxis

Check if Iceland has car sharing at the airport. Often they'll be tons of cars parked at the airport that are half the price of taking a taxi into the city. In most instances, you register your driving licence on an app and scan the code on the car to get going.

Checking Bags

Sometimes you need to check bags. If you do, put an AirTag inside. That way, you'll be about to see when you land where your bag is. This saves you the nail biting wait at baggage claim. And if worse comes to worst, and you see your bag is actually in another city, you can calmly stroll over to customer services and show them where your bag is.

Is it cheaper and more convenient to send your bags ahead?

Before you check your bags, check if it's cheaper to send them ahead of you with sendmybag.com obviously if you're staying in an Airbnb, you'll need to ask the hosts permission or you can time them to arrive the day after you. Hotels are normally very amenable.

What Credit Card Gives The Best Air Miles?

You can slash the cost of flights just for spending on a piece of plastic.

LET'S TALK ABOUT DEBT

Before we go into the best cards for each country, let's first talk about debt. The US system offers the best and biggest rewards. Why? Because they rely on the fact that many people living in the US will not pay their cards in full and the card will earn the bank significant interest payments. Other countries have a very different attitude towards money, debt, and saving than Americans. Thus in Germany and Austria the offerings aren't as favourable as the UK, Iceland and Australia, where debt culture is more widely embraced. The takeaway here is this: **Only spend on one of these cards when you have set-up an automatic total monthly balance repayment. Don't let banks profit from your lizard brain!**

The best air-mile credit cards for those living in the UK

Amex Preferred Rewards Gold comes out top for those living in the UK for 2024.

Here are the benefits:

- 20,000-point bonus on £3,000 spend in first three months. These can be used towards flights with British Airways, Virgin Atlantic, Emirates and Etihad, and often other rewards, such as hotel stays and car hire.
- 1 point per £1 spent
- 1 point = 1 airline point
- Two free visits a year to airport lounges
- No fee in year one, then £140/yr

The downside:

- Fail to repay fully and it's 59.9% rep APR interest, incl fee

You'll need to cancel before the £140/yr fee kicks in year two if you want to avoid it.

The best air-mile credit cards for those living in Canada

Aeroplan is the superior rewards program in Canada. The card has a high earn rate for Aeroplan Points, generating 1.5 points per $1 spent on eligible purchases. Look at the specifics of the eligible purchases https://www.aircanada.com/ca/en/aco/home/aeroplan/earn.html. If you're not spending on these things AMEX's Membership Rewards program offers you the best returns in Canada.

The best air-mile credit cards for those living in Germany

If you have a German bank account, you can apply for a Lufthansa credit card.

Earn 50,000 award miles if you spend $3,000 in purchases and paying the annual fee, both within the first 90 days.

Earn 2 award miles per $1 spent on ticket purchases directly from Miles & More integrated airline partners.

Earn 1 award mile per $1 spent on all other purchases.

The downsides

the €89 annual fee

Limited to fly with Lufthansa and its partners but you can capitalise on perks like the companion pass and airport lounge vouchers.

You need excellent credit to get this card.

The best air-mile credit cards for those living in Austria

"In Austria, Miles & More offers you a special credit card. You get miles for each purchase with the credit card. The Miles & More program calculates miles earned based on the distance flown and booking class. For European flights, the booking class is a flat rate. For intercontinental flights, mileage is calculated by multiplying the booking class by the distance flown." They offer a calculator so you can see how many points you could earn: https://www.miles-and-more.com/at/en/earn/airlines/mileage-calculator.html

The best air-mile credit cards for those living in Iceland:

"The American Express card is the best known and oldest to earn miles, thanks to its membership Rewards program. When making payments with this card, points are added, which can then be exchanged for miles from airlines such as Iberia, Air Europa, Emirates or Alitalia." More information is available here: https://www.americanexpress.com/es-es/

The best air-mile credit cards for those living in Australia

ANZ Rewards Black comes out top for 2024.

180,000 bonus ANZ Reward Points (can get an $800 gift card) and $0 annual fee for the first year with the ANZ Rewards Black
Points Per Spend: 1 Velocity point on purchases of up to $5,000 per statement period and 0.5 Velocity points thereafter.
Annual Fee: $0 in the first year, then $375 after.
Ns no set minimum income required, however, there is a minimum credit limit of $15,000 on this card.

Here are some ways you can hack points onto this card: https://www.pointhacks.com.au/credit-cards/anz-rewards-black-guide/

The best air-mile credit card solution for those living in the USA with a POOR credit score

The downside to Airline Mile cards is that they require good or excellent credit scores, meaning 690 or higher.

If you have bad credit and want to use credit card air lines you will need to rebuild your credit poor. The Credit One Bank® Platinum Visa® for Rebuilding Credit is a good credit card for people with bad credit who don't want to place a deposit on a secured card. The Credit One Platinum Visa offers a $300 credit limit, rewards, and the potential for credit-limit increases, which in time will help rebuild your score.

PLEASE don't sign-up for any of these cards if you can't trust yourself to repay it in full monthly. This will only lead to stress for you.

Frequent Flyer Memberships

"Points" and "miles" are often used interchangeably, but they're usually two very different things. Maximise and diversify your rewards by utilising both.

A frequent-flyer program (FFP) is a loyalty program offered by an airline. They are designed to encourage airline customers to fly more to accumulate points (also called miles, kilometres, or segments) which can be redeemed for air travel or other rewards.

You can sign up with any FFP program for free. There are three major airline alliances in the world: Oneworld, SkyTeam and Star Alliance. I am with One World https://www.oneworld.com/members because the points can be accrued and used for most flights.

The best return on your points is to use them for international business or first class flights with lie-flat seats. You would need 3 times more miles compared to an economy flight, but if you paid cash, you'd pay 5 - 10 times more than the cost of the economy flight, so it really pays to use your points only for upgrades. The worst value for your miles is to buy an economy seat or worse, a gift from the airlines gift-shop.

Sign up for a family/household account to pool miles together. If you share a common address, you can claim the miles with most airlines. You can use AwardWallet to keep track of your miles. Remember that they only last for 2 years, so use them before they expire.

How to get 70% off a Cruise

An average cruise can set you back $4,000. If you dream of cruising the oceans, but find the pricing too high, look at repositioning cruises. You can save as much as 70% by taking a cruise which takes the boat back to its home port.

These one-way itineraries take place during low cruise seasons when ships have to reposition themselves to locations where there's warmer weather.

To find a repositioning cruise, go to vacationstogo.com/repositioning_cruises.cfm. This simple and often overlooked booking trick is great for avoiding long flights with children and can save you so much money!

It's worth noting we don't have any affiliations with any travel service or provider. The links we suggest are chosen based on our experience of finding the best deals.

Relaxing at the Airport

The best way to relax at the airport is in a lounge where they provide free food, drinks, comfortable chairs, luxurious amenities (many have showers) and, if you're lucky, a peaceful ambience. If you're there for a longer time, look for Airport Cubicles, sleep pods which charge by the hour.

You can use your FFP Card (Frequent Flyer Memberships) to get into select lounges for free. Check your eligibility before you pay.

If you're travelling a lot, I'd recommend investing in a Priority Pass for the airport.

It includes 850-plus airport lounges around the world. The cost is $99 for the year and $27 per lounge visit or you can pay $399 for the year all inclusive.

If you need a lounge for a one-off day, you can get a Day Pass. Buy it online for a discount, it always works out cheaper than buying at the airport. Use www.LoungePass.com.

Lounges are also great if you're travelling with kids, as they're normally free for kids and will definitely cost you less than snacks for your little ones. The rule is that kids should be seen and not heard, so consider this before taking an overly excited child who wants to run around, or you might be asked to leave even after you've paid.

How to spend money

Bank ATM fees vary from $2.50 per transaction to as high as $5 or more, depending on the ATM and the country. You can completely skip those fees by paying with card and using a card which can hold multiple currencies.

Budget travel hacking begins with a strategy to spend without fees. Your individual strategy depends on the country you legally reside in as to what cards are available. Happily there are some fin-tech solutions which can save you thousands on those pesky ATM withdrawal fees and are widely available globally. Here are a selection of cards you can pre-charge with currency for Iceland:

N26

N26 is a 12-year-old digital bank. I have been using them for over 6 years. The key advantage is fee-free card transactions abroad. They have a very elegant app, where you can check your timeline for all transactions listed in real time or manage your in-app security anywhere. The card you receive is a Mastercard so you can use it everywhere. If you lose the card, you don't have to call anyone, just open the app and swipe 'lock card'. It puts your purchases into a graph automatically so you can see what you spend on. You can open an account from abroad entirely online, all you need is your passport and a camera n26.com

Revolut

Revolut is a multi-currency account that allows you to hold and exchange 29 currencies and spend fee-free abroad. It's a UK based neobank, but accepts customers from all over the world.

Wise debit card

If you're going to be in one place for a long time, the Wise debit card is like having your travel money on a card – it lets you spend money at the real exchange rate.

Monzo

Monzo is good if your UK based. They offer a fee-free UK account. Fee-free international money transfers and fee-free spending abroad.

The downside

The cards above are debit cards, meaning you need to have money in those accounts to spend it. This comes with one big downside: safety. Credit card issuers' have "zero liability" meaning you're not liable for unauthorised charges. All the cards listed above do provide cover for unauthorised charges but times vary greatly in how quickly you'd get your money back if it were stolen.

The best option is to check in your country to see which credit cards are the best for travelling and set up monthly payments to repay the whole amount so you don't pay unnecessary interest. In the USA, Schwab regularly ranks at the top for travel credit cards. Credit cards are always the safer option when abroad simply because you get your money back faster if its stolen and if you're renting cars, most will give you free insurance when you book the car rental using the card, saving you money.

Always withdraw money; never exchange.

Money exchanges, whether they be on the streets or in the airports will NEVER give you a good exchange rate. Do not bring bundles of cash. Instead, withdraw local currency from the ATM as needed and try to use only free ATMs. Many in airports charge you a fee to withdraw cash. Look for bigger ATMs attached to banks to avoid this.

Recap

- Take cash from local, non-charging ATMs for the best rates.

- Never change at airport exchange desks unless you absolutely have to, then just change just enough to be able get to a bank ATM.

- Bring a spare credit card for emergencies.

- Split cash in various places on your person (pockets, shoes) and in your luggage. It's never sensible to keep your cash or cards all in one place.

- In higher risk areas, use a money belt under your clothes or put $50 in your shoe or bra.

Revolut
Revolut is a multi-currency account that allows you to hold and exchange 29 currencies and spend fee-free abroad. It's a UK based neobank, but accepts customers from all over the world.

Wise debit card
If you're going to be in one place for a long time the Wise debit card is like having your travel money on a card – it lets you spend money at the real exchange rate.

Monzo
Monzo is good if your UK based. They offer a fee-free UK account. Fee-free international money transfers and fee-free spending abroad.

The downside

The cards above are debit cards, meaning you need to have money in those accounts to spend it. This comes with one big downside: safety. Credit card issuers' have "zero liability" meaning you're not liable for unauthorised charges. All of the cards listed above do provide cover for unauthorised charges but times vary greatly in how quickly you'd get your money back if it were stolen.

The best option is to check in your country to see which credit cards are the best for travelling and set up monthly payments to repay the whole amount so you don't pay unnecessary interest. In the USA, Schwab[4] regularly ranks at the top for travel credit cards. Credit cards are always the safer option when abroad simply because you get your money back faster if its stolen and if you're renting cars, most will give you free insurance when you book the car rental using the card, saving you money.

Always withdraw money; never exchange.

Money exchanges whether they be on the streets or in the airports will NEVER give you a good exchange rate. Do not bring bundles of cash. Instead withdraw local currency from the ATM as needed and try to use only free ATM's. Many in airports charge you a fee to withdraw cash. Look for bigger ATM's attached to banks to avoid this.

Recap

- Take cash from local, non-charging ATMs for the best rates.
- Never change at airport exchange desks unless you absolutely have to, then just change just enough to be able get to a bank ATM.
- Bring a spare credit card for emergencies.
- Split cash in various places on your person (pockets, shoes) and in your luggage. Its never sensible to keep your cash or cards all in one place.
- In higher risk areas, use a money belt under your clothes or put $50 in your shoe or bra.

---

[4] Charles Schwab High Yield Checking accounts refund every single ATM fee worldwide, require no minimum balance and have no monthly fee.

How NOT to be ripped off

"One of the great things about travel is that you find out how many good, kind people ther e are."
— Edith Wharton

The quote above may seem ill placed in a chapter entitled how not to be ripped off, but I included it to remind you that the vast majority of people do not want to rip you off. In fact, scammers are normally limited to three situations:

1. Around heavily visited attractions - these places are targeted purposively due to sheer footfall. Many criminals believe ripping people off is simply a numbers game.

2. In cities or countries with low-salaries or communist ideologies. If they can't make money in the country, they seek to scam foreigners. If you have travelled to India, Morocco or Cuba you will have observed this phenomenon.

3. When you are stuck and the person helping you know you have limited options.

Scammers know that most people will avoid confrontation. Don't feel bad about utterly ignoring someone and saying no. Here are six strategies to avoid being ripped off:

1. **Never ever agree to pay as much as you want. Always decide on a price before.**

Whoever you're dealing with is trained to tell you, they are uninterested in money. This is a trap. If you let people do this they will ask for MUCH MORE money at the end, and because you have used there service, you will feel obliged to pay. This is a conman's trick and nothing more.

2. Pack light

You can move faster and easier. If you take heavy luggage, you will end up taking taxis which are comparatively very costly over time.

3. NEVER use the airport taxi service. Plan to use public transport before you reach the airport.

4. Don't buy a sim card from the airport. Buy from the local supermarkets it will cost 50% less.

5. Eat at local restaurants serving regional food

Food defines culture. Exploring all delights available to the palate doesn't need to cost enormous sums.

6. Ask the locals what something should cost, and try not to pay over that.

7. If you find yourself with limited options. e.g. your taxi dumps you on the side of the road because you refuse to pay more (common in India and parts of South America) don't act desperate and negotiate as if you have other options or you will be extorted.

8. Don't blindly rely on social media[5]

Let's say you post in a Facebook group that you want tips for travelling to The Maldives. A lot of the comments you will receive come from guides, hosts and restaurants doing their own promotion. It's estimated that 50% or more of Facebook's current monthly active users are fake. And what's worse, a recent study found Social media platforms leave 95% of reported fake accounts up. These accounts are the digital versions of the men who hang around the Grand Palace in Bangkok telling tourists its closed, to divert you to shops where they will receive a commission for bringing you.

It can also be the case that genuine comments come from people who have totally different interests, beliefs and yes, budgets to yours. Make your experience your own and don't believe every comment you read.

Bottom line: use caution when accepting recommendations on social media and always fact-check with your own research.

Small tweaks on the road add up to big differences in your bank balance

Take advantage of other hotel amenities

If you fancy a swim but you're nowhere near the ocean, try the nearest hotel with a pool. As long as you buy a drink, the hotel staff will probably grant you access.

Fill up your mini bar for free.

Fill up your mini bar for free by storing things from the breakfast bar or grocery shop in your mini bar to give you a greater selection of drinks and food without the hefty price tag.

Save yourself some ironing

Use the steam from the shower to get rid of wrinkles in clothing. If something is creased, leave it trapped with the steam in the bathroom overnight for even better results.

See somewhere else for free

Opt for long stopovers, allowing you to experience another city without spending much money.

Wear your heaviest clothes

On the plane to save weight in your pack, allowing you to bring more with you. Big coats can then be used as pillows to make your flight more comfortable.

Don't get lost while you're away.

Find where you want to go using Google Maps, then type 'OK Maps' into the search bar to store this information for offline viewing.

---

[5] https://arstechnica.com/tech-policy/2019/12/social-media-platforms-leave-95-of-reported-fake-accounts-up-study-finds/

Use car renting services

Share Now or Car2Go allow you to hire a car for 2 hours for $25 in a lot of European countries.

Share Rides

Use sites like blablacar.com to find others who are driving in your direction. It can be 80% cheaper than normal transport. Just check the drivers reviews.

Use free gym passes

Get a free gym day pass by googling the name of a local gym and free day pass.

When asked by people providing you a service where you are from..

If there's no price list for the service you are asking for, when asked where you are from, Say you are from a lesser-known poorer country. I normally say Macedonia, and if they don't know where it is, add it's a poor country. If you say UK, USA, the majority of Europe bar the well-known poorer countries taxi drivers, tour operators etc will match the price to what they think you pay at home.

Set-up a New Uber/ other car hailing app account for discounts

By googling you can find offers with $50 free for new users in most cities for Uber/ Lyft/ Bolt and alike. Just set up a new gmail.com email account to take advantage.

Where and How to Make Friends

"People don't take trips, trips take people." – John Steinbeck

Become popular at the airport

Want to become popular at the airport? Pack a power bar with multiple outlets and just see how many friends you can make. It's amazing how many people forget their chargers, or who packed them in the luggage that they checked in.

Stay in Hostels

First of all, Hostels don't have to be shared dorms, and they cater to a much wider demographic than is assumed. Hostels are a better environment for meeting people than hotels, and more importantly, they tended to open up excursion opportunities that further opened up that opportunity.

Or take up a hobby

If hostels are a definite no-no for you; find an interest. Take up a hobby where you will meet people. I've dived for years and the nature of diving is you're always paired up with a dive buddy. I met a lot of interesting people that way.

Small tweaks on the road add up to big differences in your bank balance

Take advantage of other hotel's amenities

If you fancy a swim but you're nowhere near the ocean, try the nearest hotel with a pool. As long as you buy a drink, the hotel staff will likely grant you access.

Fill up your mini bar for free.

Fill up your mini bar for free by storing things from the breakfast bar or grocery shop in your mini bar to give you a greater selection of drinks and food without the hefty price tag.

Save yourself some ironing

Use the steam from the shower to get rid of wrinkles in clothing. If something is creased, leave it trapped with the steam in the bathroom overnight for even better results.

See somewhere else for free

Opt for long stopovers, allowing you to experience another city without spending much money.

Wear your heaviest clothes

on the plane to save weight in your pack, allowing you to bring more with you. Big coats can then be used as pillows to make your flight more comfortable.

Don't get lost while you're away.

Find where you want to go using Google Maps, then type 'OK Maps' into the search bar to store this information for offline viewing.

Use car renting services

Share Now or Car2Go allow you to hire a car for 2 hours for $25 in a lot of Europe.

Share Rides

Use sites like blablacar.com to find others who are driving in your direction. It can be 80% cheaper than normal transport. Just check the drivers reviews.

Use free gym passes

Get a free gym day pass by googling the name of a local gym and free day pass.

When asked by people providing you a service where you are from..

If there's no price list for the service you are asking for, when asked where you are from, Say you are from a lesser-known poorer country. I normally say Macedonia, and if they don't know where it is, add it's a poor country.If you say UK, USA, the majority of Europe bar the well-known poorer countries taxi drivers, tour operators etc will match the price to what they think you pay at home.

Set-up a New Uber/ other car hailing app account for discounts

By googling you can find offers with $50 free for new users in most cities for Uber/ Lyft/ Bolt and alike. Just set up a new gmail.com email account to take advantage.

Where and How to Make Friends

"People don't take trips, trips take people." – John Steinbeck

Become popular at the airport

Want to become popular at the airport? Pack a power bar with multiple outlets and just see how many friends you can make. It's amazing how many people forget their chargers, or who packed them in the luggage that they checked in.

Stay in Hostels

First of all, Hostels don't have to be shared dorms, and they cater to a much wider demographic than is assumed. Hostels are a better environment for meeting people than hotels, and more importantly they tended to open up excursion opportunities that further opened up that opportunity.

Or take up a hobby

If hostels are a definite no-no for you; find an interest. Take up a hobby where you will meet people. I've dived for years and the nature of diving is you're always paired up with a dive buddy. I met a lot of interesting people that way.

When unpleasantries come your way...

We all have our good and bad days travelling, and on a bad day you can feel like just taking a flight home. Here are some ways to overcome common travel problems:

Anxiety when flying

It has been over 40 years since a plane has been brought down by turbulence. Repeat that number to yourself: 40 years! Planes are built to withstand lighting strikes, extreme storms and ultimately can adjust course to get out of their way. Landing and take-off are when the most accidents happen, but you have statistically three times the chance of winning a huge jackpot lottery, then you do of dying in a plane crash.

If you feel afraid on the flight, focus on your breathing saying the word 'smooth' over and over until the flight is smooth. Always check the airline safety record on airlinerating.com I was surprised to learn Ryanair and Easyjet as much less safe than Wizz Air according to those ratings because they sell similarly priced flights. If there is extreme turbulence, I feel much better knowing I'm in a 7 star safety plane.

Wanting to sleep instead of seeing new places

This is a common problem. Just relax, there's little point doing fun things when you feel tired. Factor in jet-lag to your travel plans. When you're rested and alert you'll enjoy your new temporary home much more. Many people hate the first week of a long-trip because of jet-lag and often blame this on their first destination, but its rarely true. Ask travellers who 'hate' a particular place and you will see that very often they either had jet-lag or an unpleasant journey there.

Going over budget

Come back from a trip to a monster credit card bill? Hopefully, this guide has prevented you from returning to an unwanted bill. Of course, there are costs that can creep up and this is a reminder about how to prevent them making their way on to your credit card bill:

- To and from the airport. Solution: leave adequate time and take the cheapest method - book before.

- Baggage. Solution: take hand luggage and post things you might need to yourself.

- Eating out. Solution: go to cheap eats places and suggest those to friends.

- Parking. Solution: use apps to find free parking

- Tipping. Solution Leave a modest tip and tell the server you will write them a nice review.

- Souvenirs. Solution: fridge magnets only.

- Giving to the poor. (This one still gets me, but if you're giving away $10 a day - it adds up) Solution: volunteer your time instead and recognise that in tourist destinations many beggars are run by organised crime gangs.

Price v Comfort

I love traveling. I don't love struggling. I like decent accommodation, being able to eat properly and see places and enjoy. I am never in the mood for low-cost airlines or crappy transfers, so here's what I do to save money.

- Avoid organised tours unless you are going to a place where safety is a real issue. They are expensive and constrain your wanderlust to typical things. I only recommend them in Algeria, Iran and Papua New Guinea - where language and gender views pose serious problems all cured by a reputable tour organiser.

- Eat what the locals do.

- Cook in your Airbnb/ hostel where restaurants are expensive.

- Shop at local markets.

- Spend time choosing your flight, and check the operator on arilineratings.com

- Mix up hostels and Airbnbs. Hostels for meeting people, Airbnb for relaxing and feeling 'at home'.

Not knowing where free toilets are

Use Toilet Finder - https://play.google.com/store/apps/details?id=com.bto.toilet&hl=en

Your Airbnb is awful

Airbnb customer service is notoriously bad. Help yourself out. Try to sort things out with the host, but if you can't, take photos of everything e.g bed, bathroom, mess, doors, contact them within 24 hours. Tell them you had to leave and pay for new accommodation. Ask politely for a full refund including booking fees. With photographic evidence and your new accommodation receipt, they can't refuse.

The airline loses your bag

Go to the Luggage desk before leaving the airport and report the bag missing. Hopefully you've headed the advice to put an AirTag in your checked bag and you can show them where to find your bag. Most airlines will give you an overnight bag, ask where you're staying and return the bag to you within three days. It's extremely rare for Airlines to lose your bag due to technological innovation, but if that happens you should submit an insurance claim after the three days is up, including receipts for everything you had to buy in the interim.

Your travel companion lets you down

Whether it's a breakup or a friend cancelling, it sucks and can ramp up costs. The easiest solution to finding a new travel companion is to go to a well-reviewed hostel and find someone you want to travel with. You should spend at least three days getting to know this person before you suggest travelling together. Finding someone in person is always better than finding someone online, because you can get a better idea of whether you will have a smooth journey together. Travel can make or break friendships.

Culture shock

I had one of the strongest culture shocks while spending 6 months in Japan. It was overwhelming how much I had to prepare when I went outside of the door (googling words and sentences what to use, where to go, which station and train line to use, what is this food called in Japanese and how does its look etc.). I was so tired constantly but in the end I just let go and went with my extremely bad Japanese. If you feel culture shocked its because your brain is referencing your surroundings to what you know. Stop comparing, have Google translate downloaded and relax.

Your Car rental insurance is crazy expensive

I always use carrentals.com and book with a credit card. Most credit cards will give you free insurance for the car, so you don't need to pay the extra. Some unsavoury companies will bump the price up when you arrive. Ask to speak to a manager. If this doesn't resolve, it google "consumer ombudsman for NAME OF COUNTRY." and seek an immediate full refund on the balance difference you paid. It is illegal in most countries to alter the price of a rental car when the person arrives to pickup a pre-arranged car.

A note on Car Rental Insurance

Always always always rent a car with a credit card that has rental vehicle coverage built into the card and is automatically applied when you rent a car. Then there's no need to buy additional rental insurance (check with your card on the coverage they protect some exclude collision coverage). Do yourself a favour when you step up to the desk to rent the car tell the agent you're already covered and won't be buying anything today. They work on commission and you'll save time and your patience avoiding the upselling.

You're sick

First off ALWAYS, purchase travel insurance. Including emergency transport up to $500k even to back home, which is usually less than $10 additional. I use https://www.comparethemarket.com/travel-insurance/ to find the best days. If I am sick I normally check into a hotel with room service and ride it out.

Make a Medication Travel Kit

Take travel sized medications with you:

- Antidiarrheal medication (for example, bismuth subsalicylate, loperamide)

- Medicine for pain or fever (such as acetaminophen, aspirin, or ibuprofen)

- Throat Lozenges

Save yourself from most travel related hassles

- Do not make jokes with immigration and customs staff. A misunderstanding can lead to HUGE fines.

- Book the most direct flight you can find nonstop if possible.

- Carry a US$50 bill for emergency cash. I have entered a country and all ATM and credit card systems were down. US$ can be exchanged nearly anywhere in the world and is useful in extreme situations, but where possible don't exchange, as you will lose money.

- Check, and recheck, required visas and such BEFORE the day of your trip. Some countries, for instance, require a ticket out of the country in order to enter. Others, like the US and Australia, require electronic authorisation in advance.

- Airport security is asinine and inconsistent around the world. Keep this in mind when connecting flights. Always leave at least 2 hours for international connections or international to domestic. In Stansted for example, they force you to buy one of their plastic bags, and remove your liquids from your own plastic bag…. just to make money from you. And this adds to the time it will take to get through security, so lines are long.

- Wiki travel is perfect to use for a lay of the land.

- Expensive luggage rarely lasts longer than cheap luggage, in my experience. Fancy leather bags are toast with air travel.

Food

- When it comes to food, eat in local restaurants, not tourist-geared joints. Any place with the menu in three or more languages is going to be overpriced.

- Take a spork - a knife, spoon and fork all in one.

Water Bottle

Take a water bottle with a filter. We love these ones from Water to Go.

Empty it before airport security and separate the bottle and filter as some airport people will try and claim it has liquids…

Bug Sprays

If you're heading somewhere tropical spray your clothes with Permethrin before you travel. It lasts 40 washes and saves space in your bag. A 'Bite Away' zapper can be used after the bite to totally erase it. It cuts down on the itching and erases the bite from your skin.

Order free mini's

Don't buy those expensive travel sized toiletries, order travel sized freebies online. This gives you the opportunity to try brands you've never used before, and who knows, you might even find your new favourite soap.

Take a waterproof bag

If you're travelling alone you can swim without worrying about your phone, wallet and passport laying on the beach.

You can also use it as a source of entertainment on those ultra budget flights.

Make a private entertainment centre anywhere

Always take an eye-mask, earplugs, a scarf and a kindle reader - so you can sleep and entertain yourself anywhere!

The best Travel Gadgets

The door alarm

If you're nervous and staying in private rooms or airbnbs take a door alarm. For those times when you just don't feel safe, it can help you fall asleep. You can get tiny ones for less than $10 from Online Retailers: https://www.Online Retailers.com/Travel-door-alarm/s?k=Travel+door+alarm

Smart Blanket

Online Retailers sells a 6 in 1 heating blanket that is very useful for cold plane or bus trips. Its great if you have poor circulation as it becomes a detachable Foot Warmer: Online Retailers http://amzn.to/2hTYIOP I paid $49.00.

The coat that becomes a tent

https://www.adiff.com/products/tent-jacket. This is great if you're going to be doing a lot of camping.

Clever Tank Top with Secret Pockets

Keep your valuables safe in this top. Perfect for all climates.

on Online Retailers for $39.90

Optical Camera Lens for Smartphones and Tablets

Leave your bulky camera at home. Turn your device into a high-performance camera. Buy on Online Retailers for $9.95

Travel-sized Wireless Router with USB Media Storage

Convert any wired network to a wireless network. Buy on Online Retailers for $17.99

Buy a Scrubba Bag to wash your clothes on the go

Or a cheaper imitable. You can wash your clothes on the go.

Hacks for Families

Rent an Airbnb apartment so you can cook

Apartments are much better for families, as you have all the amenities you'd have at home. They are normally cheaper per person too. We are the first travel guide publisher to include Airbnb's in our recommendations if you think any of these need updating you can email me at philgtang@gmail.com

Shop at local markets

Eat seasonal products and local products. Get closer to the local market and observe the prices and the offer. What you can find more easily, will be the cheapest.

Take Free Tours

Download free podcast tours of the destination you are visiting. The podcast will tell you where to start, where to go, and what to look for. Often you can find multiple podcast tours of the same place. Listen to all of them if you like, each one will tell you a little something new.

Pack Extra Ear Phones

If you go on a museum tour, they often have audio guides. Instead of having to rent one for each person, take some extra earphones. Most audio tour devices have a place to plug in a second set.

Buy Souvenirs Ahead of Time

If you are buying souvenirs somewhere touristy, you are paying a premium price. By ordering the same exact products online, you can save a lot of money.

Use Cheap Transportation

Do as the locals do, including weekly passes.

Carry Reusable Water Bottles

Spending money on water and other beverages can quickly add up. Instead of paying for drinks, take some refillable water bottles.

Combine Attractions

Many major cities offer ticket bundles where one price gets you into 5 or 6 popular attractions. You will need to plan ahead of time to decide what things you plan to do on vacation and see if they are selling these activities together.

Pack Snacks

Granola bars, apples, baby carrots, bananas, cheese crackers, juice boxes, pretzels, fruit snacks, apple sauce, grapes, and veggie chips.

Stick to Carry-On Bags

Do not pay to check a large bag. Even a small child can pull a carry-on.

Visit free art galleries and museums

Just google the name + free days.

Eat Street Food

There's a lot of unnecessary fear around this. You can watch the food prepared. Go for the stands that have a steady queue.

Travel Gadgets for Families

Dropcam

Are what-if scenarios playing out in your head? Then you need Dropcam.

'Dropcam HD Internet Wi-Fi Video Monitoring Cameras help you watch what you love from anywhere. In less than a minute, you'll have it setup and securely streaming video to you over your home Wi-Fi. Watch what you love while away with Dropcam HD.'

Approximate Price: $139

Kelty-Child-Carrier

Voted as one of the best hiking essentials if you're traveling with kids and can carry a child up to 18kg.

Jetkids Bedbox

No more giving up your own personal space on the plane with this suitcase that becomes a bed.

How I got hooked on luxury on a budget travelling

'We're on holiday' is what my dad used to say to justify getting us in so much debt we lost our home and all our things when I was 11. We moved from the suburban bliss of Hemel Hempstead to a run down council estate in inner-city London, near my dad's new job as a refuge collector, a fancy word for dustbin man. I lost all my school friends while watching my dad go through a nervous breakdown.

My dad loved walking up a hotel lobby desk without a care in the world. So much so, that he booked overpriced holidays on credit cards. A lot of holidays. As it turned out, we couldn't afford any of them. In the end, my dad had no choice but to declare bankruptcy. When my mum realised, he'd racked up so much debt our family unit dissolved. A neat and perhaps as painless a summary of events that lead me to my life's passion: budget travel that doesn't compromise on fun, safety or comfort.

I started travelling full-time at the age of 18. I wrote the first Super Cheap Insider guide for friends visiting Norway - which I did for a month on less than $250. When sales reached 10,000 I decided to form the Super Cheap Insider Guides company. As I know from first-hand experience debt can be a noose around our necks, and saying 'oh come on, we're on vacation' isn't a get out of jail free card. In fact, its the reverse of what travel is supposed to bring you - freedom.

Before I embarked upon writing Super Cheap Insider guides, many, many people told me that my dream was impossible. Travelling on a budget could never be comfortable. I hope this guide has proved to you what I have known for a long-time: budget travel can feel luxurious when you know and use the insider hacks.

And apologies if I depressed you with my tale of woe. My dad is now happily remarried and works as a chef in Iceland at a fancy hotel - the kind he used to take us to!

A final word...

There's a simple system you can use to think about budget travel. In life, we can choose two of the following: cheap, fast, or quality. So if you want it Cheap and fast you will get a lower quality service. Fast-food is the perfect example. The system holds true for purchasing anything while travelling. I always choose cheap and quality, except at times where I am really limited on time. Normally, you can make small tweaks to make this work for you. Ultimately, you must make choices about what's most important to you and heed your heart's desires.

'Your heart is the most powerful muscle in your body. Do what it says.' Jen Sincero

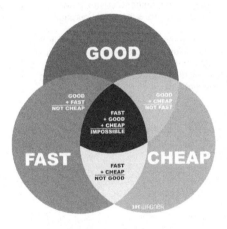

If you've found this book useful, please select some stars, it would mean genuinely make my day to see I've helped you.

Copyright

Published in Great Britain in 2024 by Super Cheap Insider Guides LTD.

Copyright © 2024 Super Cheap Insider Guides LTD.

The right of Phil G A Tang to be identified as the Author of the Work has been asserted in accordance with the Copyright, Designs and Patents Act 1988.

All rights reserved.

Made in the USA
Columbia, SC
26 December 2024

50654316R00135